D1076893

action plan for
effective self management

'*A*' *Time*

The busy manager's action plan for effective self management

JAMES NOON

Van Nostrand Reinhold (UK) Co. Ltd

To Hilary, Ben and Hannah

Published in 1985 by
Van Nostrand Reinhold (UK) Co. Ltd
Molly Millars Lane, Wokingham, Berkshire,
England

Typeset by
Colset Private Ltd, Singapore

Printed in Great Britain by
J.W. Arrowsmith Ltd, Bristol

British Library Cataloguing in Publication Data

Noon, James
  A-time: the busy manager's action plan for
  effective self management.
  1. Management
  I. Title
  658.4   HD31

ISBN 0-442-30642-3

Contents

Preface

Today you are reading this book. Yesterday and every working day before, you devoted the majority of your time to your low priority work. In fact, if you are a typical manager you will have devoted only 30–40% of your time to the things that are the most important in your job.

Your potential to achieve more in your job and your career is great. You can gain at least 10% increase in performance consistently and you can also save up to 20% of your time in your job. You can convert this time into better performance.

How can you gain this extra potential? Firstly you need to examine how you are presently managing yourself and how you are managing your time. This book will show you how. Secondly you need to establish some golden rules about your self management and some disciplines for using your time more effectively. Your aim is to devote at least 50% of your time to your top priority work. This book will guide you through the golden rules and tell you about 'A' time which will give you the technique for controlling your time at work for top performance.

The book has been written for managers of all ages and all levels of seniority. Whatever your function or whatever your type of organization, whether it be private or public, the golden rules will apply. The golden rules are all practical and common sense and they are written for the manager who wants to take a little time to manage his or her time more effectively.

The book is written for even the busiest of managers. The last chapter is a complete summary of all the key points, key actions and key disciplines that you need. The last chapter is the book within the book. The other chapters will give the detail and also provide you with the techniques and evaluation forms that will give you a great insight into your personal self management and time management.

Acknowledgements

Warm thanks to the many thousands of managers I have worked with, talked to and observed. They are a constant source of curiosity, surprise and good management practice.

Many thanks also to my colleagues at Henley – The Management College and International Thomson Organisation. They always demonstrate great patience and support.

Finally, many thanks to Stephanie Mathews, my secretary, who not only types the manuscripts, but is the constant example for the effective secretary.

James Noon
Business Time/System
Knightway House
20 Soho Square
LONDON W1V 6DT

Introduction

Throughout this book many references are made to 'A' time or time spent on 'A' priority work. What is 'A' time?

'A' time is both a philosophy of working and a technique of work that ensures that your energy, skill and commitment are focused on achieving high quality, top priority work. This philosophy and technique are what I call self management — that is managing yourself for higher achievement.

I developed the concept of self management and 'A' time as a practical solution to a very practical problem that all managers face every day of their working lives — ensuring that important work is completed *each day*.

From my research, observation and working with many thousands of managers world-wide, I became convinced that two factors interfere with the completion of important work *on time*. The first factor is concerned with a commitment to a high achieving style of management. The second factor is concerned with a manager's tendency to abdicate control over his or her diary and work-scheduling. Both these factors combine to produce low productivity and an inconsistent approach to working.

The philosophy of self-management is concerned with developing a style of management based on a few golden rules that help to keep a consistent focus on important work and effectively managing people. The technique of self-management or 'A' time is simply the reservation of blocks of time AHEAD, by about four weeks, to ensure that time is AVAILABLE for important work.

What key action points typify the style and technique of the self manager? He or she:

(1) Says YES very enthusiastically to work, but says NO, very effectively, when saying YES could substantially affect the completion of high priority work.

(2) Controls managerial procrastination by starting work early and by concentrating on important work FIRST. Delay is the major enemy of the self manager.

(3) Endeavours to control work stress, not by esoteric methods, but by identifying, confronting and responding to the source of stress.

(4) Has a strong vision of what is needed to be achieved in his or her job and translates this vision into action by scheduling KNOWN and IMPORTANT work AHEAD.

(5) Has a very positive and flexible approach to work and time planning in order to balance the time needed for REACTION and that needed for PLANNED ACTIVITY.

(6) Manages priorities by identifying AHEAD the sensitive time when priority problems are likely to occur.

(7) Controls his or her diary and work schedule such that time is available for KNOWN and IMPORTANT work. He or she also has very positive daily attitudes and disciplines to control time for important work.

(8) Plans and controls meetings with an emphasis on ACTION.

(9) Carefully plans and briefs delegation of tasks and very effectively follows up on tasks.

(10) Develops teams of people by an emphasis on priorities, direction, involvement and harmony and keeps his or her team focused on success.

(11) Works very effectively with his or her secretary and administrative support staff and gives priority to this support function.

(12) Is RUTHLESS and QUICK with business reading, business writing, paperwork and routine work.

Assessing your work style

The way that you think about life and work will affect the way you think about your job performance and your time management. Your life, performance and time are clearly very closely linked together and each affects the other to determine what you have achieved so far and what you will achieve in the future.

In this chapter we begin the process of understanding how we can manage our personal performance and time management. This process begins with an assessment of your basic attitudes and behaviour towards your job and time. The chapter will highlight your basic approach to your performance and time and enable you to establish a general strategy for improving your performance. In the subsequent chapters, we will assess your time and performance management in more detail.

What you achieve and how you use time in your pursuit of achievements depends very much upon four key concepts coming together into an effective whole for you, and you alone. These four key concepts are:

(1) How you manage your Work Behaviour.
(2) How you manage your Work Planning.
(3) How you manage your Tendency to Procrastinate.
(4) How you manage Work Stress.

These four concepts are the raw material of your personal performance and time management. To see these ideas in action, let us look at the case example of John Baker. After the case example we will develop the ideas further.

CASE EXAMPLE: JOHN BAKER

There were many things in John's job that gave him pleasure but he reserved the most pleasure for getting things done. Achievement as a thing in itself was a key goal for John. In many respects, John needed a high level of achievement because his job, as a Production Manager in a factory that was growing very rapidly, did demand a very high commitment from John and all its personnel.

John was a man whom you would describe as 'quick'. He seemed to talk quickly, move quickly and hurry along conversations and meetings. Although very intolerant of interruption to himself, he was often the person who interrupted the most as people were developing their ideas and arguments. On one such occasion of interruption at a scheduling meeting, Barry Copeman, the Purchasing Manager of many years' standing, accused John of 'hurry sickness'. John was just able to control his aggressive feelings and wished he could challenge Barry on his achievements for the company compared with his own.

Just as John was quick to speak and quick to anger, he was also quick to say yes. In many respects this was seen as a redeeming attribute in him. He loved to handle many jobs at the same time and he was quite capable of keeping his concentration and energy directed to all his tasks until they were finished and new replacement tasks were given to him. Of course, as you would expect of a man who accepted too much, there were a few occasions when a task was not completed on time or it was below quality. However, John was generally able to justify to himself an error like this on the basis of his overall achievements across his job.

Although planning was a very important technical component of his job as a Production Manager, John didn't really have the time or the inclination to plan his own job or to consider how time could be used effectively. It had often been suggested to him that more planning would help him to have a broader view of his job and, in time, this would improve his overall job effectiveness. John's normal reaction to these comments was to increase his efforts so that he could prove how he could achieve more, not through planning, but through sheer hard work. The criticism of 'fire-fighting' which was sometimes levelled against John was, in John's view, naive because he considered that the very nature of production would generate many incidents that needed to be dealt with as they arose. It was pointless to plan because everything had to be done and generally it had to be done right away.

In many respects John felt he was overloaded with work but this had to be accepted because of the growth in the company. He wasn't always confident about what he was expected to achieve in the eyes of his boss nor was he confident that he was getting the best from his subordinates. Also on many occasions he found he had to implement decisions that he had not been involved with. John didn't feel stressed at work but he often felt irritable and on more than a few occasions he had suffered from insomnia. John's wife, Ann, felt that he should take things a little easier and spend more time with the children.

For all intents and purposes, John appeared to be a successful manager. He appeared to achieve what was expected of him, he was very loyal and willing to extend himself for the company and his rapid, aggressive ways were to be accommodated by his fellow managers and subordinates. This was the general view of John and it had been this view for the three years he had held the job as Production Manager. The first signs of change in this view came when John missed two consecutive and important production deadlines for a new customer and the Manufacturing Director began to think a basic but critical question: 'If John Baker was so concerned about achievement, why was his performance only average and not significantly higher as you would expect from a man who appeared to work very hard and long?'

When we review the case of John Baker, we find a number of issues have been raised. Unfortunately these issues are more common than we would expect at first sight of the case; John Baker's problems are only slightly more dramatic than the problems many people and managers face at work. The first issue is that John's basic work style seems to permeate all his activities and decisions. His rush to achieve colours his life style, how he communicates, how he manages people and how he controls his emotions. John seems driven by time and he appears to have very little flexibility around this basic work behaviour pattern. John appears to be out of control of his job. All his activities appear to control him and yet he will accept any new activity so that he can continue to be driven by time. Time and job are the clear masters of John and this raises the second issue. John's view of his job is that to plan is to question the essential nature of his performance and achievement. His present condition, although not highly effective, is more comfortable than a newer, more relaxed and effective work style and load.

Finally, the third issue is beginning to raise itself. John does miss some deadlines and it will be only a matter of time before major errors are committed. John is not a selective man in his work and you are likely to find that equal priority has been given to the production deadline for the new order as for (say) a spare parts listing for a new machine. You are equally likely to find with John that the trivia of his job provide the most effective way for him to procrastinate on the major activities and projects that he is responsible for. The trivia, the crises, the interruptions to his day, the wasted energy of his aggression and his impatience for others are all essential for John so that he can continue to struggle for his achievements even against the odds. Very naturally, John is under stress but is failing to recognize the signs or the effects they are having upon his job and life. Let us now look at all these issues in more detail.

Time and work behaviour

The very qualities that help to make a person a success — independence and drive — are also the qualities that, if not properly managed by the person, can lead to failure and deterioration in competency. In the case example of John Baker, the drive to achieve could become the drive to failure due to a lack of self-awareness and management on his part. What is the background to these drives and work behaviour and how do they affect time management?

About 30 years ago, cardiologists Meyer Friedman and Ray Rosenman began investigating the connection between behaviour and heart disease. Between 1960 and 1970 they completed a major study and they categorized a type of behaviour which was highly associated with coronary heart disease. They called this behaviour Type A. As a contrast, they categorized a type of behaviour which was less likely to be associated with coronary heart disease. They called this behaviour Type B. The work of Friedman and Rosenman has had an important impact upon our knowledge of how people behave at work.

Type A and Type B behaviours have a very important bearing upon a person's approach to time management. Often Type A and Type B behaviours are a manifestation of deeply held drives and motivations and these have an impact on how time is perceived and used. Type A behaviour is action-driven; a person exhibiting this behaviour is relatively aggressive and appears to be involved in a struggle to achieve more in less time. By way of contrast, Type B is relatively unhurried, relaxed and calm and is not struggling to achieve more in less time. Very rarely is a person wholly Type A or Type B. As a general rule a person will be a mix of the two types, but with a tendency towards either A or B. Although the point is often misunderstood, Type A behaviour is not always associated with success. There is a tendency to perceive Type A behaviour as successful behaviour because it is very concerned with achievement and drive. However, sometimes Type B behaviour is more successful, particularly in situations which require qualities of calm, selectivity and the ability to handle qualitative issues. As a guide to Type A and Type B behaviour, the two case examples of George Manners and John Mortimer highlight the differences.

CASE EXAMPLE: GEORGE MANNERS

George Manners is a typical Type A. George has 'hurry sickness'; he sees success as wholly dependent upon achieving more and more goals. He often tries to do many things at the same time. He will dictate a letter while getting a telephone number or he will think through a problem while somebody is trying to ask him for advice. Because George likes to achieve a great deal, he tries to get more into each day. He often creates his own deadlines, even when they are not required, and he will strive very hard to meet his own deadline. To make absolutely sure he has achieved, he prefers to measure this output in numbers and very rarely will he consider qualitative issues. 'Ideas, abstract thoughts and concepts are all very well but can I use them to get the job done?' This is a constant question in George' mind.

George is very confident and he gives the impression of being self-assured, but below the surface he does have self-doubts. Sometimes these doubts can be very positive for George because they check his actions and decisions. However, sometimes they can be negative and then these doubts can lead to some insecurity. George is very competitive and he likes to challenge other people's ideas and decisions. Sometimes, however, he does feel very aggressive towards people and he tries hard to control his feelings of hostility which try to rise to the surface. He can be very impatient and will often give a short answer to people he does not need or respect. One of George's favourite pastimes is to interrupt the ideas and speech of his subordinates.

George often becomes frustrated with what he has achieved and he prefers to work harder for future achievements than take satisfaction from the present. This often means he does not relax; on the occasions when he can relax, he often feels guilty about it and seeks to work harder to make up for the lost time.

Generally, George has narrow interests because much of what he is interested in is, in fact, related to his work. His social life seems to revolve around work colleagues and his reading interests are now very few, apart from magazines, newspapers and work journals. George often thinks he has too little time to devote to his personal life and that fresh interests are a luxury. These time problems are not just reserved for his leisure interests; when George is at work he does feel the pressure of time and he is constantly trying to get more done in less time.

George does not control his workload and he is generally willing to take on any project or task at hand. Because of this he has very little time to plan his work or time and he believes that 'energy' and not planning is the best way to achieve. George certainly works hard but very rarely does he work smart! Just as the 'hurry sickness' penetrates all his life and work, it also shows in his physical style. George is a quick thinker and speaker and on occasions he can be so rapid in his movements and gestures that observers find it distracting. Without doubt, George thinks he is going somewhere fast!

CASE EXAMPLE: JOHN MORTIMER

Compared to George Manners, John Mortimer is a typical Type B. He can be so relaxed about his life and work that on occasions he can be infuriating to others. John does not believe success depends upon achieving more goals; he prefers to consider success as a result of many different influences in life, only a few of which are under his control. He very rarely tries to do two activities at the same time and he certainly does not work to a deadline unless it is absolutely necessary. In fact deadlines are not in favour with John and he tries hard not to have any in his work. For John, the quality of work is very important and particularly the satisfaction he can get from his own work. He likes to deal in qualitative issues, and abstract ideas and concepts are important in his thinking. John does have good ideas, but often they are seen to be too abstract and not specific to the job at hand. The present day is very important to John and he gets great satisfaction from his present surroundings and achievements.

John is not particularly confident or self-assured and he is prone to rely heavily upon the acceptance of himself by others. He likes to feel affiliated to people and he feels no competition or challenge from other people's ideas and decisions. If John has to submerge his own views, then this is quite acceptable to him and he feels very little aggression towards others at work. In many respects, John appears to be well liked by others, he certainly does not feel impatience towards them, and he very rarely interrupts. However, he very rarely stimulates the ideas of others and, in many ways, he contributes less than he should to the health and achievements of the work team.

John is very relaxed about life and work, and often his life can just drift by. On many occasions John has been criticized for being too relaxed, almost complacent about things. He has many interests in life outside work and, in the main, his social life is made up of people from outside this work. John's view of time is that it is not important and he often tries to ensure that work is managed so that it has little impact or urgency.

Because the work pressures and load are lower than average,

John does not feel the need to plan because most of what he wants to achieve can be easily accommodated in his relaxed work style. John's physical style is slow. He considers things for a long time and he takes his time to make his point. He is generally slower in his movements and gestures than average. John is quite happy to go somewhere, but slowly.

You can see from the case examples of George Manners and John Mortimer that they have contrasting types of work behaviour. Neither the Type A or the Type B is a preferable work style because both have their strengths and weaknesses. However, work behaviour does have an impact upon time management and personal performance. As you can imagine, Type As have different performance and time problems from Type Bs.

ACTION POINTS FOR TYPE A BEHAVIOUR

What are the implications of work behaviour on personal performance and time management? People with a tendency towards Type A behaviour are inclined to meet their problems at the works control level. They tend to accept more and more activities than they can cope with and to want to do their own work rather than delegate it. They often resist any form of work or time planning because of a lack of inclination and what they perceive as a lack of time. The end result is that people with Type A tendencies are generally submerged within their work and are often trying very hard to keep on top of it. Bad habits, crises and fire-fighting are all acceptable because they reinforce the position rather than alleviate it. They very rarely identify the most important areas of their work and they tend not to give any form of priority to the different aspects or areas of their job.

Because a Type A tendency is an orientation to the volume of work, then quantity is more important than quality. Getting a job finished is more important than getting the job finished well. There is always a tendency to accept lower quality goals than should be the case and in many respects, the Type A tendency can lead to under-achievement at the quality level. Often a Type A is narrow in outlook and this affects the quality of solutions to problems and the richness of ideas.

Another of the potential weak areas of the Type A is a lack of sensitivity and appreciation of the contributions of other people. People with Type A tendencies can often be too independent and driving to be concerned with developing their interpersonal skills. Therefore, in many respects, their work team as a whole can under-achieve. Finally, the person with Type A tendencies is not necessarily a satisfied worker. There are many sub-

merged emotions and frustrations which impede proper and consistent performance. Often the sense of achievement, which is the primary drive, is short-lived and fleeting. His performance can be erratic and, if not properly self-managed, this independence and drive can become damaging attributes. The key action points for Type As and people with Type A tendencies are:

(1) Work hard at creating performance goals, activities and priorities. Decide on what you are going to achieve and stick to this and no more. Learn to say No!
(2) Begin to plan your work and time more effectively. Take active control over your workload and plan to do less but delegate more. Learn to stop doing too much!
(3) Begin to set higher quality goals and be prepared to measure yourself by qualitative factors and not only by numbers. Learn to let the richness of your ideas and abstract concepts have more impact upon your work.
(4) Learn to relax with yourself! You no longer have to prove how good you are or how much you can achieve. Take more pleasure from what you have achieved so far and this satisfaction will stimulate far higher achievements in the future.
(5) Keep your sense of independence and drive active but positive. Manage it well so it does not work against you and your work team. Don't forget that independence and drive can damage you if not properly managed.
(6) Don't dampen the contributions of others; give people more space and flexibility and you will achieve far higher teamwork and output. Work with people, not against them!

ACTION POINTS FOR TYPE B BEHAVIOUR

People with a tendency toward Type B behaviour are inclined to meet their problems at the under-achievement level. The drive for output is low compared with that of a typical Type A; they have a tendency to organize and screen their workload so that it never places pressure upon them. They can create strong barriers around their work so that observations from outsiders are restricted. Complacency can become a major negative factor in the Type B behaviour. Because of the low workload pressure, there is very little need to plan work performance and time. With Type Bs, there is always more time than is required and there is always a tendency to waste time or procrastinate. The lack of pressure can lead to disorganization at the personal level rather than excessive neatness and organization.

Type Bs tend to be quality orientated in their work. Numbers are less important to them than finishing a job at a quality level which is acceptable to them, irrespective of whether the quality is too high for the job at hand, impractical or too costly. Often the Type B is too broad in outlook and this can affect the practicality and relevance of his ideas and solutions. One of the potential areas of weakness is the under-achievement in the work team. Although the Type B will seek good relationships with people, and generally this will be an important issue for him, there is a tendency for the high affiliation to colour the achievement of individuals and the team, and team decisions can be reflections of the team's weakest member or lowest common denominator. Finally the person with Type B tendencies can be too self-satisfied and complacent a worker. He has little frustration with his present situation and is quite happy to remain in his present position. The key action points for Type Bs and people with Type B tendencies are:

(1) Work hard at stretching performance goals, activities and priorities. Decide on what you want to do and drive harder to achieve these goals. Don't procrastinate. Do it now!

(2) Begin to plan your work and time more effectively. As your workload increases you will need to plan and organize yourself. Actively seek more work and organize it well.

(3) Begin to set higher quantity goals and be prepared to measure yourself by numbers and output. Learn to bring your ideas down to concrete reality and concentrate on the job at hand. Translate your thoughts into measurable action!

(4) Review your strengths and weaknesses as a manager of people. Are you allowing too much freedom and discussion in your team and is the team under-achieving?

Now that you know a little more about work behaviour, find out about *your* work behaviour *by completing* Worksheet 1.1. When you have finished the worksheet return to the **action points** and note down the action most appropriate to you. You will need your notes later so record them now.

Worksheet 1.1   Work behaviour

Consider the factors below and circle a number that best represents your work behaviour. For example if you think that your success depends very much upon driving hard for results (factor 1) then circle 1. If you think your success only moderately depends upon your drive for results then circle 2. If you think your success doesn't necessarily depend upon your drive for results then circle 3. If you think that success doesn't depend on drive then circle 4 and if you think that your success doesn't depend on your drive at all and depends upon other factors then rate yourself 5.

(1) For me success depends upon driving hard for results. I set my goals and I drive hard to achieve on time.   1 2 3 4 5   For me success depends upon many factors apart from my goals.

(2) I often do many things at the same time.   1 2 3 4 5   I always do one thing at a time.

(3) I prefer that my work is measurable and I prefer numbers as the measure.   1 2 3 4 5   I don't mind if my work is measurable but I prefer qualitative measures.

(4) I am seen as very confident and self-assured. I believe this is an important part of my personality.   1 2 3 4 5   Although I am confident and self-assured I don't think I am necessarily seen in this way.

(5) I get most satisfaction from achieving things which will give me a better future.   1 2 3 4 5   I get most satisfaction from achieving things that will give me a better present.

(6) I am very competitive and I often challenge people, ideas and decisions.   1 2 3 4 5   I don't feel particularly competitive and I rarely challenge people, ideas or decisions.

(7) I often feel aggressive and I have to control any hostile feelings.   1 2 3 4 5   I very rarely feel aggressive and I have no submerged hostile feelings.

(8) I often become impatient with people and I am prone to interrupt them.   1 2 3 4 5   I very rarely become impatient with people and I always allow a person plenty of time to finish their speaking.

(9) I have difficulty in relaxing and even when I do I sometimes feel guilty.   1 2 3 4 5   I have no difficulty at all in relaxing and I never feel guilty about it.

(10) I often feel the pressure of time and deadlines.   1 2 3 4 5   I very rarely feel the pressure of time and deadlines.

Assessment: When you have circled a number for each factor on the worksheet, then add your numbers and divide by 10. If you have a number between 1.0 and 1.4 then you are clear Type A. A number between 1.5 and 2.4 shows you have strong tendency to Type A behaviour. If your number is between 2.5 and 3.5 then you are neither Type A or Type B. A number between 3.6 and 4.5 means you have a strong tendency towards Type B and a number between 4.6 and 5.0 means you are clearly Type B in work behaviour.

Time and planning

In the last section we found that the need to plan your work and time was a key action point for both Types A and B. As you work your way through this book, you will find that we stress the need to plan your performance and time in a very flexible and creative manner. We believe that the ability to plan in this way is the key to achieving substantial performance gains and control over time. Building on this, it is very important that your thinking about planning is positive. In this section, we are going to highlight a few important ideas about planning and to establish your basic attitude toward planning.

Firstly what do we mean by planning? This book is concerned with your job and time at work and how these may be managed more effectively. Planning in our context means how you go about planning your job and its performance goals. In addition, we refer to planning as applied to personal organization and effectiveness at the day-to-day level and we also refer to planning in the sense of how your time is managed at a daily level and in the longer term.

Often the need to plan is recognized but, when confronted with the methods and means, some people will shy away from practising planning. In many ways they may choose more comfortable habits of working even while accepting that they are less effective.

Planning means deciding in advance what to do; how to do it; and who is to do it. Planning bridges the gap from where we are now to where we want to be in the future. The purpose of planning is not to predict the future but to assist you to achieve your goals in the future.

Planning helps you to organize your actions, decisions and resources in such a way that you can respond to change in a positive and creative way and still remain on target to achieve your goals. In the strictest sense of the word, planning is an extremely creative process that has the flexibility to cope with change. A plan that does not have flexibility is useless.

The essential purpose of a plan is to achieve a goal. If this is the case, how does the process of planning ensure that goals are achieved?

(1) Because planning is a creative and flexible process that copes with change, the planning process concentrates on ensuring that the goals set are, in fact, realistic and achievable, and that they are reviewed in the light of changing circumstances. In fact the more the circumstances are changing, the more planning becomes imperative.

(2) Because planning is directed towards goals, the goals must be identified and capable of being defined. This helps to make goals communicable and to co-ordinate your efforts and activities with other people's.

(3) Planning emphasises commitment and effective operations. A sound plan will help to schedule resources, co-ordinate activities and lead to the most economic use of all resources (including time).

(4) Planning tends to ensure that personal performance goals are achieved, because it allows for activities to be monitored and controlled against the overall plan and for corrective decisions to be taken if required.

Although planning has many benefits, you do find that some people will reject planning. They believe that planning will restrict their freedom of action and choice: In fact, planning increases one's freedom by allowing more time and resources to be used in other ways. Some people reject planning because they believe plans are 'full of numbers' which they can't understand and are rigid and unproductive; in fact, planning (as we develop the concept in this book) has few numbers and is based mainly upon a qualitative assessment of situations and on personal judgements and experiences. You will also find that planning is flexible and highly productive in relation to your effort and time.

Probably the most common reason for rejecting planning is that people believe it to be detailed and taxing and they do not have the capability to think to the level of detail which they believe is needed. In fact, planning is based upon *Key Factors* and not details. Indeed it is important to remain at the key factor level so that plans can be co-ordinated and an overview of progress maintained.

Although people will accept or reject planning for different reasons, here are some general reasons why planning fails:

— Some people lack commitment to their plans. They let today's problems push aside tomorrow's opportunities and they see crises and fire-fighting as a natural part of their job.
— Some people do not have a general strategy for their job and do not see the need to plan. In fact they lack an overview of their job and see it in a narrow light with short time scales.
— Some people have difficulty in setting achievable goals and so the planning process fails for them. In these cases the person needs a simple system for establishing performance goals.
— Some people over-plan and become bogged down in detail and procrastination. Generally people

who are over-planning lose sight of the purpose of planning and suffer from the well-known planners' disease 'paralysis by analysis'.
— Some people rely too heavily upon prior experiences. In these circumstances they do not have the capability of changing to meet new conditions. There is not doubt that experience is a great teacher, but it is precisely because experience is so powerful that you must not become short-sighted about it.
— Some people resist the change which planning implies. Planning may mean new roles and activities or new disciplines and working relationships. Some of the new ideas may be threatening and there is a tendency to resist any change and the plans that may bring it about.

Each of these reasons for failure in planning are perfectly normal and to be expected. However, the reasons for failure do seem to indicate a lack of vision and positive attitude to one's job and/or a lack of skill in implementing the planning systems. Clearly, if a person has no ability to plan their job or has little commitment to implementing their plans, there is very little that anyone can do about it. However these people are few and the vast majority of people at work can benefit from simple and flexible planning. To develop a positive attitude towards planning, the following golden rules will help you towards a stage where planning is an habitual activity and high performance a natural outcome.

THE GOLDEN RULES

(1) You must commit yourself to planning and implementing your plans. You need to inform people who are affected by your planning that you are committed to a planning system.
(2) You must use a planning system that is simple and practical. It needs to allow you to use your natural vision and creativity in a flexible way.
(3) You must organize yourself for planning. You need to establish performance goals and you need to 'do' your plan. Plans, actions and outcomes must be related and active.
(4) You must be definite about your plans and communicate what you intend to achieve by the plan. You need to get your own ideas straight and then let other people know what is to be achieved.
(5) You must link your long-term plans with your short-term plans. What you want to achieve in a year must be capable of being expressed as definite activity which can be done now.
(6) You must accept change and benefit from it. Change is acceptable if you plan it and become involved in it. Always seek the benefits of change for you and then plan to achieve them.

What are your attitudes towards planning? Complete Worksheet 1.2 and establish your basic attitude. When you have finished the worksheet review the section above on difficulties in planning and the golden rules and note down your broad strategy for dealing with any negative attitudes you have uncovered in the worksheet. Again you'll need your notes later so do it now!

Worksheet 1.2 Planning attitude

Consider each of the factors below and circle a number which represents your particular attitude. Remember the purpose of this indicator is to highlight your general attitudes towards planning. This guide is for your personal use, so be honest with yourself.

(1) There is no need to plan in my job and I can achieve as much as I wish without a plan.   1 2 3 4 5   I believe I need to plan in my job and my achievements depend upon my planning capability.

(2) I find that planning restricts my freedom of choice and action.   1 2 3 4 5   I find that planning allows me to be more creative and often highlights actions to take which may not have occurred with my plan.

(3) Planning does not suit my style of work.   1 2 3 4 5   Planning suits my style of work and I welcome the disciplines it provides.

(4) Planning cannot cope with the day-to-day pressures and changes.   1 2 3 4 5   My planning helps me to sort out the priorities of my day and to cope with change.

(5) Planning doesn't take into account my experience and judgement.   1 2 3 4 5   Planning is my experience and judgement but in an organised framework.

(6) Planning is too detailed and complicated.   1 2 3 4 5   Planning is concerned with key factors and issues.

(7) Planning requires too much time.   1 2 3 4 5   Planning saves time overall but I need to invest time in my planning at the beginning.

(8) Planning requires too much commitment.   1 2 3 4 5   I find that planning makes things clearer and I can then commit myself to my plan.

(9) Planning shows up my weaknesses and it might imply I have to change.   1 2 3 4 5   Planning shows up my weaknesses and my strengths and normally I can foresee change ahead.

(10) I have used planning in the past but it wasn't really successful for me.   1 2 3 4 5   I plan because I have made it successful for me.

Assessment: When you have circled a number for each factor on the worksheet, add the numbers and divide by 10. If you have a number between 1.0 and 1.4 then you have a highly negative attitude towards planning and probably all your past attempts have proved unsuccessful. If you have a number between 1.5 and 2.4 then you are negative about planning and you have had difficulty with coping with any past planning problems. If you have a number between 2.5 and 3.5 then you are neither negative nor positive in attitude and are still seeking the benefits of planning. If you have a number between 3.6 and 4.5 then you are positive in attitude and receive benefits from planning. You are probably still dealing with a few problem areas. If you are between 4.6 and 5.0 then you are highly positive and achieving the full benefits of planning in your job.

Time and procrastination

So far we have considered how our work behaviour affects our performance and time management and how we need to plan for higher performance and effective use of time. In many respects the Type A and B behaviour are an indication of our drives forward (Type A is far higher than Type B), while positive thinking on personal planning indicates our ability to do the job at hand. The third factor to consider is our capability to overcome the delays and impediments which face us or which we place in front of ourselves, and to carry our planning through to achievement. Just as we have a drive forwards to achieve, we have a check and balance in our drive 'backwards' through our natural procrastination. The essential role of procrastination is to control the strong forward drives so that we don't burn ourselves out like shooting stars! However, procrastination needs to be managed because it can be a strong impediment in our achievement potential and performance.

Procrastination is a common problem which is now becoming widely recognized as a significant impediment to work performance. We all like to procrastinate and often it can be as positive as it can be negative. We all put off unpleasant tasks, particularly if they involve people. We all avoid making sensitive and emotionally disturbing telephone calls. We dislike having to tell a customer something when we do not believe it ourselves. We all avoid the very large projects or tasks which do not fit naturally into our day-to-day work pattern. We also avoid the unfamiliar activity when we do not really know what the outcome could be or what to do if a mistake arises. In principle we are all just as good at not doing something as we are doing something else. This natural drive to delay is our natural procrastination.

For most of us the drive to procrastinate does not create too much of a problem. It will delay a project which can have bad consequences or it can result in a lower quality of output because we have had to rush the job at the last minute. Although the normal results of procrastination can be very damaging to one's job, there is always a possibility that normal procrastination can be a very creative way of delaying work in order to achieve a better outcome. The main point being made here is that we need to keep a very open mind about normal procrastination because its positive side can be very beneficial to our work. However there is another level of procrastination from which we also suffer. This is a level of procrastination which is deeply embedded in our behaviour and generally this has a negative effect. This can take many forms.

Procrastination can take the form of self-doubt. In these circumstances, a person may doubt their own capability despite their professional competence and ability to do a good job. Work is avoided because the person wishes to avoid the results of the work which they feel will further damage their self-esteem. In many respects procrastination takes the form of fear of failure. A very common situation which provokes this procrastination is when the task at hand involves public exposure, such as speech-making or writing to the public at large. Although we all have a fear of failure in public situations as a natural defence mechanism, it is necessary to analyse whether this is positive or negative in terms of our work performance.

Another form of procrastination is the search for perfection. Again procrastination is being used as a mechanism to avoid failure. Perfectionists set impossibly high standards of output and will strive to achieve these standards. The outcome is that they will always be short of better information, better resources, more time, better trained staff, more creative ideas; in sum they will always need something before a goal can be achieved and consequently it is never achieved. In effect, the perfectionist is not achieving the goal in order to avoid the fear of failure at the very high standards that have been set.

A third form of procrastinator is the rebel. The rebel procrastinators always seek to express defiance of others and to demonstrate their self-control and determination over people and the environment. The manifestation of the rebel procrastinators is the last minute deadline; the large tasks attempted in short time periods. In many respects the rebel needs constant crises and problems, which can be solved in order to show the control over events. In reality, the rebel lacks sensitivity and often the work performance is under-achieved because the time is constantly filled with trivia and short-term results. Deadlines are missed and large projects are low in quality because the rebel procrastinators concentrates on the little things at the expense of the big things. Often Type A behaviour is prone to rebel procrastination, such that they are completely overwhelmed by the trivia of their jobs and they need to work harder and harder to keep up with it.

A fourth form of procrastination is that of the excessive socializer. Here the procrastinator delays the start or finish of activities by involving themself in gossip, lengthy non-work-related conversations, or trips around the office and factory floor to seek distractions or trivial tasks.

A fifth form of procrastinator is the daydreamer. Very often he lacks the concentration and mental discipline to focus upon top priority work. There is always a distraction to break concentration and never a commitment and drive to finish the task. Day dreams take many forms — future career, promotion, mistakes, home and family, social events or sexual fantasy. Whatever the work these distractions are always available for a quick daydream!

Finally, the sixth form of procrastination is the priority inverter. This is a very typical form of procrastination which all managers suffer from. It is typified by putting low priority work in front of high priority work. Very often this happens at the beginning of the working day when a manager erroneously decides to 'get rid of' the minor tasks so that he can concentrate on the 'big' tasks of the day. However the low priority tasks take more time than expected, other minor tasks enter the day and the high priority work eventually is started in the afternoon. As you expect it is not completely finished and is left until the next morning. However the next morning brings exactly the same priority inversion and finally the high priority task is completed in the afternoon — one day later than it could have been!!

All the various forms of procrastination, whether it be natural and creative or deeply embedded in our work style — as in the case of the doubter, the perfectionist, the rebel or the excessive socializer — are perfectly plausible reasons, but more often than not they are excuses to avoid failure in the eyes of ourselves and others.

ACTION POINTS FOR THE PROCRASTINATOR

We have mentioned that procrastination is a very common, and indeed natural, problem. How can we deal with it in an effective manner? Here are a number of golden rules which will help you to overcome any problem you might have.

(1) Accept that procrastination is common and that you are not unique (or the worst procrastinator!) and that we procrastinate because we fear failure.

Fearing failure is perfectly normal and generally there is no real foundation for our feelings. This means you can solve your problems.

(2) Procrastination tends to have a common theme or foundations to its manifestation in individuals. You only procrastinate on certain actions or in certain situations. This means the problem is smaller than you think.

(3) Procrastination is solved by doing little things in your area of procrastination. When you know where your weak areas are, then you need to concentrate on these, persevere and discipline yourself. This means that the Do It Now! technique can be very powerful when you know where to focus your effort.

(4) Always be positive in the face of procrastination. Reward yourself when you succeed and boost your morale when you need to do so.

(5) Get into the Single Handling thinking which means you are going to do the job once, and once only. You will pick the job up and finish it before you put it down again.

(6) Never put low priority work in front of high priority work.

(7) Keep your socializing down to the level of good working relationship, but no more.

(8) A very powerful discipline for effective self management is the 'Start Time' philosophy. Scheduling the *start* of work and not just the *finish* leads to better planning and personal organization as well as keeping procrastination firmly under control.

Are you a procrastinator? Complete Worksheet 1.3, establish your overall score and highlight the key factors at the root of your procrastination. After you have completed the worksheet return to the action points and make a positive commitment to the techniques of 'Do It Now!', 'Single Handling' and Start Times. Don't forget to make your notes in preparation for use later.

Worksheet 1.3   Procrastination

Consider each of the factors below and circle a number which represents your particular behaviour. Remember there are no right or wrong answers to the procrastination indicator and its purpose is to give a general guide to your behaviour. This guide is for your personal use, so be honest with yourself.

(1) I always clean and tidy my desk whenever I have to start a difficult job.   1   2   3   4   5   Whenever I start a difficult job I rarely feel the need to clear and tidy my desk.

(2) Even when a job is going well I often doubt whether I will be able to complete it satisfactorily.   1   2   3   4   5   I am always confident that I will be able to produce a good job.

(3) I am often guilty of delaying putting a sound plan into action.   1   2   3   4   5   I never delay in putting a sound plan into action.

(4) I am very fond of flirting at work or chatting and gossiping or wandering around when I have no reason to do so.   1   2   3   4   5   All the things I do at work are related to getting my job done. Flirting, chatting and wandering around are kept to a minimum.

(5) I always have to concentrate hard and discipline myself to get started on a job.   1   2   3   4   5   I start jobs very easily and naturally. I always start early.

(6) On many occasions I have avoided unpleasant, difficult, unfamiliar or emotionally upsetting jobs.   1   2   3   4   5   Whenever I am faced with unpleasant, difficult, unfamiliar or upsetting jobs I just get on with it without delay.

(7) I am often guilty of putting unimportant jobs in front of important jobs even when I know it is risky to do so.   1   2   3   4   5   I never put an unimportant job in front of an important job unless I have a sound reason for doing so.

(8) I often delay a job because I fear I will make a mistake.   1   2   3   4   5   I never delay a job because of the fear of making a mistake.

(9) When I miss a deadline it is normally because I have delayed on the job.   1   2   3   4   5   I very rarely miss a deadline because of my delay.

(10) I often leave difficult jobs until the last minute or the end of the day.   1   2   3   4   5   I generally plan my jobs well in advance and normally I do all the important work early in the day or when I am at my best.

Assessment: When you have circled a number for each factor on the worksheet, add the numbers and divide by 10. If you have a number between 1.0 and 1.4 then you are very prone to procrastination and your performance is being seriously impaired. A number between 1.5 and 2.4 means you have a strong tendency to procrastinate and work below your potential. A number between 2.5 and 3.5 means you are fully aware of your tendency to procrastinate and you probably work hard to keep procrastination under control and performance up to your potential. A number between 3.6 and 4.5 means your procrastination is low and your performance is not impaired. A number between 4.6 and 5.0 means that you are free of procrastination and your performance is high.

Work stress

The final factor that affects your work style is your ability to handle work stress. Work behaviour in terms of Type A or B gives you your basic drives. Your attitude towards planning gives you your basic ability to organize your work and use your resources effectively. Your ability to cope with procrastination stops the delay in achieving your results and the flow of your work. Finally your ability to handle stress and to remain stable and productive under work pressure will determine your prolonged work stamina necessary to achieve your goals in a consistently productive manner.

Work stress is commonly understood to be the 'wear and tear' of working life. Stress is a chronic tension which if not relieved leads to a wearing down of a manager's ability to cope with the job. When stress is prolonged then it is dangerous and can lead to stress-related diseases such as ulcers, hypertension, and heart disease.

Even if related illnesses are avoided, stress can still lead to poor managerial performance. The effects of stress can be seen in low motivation, low confidence and self-esteem, poor communication, low trust and lack of involvement with work colleagues and a lack of concern for achievement.

There are many reasons why stress is a part of the manager's life. Managers face time pressures, have deadlines to meet, have people to deal with, have to achieve targets, and often they are overworked. There are many areas of stress for a manager but the three most important categories relating to time management are: work overload, the manager's role and personal relations. Let us look at these in turn:

Work overload normally breaks into two types: 'too much to do' and 'too difficult to do'. Managers who have more telephone calls, more travelling, more meetings, more deadlines, are potentially more stressed than managers who have less of these activities. Also when the quality of work output is increased significantly, over an

acceptable threshold for a manager, then confidence and self-esteem decrease. In both cases of whether it is 'too much' or 'too difficult' the manager will react positively in order to cope with the increase, but if the increase is prolonged or too excessive for the individual then stress will occur.

Interestingly, stress can also occur if a manager is underloaded. Basically this means that the right level of stimulation is necessary for an individual to avoid the stresses of underload or overload.

Dr Rosalind Forbes, a psychologist specializing in corporate stress, found that the right level of stimulation is important for a healthy managerial life (see Fig. 1.1).

Work underload leads to boredom, apathy, irritability, decrease in motivation, dullness and negative attitudes. All of these lead to low productivity. Work overload leads to apathy, strained relationships, poor judgement, lack of clarity, undecisiveness, diminished memory and recall and increased errors. Again, all of these lead to low productivity. However, when the manager has the right level of stress to act as a stimulus then we have the optimum balance where stress is very constructive and leads to high performance. In this case the signs of optimum balance are: exhilaration, high motivation, mental alertness, high energy, a realistic analysis of problems, sharp perception, sound relationships and calmness under pressure.

The *manager's role* in the organization can also potentially lead to stress. There are four main areas. The first area is when a manager has insufficient information for the job to be performed effectively. In these circumstances, managers are unclear on what is expected of them and what they should achieve. The second area is concerned with the conflicts in demands that are often placed upon them. This is often the case when a senior manager has an expectation of a job being performed in a particular way and this conflicts with the subordinate's viewpoint. Thirdly, managers manage people and this is a potential stress point. Normally managers have a high

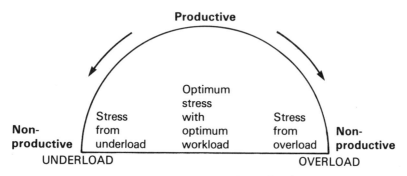

Fig. 1.1   Effect of stimulation level

workload and their performance in this workload depends upon their staff and colleagues. Lack of skill in managing people leads to low performance and stress. Fourthly, and finally, managers suffer stress when the organization for which they work is weak in structure and procedures. Managers rely upon participation in decision making and involvement with their superiors and when this is not forthcoming then stress is the outcome. There are many other aspects to this issue. Managers normally seek autonomy and discretion over their work, high consultation and good communication. Whenever any of these factors is not present then job performance is lower and stress higher. The golden rule here is that high participation leads to high performance.

A manager's *personal relationships* at work are critically important to performance and the reduction of stress. Only a small minority of managers will actively seek poor relationships and most recognize the vital importance of developing strong relationships to team performance. Your relationship with your boss is the most critical of your relationships. Poor relationships in this area lead to increased pressure for performance, more criticism and less participation and communication. Good relationships on the other hand are often typified by trust and respect, lessening of pressure for performance and an increase in participation and communication. Poor relationships with your subordinates follow a close second. In these circumstances performance is lowered through lack of concern and loyalty, low involvement and communication and the inability to delegate and control team work performance effectively. Poor relationships with colleagues are normally typified by the competition between equals. Managers are unwilling to share problems on the assumption of appearing weak and consequently the level of support and cooperation between equal managers is reduced substantially.

A self-evident feature of work stress is that not all managers are the same and each manager is likely to react differently in the same stress situations. For some managers, deadlines are a source of stimulation whereas for others they are a dread. For some managers people are a source of inspiration yet for other managers they are a source of stress. Clearly whatever aspects of stress you take, individuals will react differently to the circumstances. Nonetheless, although we are different we are also the same, inasmuch as stress, whatever its source, is a feature of managerial life. Is there a typical sort of manager behaviour that reacts generally better to stress? This is a difficult area but there are common signs that indicate three important features that appear in stress

resistant managers; realism, adaptability and sense of achievement.

Realism is a mixture of emotional stability and a willingness to seek a fair perception of a situation. When faced with a potentially stressful situation the stress resistant manager remains calm and establishes the real facts of the matter. This is neither an under or over reaction but a drive to clarify exactly what the potentially stressful situation really means. Following realism, the stress resistant manager will adapt to the changes. Resistance to accepting change is a critical factor in prolonging the stressful situation. Finally the stress resistant manager seeks to achieve success in the changed situation.

ACTION POINTS FOR THE WORK STRESSED

As we have seen above, for the manager stress is a feature of work style. By being aware of the areas where potentially stress can occur and actively arranging a work style to avoid the occurrence is probably the most effective way of coping with stress. Meditation, yoga, relaxation exercises are clearly helpful if you are inclined to these activities, but bear in mind these are all concerned with controlling the stress level as opposed to removing the causes of stress. Managers have a number of key action points for keeping stress at bay and work performance high.

(1) Seek to achieve the right work balance, not too much and not too little. A key skill in avoiding stress is to plan ahead a workload that is geared to achieving your targets, then stretch those targets a little more, then accept this level of performance and plan accordingly.
(2) It is quite amazing how many managers, even in large organizations with well designed job descriptions and appraisal procedures, are not clear on their job. Sit down with your boss and subordinates and clarify what is to be achieved and how it is to be achieved.
(3) Remember the good bosses are the bosses who actively manage the people around them. It is very commonly accepted that the good boss thinks through how to involve people in decisions, how to ensure proper participation, who allows people discretion to achieve and who establishes good formal and informal communications between people. Think about your activities last week, where could you improve on all these issues?
(4) Manage the conflicts in demands. Even the worst superior you could have will listen to a NO! if you

plan how to say NO! in a reasonable way with a reasonable description of the circumstances why NO! is necessary. As any salesman can highlight, if you put the benefits back to the boss, particularly if they are related to a higher value of output for the boss, then you are well on the way to managing the day-to-day conflicts in demand.

(5) Share your problems as well as your answers. No manager, however good he may think himself, is good enough to have all the answers. Sharing problems is a very important part of the development of good communications between people. At the end of the day a problem is solved because a team of people have cooperated.

(6) Whenever you are faced with a stress situation keep firmly in your mind: REALISM, ADAPTATION and ACHIEVEMENT. Seek to remain calm, get the facts, change to the new situation and get on with it in the new situation. Don't dig your heels in!

(7) Finally, don't forget the strength of the family at home. All the research shows that the thrusting manager who returns home to the caring spouse and family returns to thrust again the next day. Talk through with your spouse the problems as well as the successes.

Does work stress affect your job stamina? Complete Worksheet 1.4 and identify the key areas that are potentially causing stress and reducing your performance. When you have identified the factors return to the action points and note the actions that you are going to take. Don't forget you will need your notes later.

Worksheet 1.4   Work stress

Consider each of the factors below and circle a number which represents your present work situation. Remember there are no right or wrong answers to the stress indicator and its purpose is to give an insight into your present level of stress and its root sources. The guide is for your personal use, so be honest with yourself.

(1) Presently, I feel I have a low motivation to my work.

1 2 3 4 5   Presently, I feel highly motivated. I am charged with energy and I feel exhilarated.

(2) Presently, I feel low in self-esteem and somewhat depressed.

1 2 3 4 5   Presently, I feel very confident and have a high self-esteem.

(3) Presently, I feel I am under-achieving my potential.

1 2 3 4 5   Presently, I feel I am achieving a great deal at work.

(4) I often find I have too much to do and sometimes I find my work difficult.

1 2 3 4 5   I believe I have the right workload and I am confident I can cope with most problems.

(5) I feel pressured in my work.

1 2 3 4 5   I feel relaxed in my work.

(6) I am not clear on my objectives nor what is expected of me by my boss.

1 2 3 4 5   I have very clear objectives agreed with my boss.

(7) I often have to deal with conflicts in demands and I find this leads to work pressure.

1 2 3 4 5   I have to deal with conflicts in demands but normally I can resolve these to everyone's satisfaction.

(8) I don't feel involved in decisions and my boss is very much an autocrat.

1 2 3 4 5   I feel highly involved in decisions and my boss seeks high participation.

(9) I have poor relationships with my boss, colleagues and subordinates and I wish I could improve these.

1 2 3 4 5   I have very sound relationships with the people around me at work. Generally we are able to resolve differences in a reasonable way.

(10) I often find that things change so frequently that I have to 'dig my heels in' just to remain stable.

1 2 3 4 5   Things around me change frequently, but normally I can adapt and seek a new challenge in the situation.

Assessment: When you have circled a number for each of the factors on the worksheet, add the numbers and divide by 10. If your number is between 1.0 and 1.4 then you are likely to be highly stressed at work. You might feel you can cope but be warned — you are damaging your productivity. A number between 1.5 and 2.4 means you are under stress and you should take active steps to sort out the problem areas. A number between 2.5 and 3.5 means you have some stress and a few problem areas but you can probably cope with these in a reasonable way. A number between 3.6 and 4.5 means you have very little stress in your work and the occasional problem is coped with very adequately. A number between 4.6 and 5.0 means you have not only achieved the optimum stress level for your job but you are also probably a highly satisfied and achieving manager.

2

Assessing your performance

In the last chapter we established your basic work style. This chapter shows you how you can assess your performance and time management and develop your personal strategy for improvement.

Most people at work have a false impression of how they use their time at work! Many people think they spend most time on major projects and important work, yet in reality they spend most of their time on low priority work and trivia! Others believe they spend little time socializing with colleagues only to acknowledge its importance to them, when they see the large amount of time they spend on non-work related matters. Although there are some people who are very aware of their use of time, the vast majority of us generally have a false impression of exactly what we spend our time on and how this contributes to, or detracts from, our performance at work. Clearly it is very important that we establish how you perform and use your time before we can move on to how you can improve.

Our performance at work

Before we get into the detail of performance and time management assessment, let us look at some general findings about how managers work. From my own research and experience of working with many thousands of managers, there seems to be a consistent problem that emerges. This pattern is only slightly modified by the seniority of the manager and the type of organization in which he works.

Probably the most important finding is that most managers have the potential to improve their output and performance by at least 10%. Clearly the implications of this for their organizations are substantial. As you are aware, productivity is a key issue in all sectors of industry, commerce and the public services and if it were possible to build up a critical mass of managers who are committed to realizing their potential improvements in productivity then the overall productivity of our organizations would consequently improve.

Why do managers have this potential for improvement? Very broadly because managers haven't been trained, or have forgotten, to manage themselves as well as the other resources under their control. Without self management a manager will always operate at a lower level of performance than its true level.

Under this general heading of self management I have found that many managers do not plan forward to meet their goals but react on a day-to-day basis within a general framework of job strategy which they hope will be sufficient to achieve the goals. As much as a manager needs a set of job goals for the year, he or she needs a set of job goals for the day, the week and the month. Without thinking through these long term goals and how they are made up of day-to-day activities then we have no real plan nor the means of assessing the priorities of activity that the manager faces every day of his or her working life.

Secondly, many managers don't keep effective control over how their time is being used or where it is being directed. I have consistently found that managers devote only 30–40% of their time to the most important activities in their job. The vast majority of time is spent on lower priority work. I have also found that you can increase the time spent on top performance work simply by making effective use of my 'A' time technique which simply means you allocate ahead for about 4 weeks the 'A' time you require for your 'A' priority work. ('A' time will be fully discussed later.)

Thirdly, many managers overstate the crises and emergencies that occur in the day. How often have you said to yourself that you couldn't do any real work today because so many things came up in the day that had to be dealt with? My own findings suggest that only about 15% of the day is needed for coping with 'A' priority urgent work that actually arrives on the day. Very few managers will plan for this work and most will happily seek the 'comfort' of being busy whatever the priority of the work.

Fourthly, managers don't seek the opportunity to *save* time but to *use* time. I have consistently found that managers can save about 20–30% of their current time use by managing their meetings more effectively, by planning their delegation ahead, by improved planning and priorities management and by better personal organization.

What do all these findings show? Well, unless you are the exceptional manager, your personal potential for improving your performance is high and if you are working in a team of like minded and self management trained managers then the potential for your organization is also high.

Bearing in mind you have your insights on work style, i.e. your 'strategy' for performance, from Chapter 1, let us now look in detail at your 'tactics' for performance by gaining insight into the more detailed assessment of your performance and time management.

Developing your time report

To manage your time you need to know where it is going and to assess whether this use of time is an effective one or a wasted one. To establish this vital information you need to make a diary of how your time is being used. We call this diary your *Time Report*. Your Time Report is based upon a minimum of three days' record of time use. It is preferable, but not necessary, that the three days should be consecutive. It is also preferable that you choose three days that are fairly typical of your style of working. For some people this might be very difficult, but for the vast majority of people at work, you tend to find that their working days have an underlying time pattern which the time report will identify. Choose your three days sensibly: as a general rule, avoid days when you are travelling extensively, avoid the week before or

after a holiday and avoid the time when an essential member of your work team is absent from work.

A time report is a listing of activities and the times that these activities were started and finished. Apart from activity description and time, it is useful to record the day of the week and the people who were involved in the activity. If you were working alone, then record this also. The case example of Robert Ashworth shows the essential style of the time report. Robert Ashworth is the Personnel and Administration Manager for a large design engineering consultancy partnership.

CASE EXAMPLE: ROBERT ASHWORTH'S TIME REPORT

Tuesday

0830 Meeting with John Podmore (Senior Partner), to discuss new office equipment. I think this new equipment will improve the productivity of the office substantially. John believes we should commission a report.

0915 Working with Ann (Secretary). Arrange the schedule for the day. We deal with lots of correspondence but some top priority letters are still outstanding.

0945 Take telephone call from Barry Cassidy (Salesman) on arrangements for the demonstration of the new microcomputer. We agree next Wednesday at 1400. Confirm this with Ann.

0950 Begin working on report for senior partners on the engineering design staff requirements for next year. This report needs to be completed by Thursday.

1030 Telephone Robin Askins (New Business Development Manager) to enquire on the expectation for new business for next year. He is not confident about his figures but he expects a 15% reduction in new client business.

1045 Return to design staff report and build in Robin's new expectations.

1055 Interrupted by Madeleine Montgomery (Personnel Officer) who requires information on the new pension scheme we are introducing.

1125 Meeting with the Personnel Committee. I am Chairman and the meeting is to discuss manpower planning in the practice. Very good meeting but there is a substantial amount of work to be done prior to the partner's planning meeting next month.

1230 Lunch with John Podmore. Hear that Robin Askins may be having personal problems at the moment.

1400 Return to design staff report. Interrupted by various telephone calls. I handle them at the time and delay the report yet again.

1445 Prepare for Administration Committee meeting. Ask Ann for all the relevant files. Note that a number of files are missing. I should have checked this earlier in the day.

1500 Meeting with the Administration Committee. I am

Secretary to this committee. Some concern expressed about the cost of new electronic equipment and the difficulties experienced in implementing the machines.

1600 Meeting with John ?odmore to discuss the outcome of the Administration Committee. We need to be very careful with our presentation and facts if we are to introduce the new equipment.

1645 Working with Ann on correspondence.

1700 Return a number of telephone calls that have built up during today.

1720 Final look at the unfinished design staff report. I must get this finished by tomorrow.

1735 Finish

ASSESSING YOUR TIME REPORT

A time report is the basic document of time management. To assess a time report, there are four techniques which together lead to valuable insight into the way time is managed and whether personal performance is high or low. Assessing time reports is a creative process which brings together the five techniques of *Performance Assessment*; *Time Category Assessment*; *Key Time Question Assessment*; and *Preferred Day Assessment*.

Performance assessment

The first technique of time report assessment is to assess whether the performance of the day was satisfactory. Later in the book we will talk much more about performance objectives and, in particular, how they may be clarified and managed. Suffice it to say here that people at work endeavour to achieve certain objectives by performing certain activities during their day. These activities may be very simple and habitual; for example, making sure the first class mail leaves on time. Alternatively the managing director may have the task of achieving consensus on a new investment proposal. Whatever the level and position within the organization, you will find people endeavouring to perform and meet their objectives through day-to-day activities. The first technique, therefore, in time report assessment is to establish whether these activities have been successful and how the time of the day was used in these activities.

It is useful to reflect on each day of your time report and to ask yourself, 'What exactly did I wish to achieve during that day?' More often than not, people do not explicitly state their performance objectives and the resulting activities at the beginning of a day; this reflec-

tive questioning highlights what their day comprised or, more appropriately, what it should have comprised. If, by reflective questioning, we can establish the objectives of the day, then we can assess whether the activities conducted during the day were helpful in achieving these objectives. As a general rule, the day's time and effort should be devoted to achieving performance objectives.

Let us develop this point more. In any one day a person at work will undertake a number of activities. Some of these activities will be essential whilst others will be non-essential and some activities will play a supportive role in assisting other activities. For these activities we allocate priority ratings:

— *'A' Priority Activities* are highly essential activities that must be completed or progressed substantially during the day. 'A' priority activities are related directly to the performance objectives of the job. It is critical that 'A' priority activities are managed well.

— *'B' Priority Activities* are less essential activities but it is only preferable that they should be completed or progressed substantially during the day. Clearly 'B' priority activities have to be completed, but the time element is less important as the impact upon the overall performance of the job is lower.

— *'C' Priority Activities* are non-essential activities. Every job has a proportion of non-essential activities which are so minor in impact on the performance of the organization and your job that they can be disregarded, handled by other people, deferred, or screened and handled at a special low priority time.

— *'X' Priority Activities* are activities which require immediate attention as they arise during the day. Crises, emergencies, boss demands, and interruptions can all be 'X' activities. You can have 'AX', 'BX', and 'CX' activities.

Activities that support 'A' priority activity such as travelling, reading, correspondence, etc. are 'A' priority support activities.

With these priority categories of activity, we can now introduce a key principle in time management and in management generally. Vilfredo Paretto, a nineteenth century Italian economist and sociologist, made the observation that significant items in a group tended to constitute the smallest proportion of the items in the group. The Paretto principle is commonly referred to as the 80/20 principle and, in the context of time management, this suggests that 80% of our activities are responsible for only 20% of our achievements; whereas 20% of our activities are responsible for 80% of our achievements. In practical terms, this suggests that we need to free ourselves of the trivial activities of our job or complete them in the minimum amount of time. Conversely, we need to concentrate more on our 'A' priority performance objectives and 'A' priority activities. Ideally we should spend more time to achieve these activities to the highest quality and organize our time so that more 'A' priority activities can be introduced into the day's schedule. The Paretto principle tends to support the view that the majority of people are, in fact, under-achieving and that a significant reason for this under-achievement is a *lack of appreciation* of what is important in their life and *lack of selectivity* in the numerous activities undertaken.

Table 2.1 Priority rating of Robert Ashworth's activities

Activity sequence number	Activity description	Time (mins)	Priority
1	New Office Equipment meeting	45	B
2	Correspondence with Secretary	30	B
3	Micro-computer telephone call	5	C
4	Design staff report	40	A
5	New Business telephone call	15	A
6	Design staff report	10	A
7	Pension scheme interruption	20	CX
8	Personnel Committee meeting	75	B
9	Lunch	90	C
10	General telephone call interruptions	45	B and C
11	Prepare for administration meeting with Secretary	15	B
12	Administration Committee meeting	60	B
13	Administration Committee meeting de-brief	45	B
14	Correspondence with Secretary	15	B
15	Return telephone calls	20	B and C
16	Design staff report	10	A
		540	

Returning to our main discussion on Performance Assessment, we stated that we need to assess whether the performance of the day was satisfactory and whether time was used effectively in achieving this performance. Let us go back to the example of Robert Ashworth. If asked, Robert would probably identify the engineering design staff report as the 'A' priority activity of the day. This report has to be presented in a couple of days and it will be essential information in the plan of the engineering consultancy. There are many other meetings in the day as well, and Robert would have probably ranked them as 'B' priority activities. Clearly the majority of these activities were to take place because they were scheduled. However, in Robert's overall view, he would have considered these as 'preferable' activities rather than highly essential for that day. Some activities he had identified as 'C' priority — i.e. they were non-essential in Robert's view or otherwise they could have been scrapped, handled by another person or deferred to another time. Robert Ashworth's priority rating is shown in Table 2.1.

Robert was not able to complete his 'A' priority activity of the day, i.e. the design staff report was not finished, although it had progressed. From the general character of Robert's time report, we will assume that the report had not progressed as far as he would have liked. When we look at the amount of time allocated to the design staff report, we find that it amounts to about 75 minutes including a 15-minute telephone conversation seeking more facts. This is about 14% of the day's time. Ideally Robert should have allocated substantially more time to this activity and, if he had managed his day and work more effectively, it is likely that he would have found another 110 minutes from managing other activities. For example, without upsetting his main 'B' priority activities, Robert could have saved 110 minutes as shown in Table 2.2. When we added Robert's time saved to his original 75 minutes we have about 185 minutes or 34% of the working day. Not only would this be more time, it should be time that is blocked in the day so that *continuous* working time could be devoted to the activity. Continuous working time improves the quality of concentration and work output. Robert could improve this 34% to between 50% and 60% by ensuring that 'B' activities are planned and controlled well. To do this Robert would use the 'A' time technique described later.

In summary, the first technique of assessing whether performance of the day is satisfactory, shows the general effectiveness of your day and indicates very broadly how you are performing and your scope for improvement.

Table 2.2 Possible time periods saved in Robert Ashworth's day

Activity sequence no.	Activity description	Estimate of time saved (mins)
1	New Office Equipment meeting	15
3	Micro-computer telephone call	5
7	Pension Scheme interruption	20
8	Personnel Committee meeting	15
9	Lunch	15
10	General telephone call interruptions	20
13	Administration Committee meeting de-brief	15
15	Return telephone calls	5
		110

Time category assessment

The second technique builds on the first technique. In Robert Ashworth's example, we found that he could manage 'B' and 'C' priority activities so that more time was available for his 'A' priority activities. We can develop this principle into a general review of how time is spent. By categorizing your activities and adding up the time you spend on them, this will give you insight into general areas of improvement in your time management. Let us return to Robert Ashworth again: Table 2.3 shows his time categories.

Table 2.3 Robert Ashworth's time categories

Activity category	Time spent (mins)	% Day	% Category saving
Correspondence/ working with secretary	60	11	—
Meetings	225	41	8
Telephone	85	16	6
Individual work (Pension, staff report)	60	11	—
Visitors	20	4	4
Working lunch	90	17	3
	540	100	21

A number of observations can be made about Robert's time categories. He would be quite surprised to discover the amount of time he spends on the telephone and the substantial periods he spends in meetings. Clearly both these categories are necessary but, through better management of the day, better planning for shorter meetings, and delegated telephone calls, Robert is likely to find a substantial proportion of his time can be freed. Normally, by managing the categories of activities, approximately 20% of the day's time can be saved. Essentially by working to become 'crisper' in our self-management we can gain output without losing quality. This can be used for additional 'A' priority activities.

In summary, this category assessment shows you how your day is broadly structured and indicates some general areas where time can be saved so that performance overall can be improved.

Key time question assessment

The third technique requires you to take a detailed look at each of the main activities that were performed during the day. This technique is akin to a discussion about each activity and it reviews each activity in the light of five important question areas in time management. These question areas are:

(1) What was the purpose of the activity?
(2) Who were the people in the activity?
(3) How was the activity delegated?
(4) How was the activity scheduled?
(5) How was the activity timed?

Each of these question areas has a series of sub-questions aimed at probing the activity in more detail. The full list of sub-question probes are:

(1) *What was the purpose of the activity?*
    Was the activity necessary?
    Could the time spent on this activity have been better spent?
    Did the activity have the right priority rating?
(2) *Who were the people in the activity?*
    Were the people in this activity the right people to achieve its purpose?
    Was the team well organized and directed?
    Was the team spirit good?
(3) *How was the activity delegated?*
    Could this activity be delegated?
    Was this activity delegated to you?
    What impact on your time management did this delegation have?
(4) *How was the activity scheduled?*

Was this activity scheduled in advance or did it arrive at short notice?
Was the activity an interruption?
Could you have planned for this activity?

(5) *How was the activity timed?*
Was this activity conducted at the right time of the day?
Could this activity time have been used to provide more continuous time for 'A' priority activities?

The first question area 'What was the purpose of the activity?' is a very necessary one. Many days are a collection of activities that don't necessarily have a rhyme or reason. Appointments are made which are not important; visitors drop in; minor paperwork is moved from place to place. If we take the important principle of the 80/20 rule, then each main activity we perform has to relate to our performance objectives and we need to concentrate our time on these activities. The first question area therefore is very much concerned with whether the activity was a necessary one to perform and whether the time used was well spent.

The second question area 'Who were the people in the activity?' is important. In many respects the personal performance of a person at work relies upon the construction of teams of people. Many tasks cannot be achieved by single people and there is a very necessary spirit of cooperation and method of working that needs to be developed for teams to achieve their maximum output. How an individual contributes to the team, and how he uses the outcomes of team work, are both very important aspects of the overall climate for developing personal performance. For a team to be effective it needs the right people with the right experiences and skills. It also needs the right style of working and the right style of management given the task at hand. Alternatively there are many tasks that can be completed by an individual and often we do not allocate enough individual working time to our 'A' priority activities. This second question area is therefore very much concerned with how people or individuals perform their activities and whether the time was used effectively.

The third question area is 'How was the activity delegated?' There are two sides to this question. Firstly a substantial proportion of work which is presently undertaken by people not familiar with time management is, in fact, work that could be delegated. There is a tendency to think that resources are not available, or that people to whom work could be delegated are not sufficiently capable, or trained to cope, or that an activity will take longer if it is delegated. Clearly a person may not have resources but, if you think much more broadly than your subordinates, there are colleagues and even your boss to whom work can be delegated. Training subordinates to the level of capability to perform activities is a prerequisite to delegation. Generally, when trained, the delegates should not take any longer to perform the task than yourself.

The second side of the question is how activities are delegated to you. In the main you are receiving a fair proportion of your work instructions from other people; if this source of work is not managed well, then workloads can mount up and low priority work can multiply. The third question area is therefore concerned with how work comes to you and goes from you and the impact this has upon your time management.

The fourth question area 'How was the activity scheduled?' relates to your ability to plan your time. If thought through, many of your key performance goals are capable of being scheduled, as a broad framework, into your diaried activities. This planning ensures that each week or day has a balance of time allocated to 'A' priority activities. Other activities will arrive either at short notice or as interruptions; often it is these unscheduled activities that can upset even the most flexible of diaries. This is particularly the case when short notice activities are emergency 'A' priority activities. This question area is therefore concerned with how activities arise and their lead times and how this affects your time management.

Finally, the fifth question area 'How was the activity timed?' relates to how your time has been 'blocked' during the day and whether activities were done at the right time in the day. Different people work at different times during the day. Some people are very creative and productive in the morning, while others do not really get into their stride until three o'clock in the afternoon. Some people like to relax after lunch while others will have renewed energy. Each person will have their own time and productivity habits; time management needs to take these into account. Another aspect of this question is the amount of time that is allocated to an activity as a continuous block of time. Most people achieve more if they can start and finish an activity within a working period, of if they feel that they have made substantial progress within the work period. We believe that good time management should provide people with a continuous block of about 2 to 3 hours of 'A' priority time each day.

In summary, Key Time Question Assessment is very much concerned with how time is allocated within the day, how performance is affected by time, and whether work is done to the best advantage of an individual.

Let us return to Robert Ashworth and see what we can learn about Robert's time management from these question areas. Table 2.4 summarizes the key question

Table 2.4 Robert Ashworth's key time question evaluation

What was the purpose of the activity?	Who were the people in the activity?	How was the activity delegated?	How was the activity scheduled?	How was the activity timed?
1. *New Office Equipment meeting* This was a necessary meeting with a 'B' priority rating.	John Podmore, Robert Ashworth's boss. He is the right man and we will assume that the meeting was organized and team spirit was good.	This meeting probably was generated by Robert himself and he has been delegated the report. Does Robert control how much work he generates?	This was a scheduled meeting which used 45 minutes. This could have been reduced in time.	All other things being equal this is the wrong time to have an internal meeting. Assuming the opportunity, this meeting should have been timed for a different part of the day and a higher priority activity completed in its place.
2. *Correspondence with Secretary* This is a necessary activity particularly when it is used to organize the day. The activity did not achieve all its goals and probably it should have a higher priority.	Ann. Assuming that Robert and Ann got on well.	Robert could almost certainly have delegated more of his work to Ann. As a general rule an efficient secretary can manage far higher priority work and quantity of work. This also makes for better working relationships and sense of achievement.	This was a scheduled activity but more from expectation and habit than from a diaried event. Maybe Robert should schedule these early morning meetings with more purpose?	An early day schedule is always a good idea if it fits the workstyle of the two people. This activity could have been the first activity of the day and more time should have been allocated to it to ensure that high priority correspondence is completed.
3. *Micro-computer telephone call* This activity was not necessary for Robert. Although it was necessary to arrange the demonstration this could have been dealt with elsewhere.	Barry Cassidy the micro-computer salesman.	This activity should have been delegated to Ann or another person.	This was an unscheduled interruption. This could have been screened out by delegation.	This activity interfered with the work pattern of other activities.
4. *Design staff report* This is an essential 'A' priority activity.	Individual working.	No delegation.	This was not fully scheduled. It is necessary to complete the activity before a deadline but it appeared to be 'fitted in' around scheduled meetings.	This activity was not timed well. Robert should have allocated sufficient continuous time to the activity. Given Robert's style of work this time should be in the morning.

Table 2.4   cont'd

What was the purpose of the activity?	Who were the people in the activity?	How was the activity delegated?	How was the activity scheduled?	How was the activity timed?
5. *New Business telephone call* Necessary 'A' priority activity.	Robin Askins, New Business Development Manager.	No delegation.	Falls into (4) above.	Falls into (4) above.
6. *Design staff report* See 4 & 5 above.	See 4 & 5 above.	See 4 & 5 above.	See 4 & 5 above.	See 4 & 5 above.
7. *Pension Scheme interruption* Unnecessary 'C' priority activity. Although it was necessary information for Madeleine Montgomery this could have been delegated or screened.	Madeleine Montgomery, Personnel Officer. Madeleine tends to be impatient but well thought of.	No reason why Robert should be handling this. Madeleine could have referred to manuals. Ann could have screened this interruption very effectively.	Unscheduled interruption.	This activity interfered substantially with the 'A' priority design staff report and a continuous period of working.
8. *Personnel Committee meeting* Necessary 'B' priority activity that re-occurs at planned intervals.	Personnel committee. Necessary to have the right people and working spirit. Need organization and direction. Robert was chairman and meeting was good.	No delegation but work from this meeting could be delegated.	Scheduled meeting planned in advance. (Please note that no preparation time was scheduled.)	Bearing in mind the difficulty in bringing together groups of people, Robert probably had no alternative but to put this in 'A' priority time, but after lunch would have been much better.
9. *Lunch*	John Podmore.	No delegation.	Unscheduled meeting.	Valuable part of the day for developing contacts and people.
10. *General telephone calls* General calls have 'B' and 'C' priority ratings. Not necessary activities at this time.	Various people.	Delegate to Ann. As a general rule all the 'C' priority calls should be delegated and all calls screened for priority rating.	Unscheduled calls that were handled.	Calls should have been handled in low priority time at the end of the day.
11. *Prepare for admin meeting* Necessary support activity with 'B' priority rating.	Ann.	This activity should have been delegated early in the day so that relevant information could be collected. Lack of information interferes with preparation.	Unscheduled activity that should be scheduled well in advance.	From Robert's point of view committee meetings in the afternoon are fine but it did interfere with the 'A' priority design staff report.

Table 2.4 *cont'd*

What was the purpose of the activity?	Who were the people in the activity?	How was the activity delegated?	How was the activity scheduled?	How was the activity timed?
12. *Administration Committee meeting* Necessary 'B' priority activity that recurs on planned intervals.	Administration committee. Like personal committee meetings this needs planning and direction.	No delegation but work from meeting could be delegated.	Scheduled meetings planned well in advance.	From Robert's point of view this is the best time of day for this activity.
13. *Administration meeting de-brief* Necessary activity with 'B' priority rating but this was imposed by John Podmore.	John Podmore often requires a de-brief to keep himself informed.	Difficult to delegate this but an alternative means of keeping John Podmore informed would be desirable.	Unscheduled meeting at John's insistance.	This activity interfered with others. Although difficult to get out of it should have been reduced in time.
14. *Correspondence with Secretary* Necessary 'B' priority activity.	Ann. She likes to finish her day's work completely on time.	No delegation. Useful time to summarize the day and think about tomorrow and the future.	Scheduled activity.	About right in timing and duration.
15. *Return telephone calls* 'B' and 'C' priority activities.	Various people.	Many of these could be delegated or scheduled.	Unscheduled.	About right from Robert's point of view.
16. *Design staff report* See 4, 5 & 6 above.	—	—	—	—

responses against each of the main activity areas of the day. From the detailed assessment of the time report, using the Key Time Question Assessment technique, we are able to gain more substantial insight into Robert's time management problems. It is quite clear from the time report that Robert has a lot of discretion over how his time is used and also that he has sound working relationships. Both of these factors are sound foundation stones for good time management. Unfortunately Robert is not maximizing his opportunity. The Key Time Question Assessement indicates the following problem areas. See if you agree:

(1) Planning on a day-to-day basis is a key problem area. He does not plan time for 'A' priority activities but tends to fit them in around scheduled 'B' priority activities. Because of this, his 'A' priority time is broken and subject to interruption. This is the key reason why Robert has failed to achieve his

goals fully. Robert must plan for continuous 'A' priority time at the time of the day that suits him.

(2) Robert needs to delegate more work to his secretary. Much of the 'C' priority activities could have been effectively completed or screened by Ann. Robert should also devote more time to Ann and give a higher priority to his work with her.

(3) Robert does not protect his 'A' priority time. He allows visitors, telephone calls and all manner of interruptions and impositions. He tends also to plan 'B' priority activities into his 'A' priority time.

(4) Robert should manage his 'B' priority activities to take less time. Substantial gains in time could be made in this way.

(5) Robert should prepare for his meetings and ensure that these meetings are well organized, well planned and short. 'B' priority meetings should be in low priority time.

(6) Robert probably needs to manage his boss a little better. His boss tends to impose himself upon Robert and this interferes with Robert's time management.

In summary, Key Time Question Assessment provides us with an in-depth assessment of performance and time management. It shows key issues that need to be addressed if performance is to be improved.

Preferred day assessment

The idea of the preferred day assessment is both simple and important. We indicated earlier that people work at different paces at different times during the day. Some people prefer to arrive early at work and are most productive in the mornings, while others prefer the latter part of the day. Some people prefer to make their outside visits during the middle days of the working week so that Monday and Friday can always be used for office work. Some people prefer to work hard in the early part of a week, while others will not reach their highest productivity until the latter part of the week. Some people prefer a 12-hour working day while others will limit themselves to a 6½ hour contribution.

All of these various examples are indications that people have preferences for working in a particular way and at a particular time. Unless a person can accommodate these preferences into their weekly and daily schedule in a comfortable manner, then their performance will be substantially lower than their potential. Although a person has preferences, they do not have these at all costs. People are generally flexible: whenever a demand or circumstance arises which means that their preferences have to be submerged or compromised then they are usually willing to oblige. The idea of the Preferred Day is therefore a flexible one which will accommodate specific change but will return to the preference whenever the demand or circumstance has been accommodated.

Building on this idea of preference then, the various major categories of time in the day should be accommodated. These major categories of time are: 'A' priority activity time or 'A' time, secretary time, contingency time, and job planning time. A fuller explanation of 'A' time is in Chapter 8, pages 141–142; however secretary time, contingency time and job planning time need further explanation at this point.

Most people who lead an active working life have very little time to themselves. They are generally working with people, handling correspondence, in meetings, working on projects, handling work on time deadlines and so on. Whatever time they spend on thinking about their job and its future tends to be while travelling or in the evenings and at weekends. Basically reflection on work takes place when you are not working! Because most people are prepared to think about their job during their non-working time, then the need for job planning time *during* the work time is not necessary. The consequence is that people feel that time at work must be filled with activity and that *thinking* about your job is neither a legitimate use of time nor an activity.

'Job planning time' brings back to its rightful place the time you need during the working day to plan the job effectively. Another important use of 'job planning time' is the individual working time that we all need. If we have a job with substantial contact with people then time to oneself is important so that one can concentrate, not solely on job planning, but on any important objective in our job. 'Job planning time' is free time or mostly discretionary time; unless you plan to have a little 'A' priority 'job planning time' you will never be yourself and perform at a high rate.

Another important time in the day is 'contingency time'. All jobs have emergencies and features that require immediate attention as soon as they arrive. These are normal to every job and a contingency plan must be made prior to the emergency or immediate attention factor. A contingency period planned into each day is the way to make the day more productive and to protect the 'A' priority activity time. Contingency time is also when lower priority work is handled.

Another very important part of your day is the time allocated to your job planning with your secretary. Your secretary is an important member of your management team and, in the main, she can be used much more effectively. To keep your job and her job running smoothly you need to allocate a consistent time *each day* to job planning with your secretary. Normally the output of your job planning period becomes the input for your secretary time.

The final point on categories of time is that time in each category is best if it is *continuous*. A continuous block of 'A' priority activity time is more productive than the same quantity which is broken up. A continuous time of 'C' priority activity at the appropriate time of the day is more productive than the small interruptions of the day. With sound management of time, each person should aim to achieve three to four hours of continuous 'A' priority time in each day.

A typical *Preferred Day* for a manager is shown in Fig. 2.1. What this Preferred Day scheme shows is that as a preference (which will not always be possible) the manager will prefer to review his day and check it with his secretary as the first major activity. He has a preference for his highest productive period in the morning. He prefers to think about his job or spend time alone after this 'A' priority work. In the late afternoon, when he is least productive, he will schedule lower priority work. So that he can deal with emergencies and any matters that require his immediate attention — and in particular 'A' priority emergencies — he provides contingency time by extending his 'A' time into the afternoon.

As a general point it is interesting to note the popularity of 'A' time which I introduced in my previous book *Time for Success?*. In all the cases where it has been introduced, either as a corporate policy or as an individual working technique, its ability to stabilize the working day and lead to increase performance is very high. The concept has been adapted in many ways. Many organizations have a policy of a minimum of two hours' 'A' time each day for directors and senior managers. In these cases each director is allowed only to schedule top priority meetings or, if working at their desks, then no interruptions are allowed. Individual managers have introduced various ideas of 'A' time. Some allocate three hours a day in one slot while others allocate hourly slots throughout the day. Some allocate two full days a week and there are others who allocate three half days per week. In all cases where the concept has been used effectively the users report back that their time spent on 'A' priority activities has increased from about 30% to between 50% and 60%. It is important to note that what the manager controls is the 'A' time rather than the whole day. These 'A' time slots are pencilled in the diary for about four weeks ahead and both the manager and secretary ensure that only 'A' priority work enters the 'A' priority time. All other lower priority work is allocated to the remaining lower priority time slots. Try the technique and you'll see immediate benefits. Let us now return to Robert Ashworth's preferred day assessment.

Let us assume that the Preferred Day we have indicated above is that of Robert Ashworth. How is he meeting his own productivity cycle? If you refer back to Fig. 2.1 which shows Robert's day schedule and his priority ratings, we can make a number of observations.

(1) His use of secretary time is good.
(2) Within his day he has allocated to 'A', 'B' and 'C' priority activities, 14, 58 and 28% of his time respectively. As we have noted previously, this is not good. Within his 'A' priority time, which is between activities 3 and 8 inclusive, only 35% of that period is used for 'A' priority activities. To mitigate this factor, Robert has been able to allocate his time in a continuous block. As a general rule Robert is now matching his day to his preferences.
(3) Robert has job planning time within his day.

From these few observations we can see that Robert has room for improvement.

In summary, Preferred Day Assessment is a technique to match the preference of a person to their management of their performance and time. Unless there is a fair match between the high productivity period of a person's preferred 'A' priority time and the 'A' priority activities of the day, then there will be a tendency to underperform.

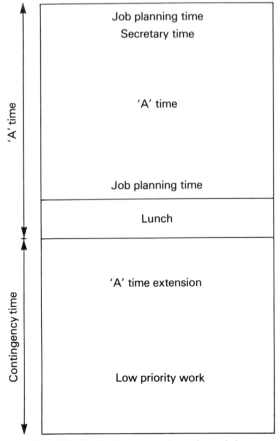

Fig. 2.1   Typical manager's preferred day

The four techniques

The four techniques of time report assessment are designed to allow different levels of insight into your performance and time management problems. Taken together they provide a very clear, in-depth picture of a person's underlying pattern of time use and performance. When the four techniques have been used then the key results can be assessed and the person's *Time Report Assessment* written. Let us consider the case example of Robert's Time Report Assessment.

CASE EXAMPLE: ROBERT ASHWORTH'S TIME REPORT — ASSESSMENT AND PERSONAL STRATEGY

Robert tends to under-achieve on his 'A' priority activities. This is mainly because he does not plan for and allocate sufficient time to his 'A' priority activities, does not carry out his 'A' priority activities in his most productive part of the day, and does not allow himself the opportunity to work *continuously* on his 'A' priority activities. Much of this additional time could be found by planning his 'B' priority activities into less productive parts of the day and making strong efforts to reduce the time allocated to these activities. Also by delegation, deferring or quickly handling his 'C' priority activities, Robert can find additional productive time. The major user of Robert's time is meetings which are generally 'B' priority activities. Robert should pay particular attention to these in terms of their time usage. These meetings should be well prepared, well planned, well organized and short. He should avoid scheduling large meetings close to each other.

Robert needs to delegate more work to his subordinates and also back to his boss. In particular he should pay more attention to his work with his secretary. The time he allocates to her should be increased and it should be given an 'A' priority rating. His secretary should handle many of the 'C' priority activities and screen out telephone calls and interruptions. She should also be briefed to protect Robert's 'A' priority time.

Robert could try to manage his boss more effectively and to assert his rights with his boss for better time management.

Robert should plan his day so that his preferences are matched to his work pattern. He needs a 'quiet time' to reflect and plan, and a 'buffer time' to allow for emergencies.

Robert needs to improve his workflow and output. His personal organization could be improved and his work with his secretary could improve this aspect substantially. Robert should also consider training in reading and writing skills.

Robert has a key strength in his working relationships with people, but he should assert his views more consistently.

Based upon the above points, these are the main factors in Robert's personal strategy for improvement:

(1) Improve planning of time and match preference to work pattern.
(2) Plan and allocate more time to 'A' priority activities.
(3) Allocate job planning time.
(4) Reduce 'B' priority activity time.
(5) Delegate, defer, handle quickly, screen 'C' priority activities.
(6) Substantially improve meetings management.
(7) Delegate.
(8) Manage the boss.
(9) Work better with secretary.
(10) Screen telephone calls and visitors.
(11) More assertion.
(12) Improve personal workspace organization.
(13) Train in reading and writing.

From Robert Ashworth's personal strategy, we can see the potential for substantial improvement in time and for substantial improvement in performance. None of the points in this personal strategy is a major issue for Robert and a little more thought and organization would realize his potential. It is clearly difficult to estimate how such time could be saved and how many more 'A' priority performance goals could be introduced into Robert's work. From working through the Robert Ashworth example, we could probably set a goal of finding another *effective* quarter of a day for Robert with a substantial improvement in performance.

3

Writing your improvement plan

In Chapter 1 we established how to assess your work style and in Chapter 2 how to assess your performance and time management. As we have mentioned previously, these are the 'strategy' and 'tactics' respectively, of your performance improvement. In this chapter we bring the assessments together and guide you through how you can write your own individual improvement plan. When you have identified your areas for improvement you can read the remaining chapters in this book which show you how you can achieve these improvements.

Writing your improvement plan is a creative process which requires you to look for general patterns of your behaviour as well as the specific improvement points. The actual process you follow is quite systematic. The case example of Keith Barclay demonstrates how Keith interprets his assessments.

CASE EXAMPLE: KEITH BARCLAY

Keith has a strong tendency towards Type 'A' behaviour. His score on the Work Behaviour Worksheet was 1.8 and when he reviewed the factors which were his strongest Type 'A' factors he found the following:

Factor 1: For me success depends upon driving hard for results. I set my own goals and I drive hard to achieve on time.

Factor 2: I often do many things at the same time.

Factor 4: I am seen as very confident and self-assured. I believe this is an important part of my personality.

Factor 9: I have difficulty in relaxing and even when I do I sometimes feel guilty.

Factor 10: I often feel the presence of time and deadlines.

Clearly Keith is in a hurry! He has very strong drives to achieve and his self-image is as an achiever. Bearing in mind the action points for Type 'A' behaviour (page 00) then the key areas for improvement are normally concerned with WORK CONTROL, DELEGATION, ALLOWING THE CONTRIBUTION OF THE WORK TEAM and PLANNING.

Keith had mixed attitudes towards job planning. His score on the Planning Attitude Worksheet was 3.3 and in many respects Keith was still seeking the benefits of planning. When he reviewed his strongest negative and positive factors he found:

Negative

Factor 1: I find that planning restricts freedom of choice and action.

Factor 3: Planning does not suit my style of work.

Factor 4: Planning cannot cope with the day-to-day pressures and changes.

Positive

Factor 1: I believe I need to plan in my job and my achievements depend upon my planning capability.

Factor 5: Planning saves time overall but I need to invest time in my planning at the beginning.

Keith has the classic dilemma. Whereas he feels that planning is necessary for his job he also feels that planning restricts his style of working and changes his time planning from 'doing' to 'thinking'. Referring to the golden rules on planning (page 8) then Keith's main improvements lie in the areas of ESTABLISHING COMMITMENT IN PLANNING, ADOPTING A FLEXIBLE PLANNING SYSTEM and ESTABLISHING THE LINK BETWEEN LONG TERM AND SHORT TERM PLANNING.

Keith is not a procrastinator. On his Procrastination Worksheet he had a score of 3.7. When he reviewed his strengths and weaknesses on the worksheet he found:

Strengths

Factor 2: I am always confident that I will be able to produce a good job.

Factor 5: I start jobs very easily and naturally.

Factor 8: I never delay a job because of the fear of making a mistake.

Weaknesses

Factor 3: I am often guilty of delaying putting a sound plan into action.

Factor 9: When I miss a deadline it's normally because I have delayed on the job.

Here again Keith faces his dilemma on planning. His confident and self-assured work behaviour naturally leads him to start early on jobs, particularly if they are short in duration but possibly when a job is of a longer term nature then delay may occur and if one deadline is missed then it could be attributable to a late start. The action points for the procrastinator (page 00) highlight that Keith needs to be aware of his procrastination on large jobs of a long-term nature and that he needs to break these down into smaller work parcels (i.e. plan) and 'DO IT NOW!' on the smaller work parcel. Bearing in mind that Keith is a Type 'A', he should also note that he is likely to be a *Rebel* type procrastinator which normally means he will arrange his work close to the deadline rather than bring it forward from the deadline. Keith's areas of improvement are: PLAN AND START LARGE JOBS EARLY and DO IT NOW!

Keith has very little stress at work and he has an optimum level of stress that stimulates his work performance. His score was 4.0. When he reviewed his factors that could account for his stress he found:

Factor 6: I am not clear on my objectives nor what is expected of me by my boss.

Factor 7: I often have to deal with conflicts in demands and I find this leads to pressure.

Factor 8: I don't feel involved in decisions and my boss is very much the autocrat.

Keith has the typical job clarity and boss relationship stress. It is likely that Keith and his boss are very similar Type 'A's. Participation and communication are low and job planning is short term. Essentially Keith is not clear on his objectives and the probable reason for this is that neither Keith nor his boss have allocated the time to think through both their objectives and to plan to involve others in their job planning.

Bring all these improvement areas together, Keith's improvement plan for the 'strategy' of his work style is:

(i) More effective work controls.
(ii) More effective delegation.
(iii) Better team management.
(iv) Relaxing with his achievements to date.
(v) Establishing a commitment to job planning.
(vi) Devising a flexible planning system for his job.
(vii) Think long-term and short-term.

(viii) Plan and start larger or long jobs early.
(ix) Do it now!
(x) Sit down with boss and clarify job objectives.
(xi) Manage his boss more effectively.

Performance plan

Let us now turn to Keith's more detailed assessment of his performance and time management based upon the four assessment technique described. Don't forget these are Keith's 'tactics' for his everyday time management.

PERFORMANCE ASSESSMENT

After assessing three days of his time log Keith found he had very typical improvement areas. The minority of his time was spent on his top priority work and the majority on his lower priority work. This had meant that some important work had progressed but not as much as Keith had hoped. When he assessed his priorities and the time spent, Keith found he could have easily boosted his 'A' time to 50% from 30% by using the 'A' time technique and controlling his lower priority work ahead by four weeks.

TIME CATEGORY ASSESSMENT

Keith found that 55% of his time was spent in meeting with an additional 18% spent on the telephone. Of the time spent in meetings, he found that more than half were under his direct control and management. Keith estimated that by his own 'crisper' management of meetings and more basic skills in handling the telephone, and more effective use secretary, he could save about 20% of this time spent in a typical day.

KEY TIME QUESTION ASSESSMENT

Keith's evaluation tended to confirm the other assessments. He needed to plan his 'A' time on a continuous pattern so that it suited his preferences for working. He needed to delegate more work to his subordinates and secretary and he also needs to control the work coming to him from his boss.

PREFERRED DAY ASSESSMENT

From this assessment Keith found he had to establish the day-to-day discipline of planning his work with his secretary and also establishing 'job planning time' in order to plan his work on a day-to-day basis. As Keith found in previous assessments this 'A' time needed to be controlled for his 'A' priority work.

Collecting together these assessments, Keith's time report read as follows:

  (i) Increase 'A' time from 30% to 50% by controlling his lower priority work.

  (ii) Save 20% more time by 'crisper' meetings and handling the telephone, and more effective use of his secretary.

  (iii) Plan to have continuous time on his 'A' priority work.

  (iv) Delegate more to his subordinates and secretary.

  (v) Manage delegation from his boss.

  (vi) Concentrate on goals, planning, priorities and diary control.

  (vii) Improve his team skills particularly in the areas of developing team spirit and team conflict resolution.

  (viii) Work on 'crisper' meetings management, through agenda planning and chairmanship.

  (ix) Give higher priority to his secretary to handle interruptions and routine work.

  (x) Establish 'job planning time'.

Final plan

Keith's final plan for improvement consists of his plan for work style and his plan for performance and time management. Naturally there is overlap between these two plans because inevitable 'strategy' and 'tactics' are interwoven. Consolidating the two plans for Keith produces his final improvement plan. This reads as follows:

  (1) More effective work control by increasing 'A' time from 30% to 50%. To achieve this I need to control my lower priority work effectively, ahead.

  (2) Save 20% of time by 'crisper' meetings and handling the telephone, and more effective use of my secretary.

  (3) More effective work control by planning for *continuous* time on my 'A' priority work.

  (4) Develop better delegation skills and delegate more to my subordinates and secretary.

  (5) Sit down with my boss and clarify my job objectives. Discuss our time management and discuss how my boss should delegate work to me.

  (6) Develop a flexible job planning system suitable for me and stay committed to it. Concentrate on objectives, planning and priorities and diary control. 'Think' and 'Do' long-term as well as short-term.

  (7) Develop team skills, particularly in the areas of team spirit and resolving team conflict.

  (8) Work on 'crisper' meetings by improving on agenda planning and chairmanship.

  (9) Give higher priority to my secretary and our joint job-planning. Let my secretary handle interruptions and all routine work.

  (10) Establish 'job planning time' for myself so that I can plan my job.

  (11) Plan and start large jobs or long jobs early.

  (12) *Do it now!* and Relax!

To establish your improvement plan, follow the worksheets on pages 32–35. It is recommended that three days should be the basis of your time log because this gives a more consistent pattern of activity. You may prefer however to do a 1-day time log. Although this will not give you a full insight into your time management, I have found from experience that in one day, if the day is chosen well, your time management pattern still emerges with careful interpretation.

Worksheet 3.1   Work behaviour

Write down your score from your Work Behaviour worksheet (Worksheet 1.1).

SCORE: _____   TYPE 'A' or 'B': _____

Write down the factors that are your strongest factors for your type. (Strong factors mean scores of 1 and 2 for Type 'A' and scores of 4 and 5 for Type 'B')

FACTOR:

FACTOR:

FACTOR:

FACTOR:

FACTOR:

FACTOR:

Based on your interpretation of the above factors and your review of the action points on page 4, what are your key areas for improvement?

IMPROVEMENT AREA 1:

IMPROVEMENT AREA 2:

IMPROVEMENT AREA 3:

Worksheet 3.2   Planning attitude

Write down your score from your Planning Attitude worksheet (Worksheet 1.2).

SCORE: _____   POSTIVE or NEGATIVE: _____

Write down your most positive attitudes and your most negative attitudes.

POSITIVE ATTITUDE:

POSITIVE ATTITUDE:

POSITIVE ATTITUDE:

NEGATIVE ATTITUDE:

NEGATIVE ATTITUDE:

NEGATIVE ATTITUDE:

Based on your interpretation of your attitudes above and golden rules and difficulties in planning on page 8, what are your key areas for attitude improvement and skill development?

IMPROVEMENT AREA 1:

IMPROVEMENT AREA 2:

IMPROVEMENT AREA 3:

Worksheet 3.3   Procrastination

Write down your score from your Procrastination worksheet (Worksheet 1.3).

SCORE: _____   DO YOU PROCRASTINATE? _____

Write down your strength and weaknesses from the factors on the worksheet.

STRONG FACTOR:

STRONG FACTOR:

STRONG FACTOR:

WEAK FACTOR:

WEAK FACTOR:

WEAK FACTOR:

When you compare your strength and weaknesses what do you find? Refer to the action points for procrastination on page 11 and identify your areas for improvement and how you intend to achieve your improvement.

IMPROVEMENT AREA 1:

IMPROVEMENT AREA 2:

IMPROVEMENT AREA 3:

Worksheet 3.4   Work stress

Write down your score from your Work Stress worksheet (Worksheet 1.4).

SCORE: _____   ARE YOU STRESSED? _____

By referring to the factors, write down the areas that are the sources of your work stress.

STRESS SOURCE 1:

STRESS SOURCE 2:

STRESS SOURCE 3:

STRESS SOURCE 4:

STRESS SOURCE 5:

Are there any common themes that run through your sources of stress, e.g. people, workload, job clarity? (Refer to pages 13–14 if you wish to refresh your memory.) Refer to the action points for work stress on page 14 and note your key areas for improvement.

IMPROVEMENT AREA 1:

IMPROVEMENT AREA 2:

IMPROVEMENT AREA 3:

Worksheet 3.5 Your work style improvement plan

Review all your improvement areas from the previous worksheets and bring these together into an overall plan. Remove any overlaps and consolidate into a single listing of key improvement areas.

MY IMPROVEMENT PLAN IS:

(1)

(2)

(3)

(4)

(5)

(6)

(7)

(8)

(9)

(10)

Worksheet 3.6 Time log briefing

This worksheet is a briefing for Worksheet 3.7 that follows.
   Worksheet 3.7 is quite straightforward but it might be useful if we highlight a few key points.

(1) At the *beginning* of each of your chosen days, make a note about what is the most important goal you need to achieve (or substantially progress) on that day. Use the space 'MAIN GOAL OF THE DAY'. At the *end* of your chosen days, make a tick against all those activities that were associated with this main goal.

(2) As you progress through each day, log the activities of the day. Description of the activities may be very brief, e.g. meetings; telephoning; individual work on major projects; correspondence; reading report; writing report; business travelling. A note on typical activity categories is at the end of this worksheet. Make a note also of the key people involved in the activity and the general level of team spirit. Log the start and finish times at the end of the day and calculate the percentage of total time spent on each activity.

(3) As you progress through each day, note against each activity the priority rating. The note on priority ratings at the end of this worksheet will give you an idea of the priority system we use in time management.

(4) As you progress through each day, make a judgement about how much time could have been saved on the activity. Clearly you cannot be precise about this time saving but make a rough assessment of potential savings if you or your colleagues had managed time more effectively. For example, if a meeting you attended was poorly chaired and people were inadequately prepared then estimate how much time could have been saved if these two factors had been corrected. You will find that as you go through the day you will see many opportunities for time saving. Please note which opportunities you identify.

(5) As you progress through each day, assess whether the activity you are working on could have been delegated to a member of your team. Please note any particular problems you might have in delegating this task (e.g. lack of resources, personnel too inexperienced, and so on).

(6) As you progress through each day, take note of any telephone interruptions or unscheduled visits. If you don't log these fully then make a fair estimate at the end of the day of the number and time spent on interruptions.

Note on Priority Ratings

'A' Priority: Very important work by which you are measured in your job. Generally this work has to be completed on time and any delay has to be avoided. 'A' Priority work is top priority work.

'B' Priority: Less important work that is related to your job but generally the work can be delayed if necessary and delay would not have high consequences.

'C' Priority: Non-important work which does not affect your job measurement directly and generally this work can be delayed, deferred, scrapped, screened out, or delegated to assistants. 'C' Priority work is your lowest priority work.

'X' Priority: This refers to work that arises as an immediate demand, emergency or crisis and which requires handling by you. 'X' priority work interrupts your day and requires some sort of action on your part. The sort of action you give it will be 'A B C' priority as above. Therefore:
   'AX': very important immediate action by you.
   'BX': less important action which can be delayed slightly or delegated.
   'CX': non-important and should be delegated.

Note on Activities Categories

Activities for managers tend to fall into a few general categories:

(1) Preparation for meetings
(2) Scheduled meetings
(3) Unscheduled or informal meetings
(4) Making and receiving telephone calls
(5) Individual work on projects
(6) Individual work on general admin/correspondence
(7) Working with your secretary
(8) Reading reports, trade journals, magazines
(9) Writing reports
(10) Business travelling
(11) Planning and thinking about your job
(12) Free time

NOTE: Meetings can range from informal meetings for supervisory staff through to annual board meetings.

TIME LOG EVALUATION

In preparation for the following assessment worksheet you will find it convenient if you consolidate your three time logs into one set of evaluations. Follow these steps.

Step 1: For the three days calculate the total percentage of time spent on your main goal activities.

Step 2: For the three days calculate the total percentage of time spent on each of the 'A B C X' priorities. Please note that your main goal activities are a sub-set of your 'A' priorities.

Step 3: For the three days calculate the total percentage of time spent in your categories of activities.

Step 4: For the three days calculate the total percentage of time that could have been saved. Please note what opportunity you had for saving time.

Step 5: For the three days calculate the total percentage of time that could have been saved through delegation. Please note any reasons why you could not have delegated.

Worksheet 3.7(a)   Day one time log

Main goal(s) of the day: (please specify)
(i)

(ii)

Sequence	Start and finish time	Activity and people description	Time taken (minutes)	% of the total day	A B C X priority (%)	Was this a main goal activity?	Estimate of time saving on this activity. How?	Could this activity be delegated? Why not?
1								
2								
3								
4								
5								
6								
7								
8								
9								
10								
11								
12								
13								
14								
15								
16								
17								
18								
19								
20								
21								
22								
23								
				A				
				B				
		Totals		C				
				X		%	%	%

Worksheet 3.7(b) Day two time log

Main goal(s) of the day: (please specify)
 (i)

(ii)

Sequence	Start and finish time	Activity and people description	Time taken (minutes)	% of the total day	A B C X priority (%)	Was this a main goal activity?	Estimate of time saving on this activity. How?	Could this activity be delegated? Why not?
1								
2								
3								
4								
5								
6								
7								
8								
9								
10								
11								
12								
13								
14								
15								
16								
17								
18								
19								
20								
21								
22								
23								
Totals					A B C X		%	%	%

Worksheet 3.7(c)   Day three time log

Main goal(s) of the day: (please specify)
  (i)

(ii)

Sequence	Start and finish time	Activity and people description	Time taken (minutes)	% of the total day	A B C X priority (%)	Was this a main goal activity?	Estimate of time saving on this activity. How?	Could this activity be delegated? Why not?
1								
2								
3								
4								
5								
6								
7								
8								
9								
10								
11								
12								
13								
14								
15								
16								
17								
18								
19								
20								
21								
22								
23								
Totals					A B C X	%	%	%

Worksheet 3.8   Performance assessment

Refer to your time logs and assess whether your main goals of each day were achieved or substantially progressed during the day.

    (i) Did you achieve your goals?

    (ii) How much time did you spend on these goals?

    (iii) Was this enough?

    (iv) What was the longest period of time you spent on your main goals? Was this enough?

    (v) Was your work on your main goals continuous or was it broke by other activities?

    (vi) If your work on main goals was broken, what was the priority of the work that broke into your main goal activity?

General Summary

What have you learnt about your performance?

Worksheet 3.9   Time category assessment

Refer to your time logs and write down the main categories of your activity and their percentage of time.

		% Time	% Time saved potential
Category	1		
	2		
	3		
	4		
	5		
	6		
	7		
	8		

Note the % time saving potential against each activity and note the main categories where you can save time.

Category	1
	2
	3
	4
	5

General Summary

What have you learnt about your present use of time?

Worksheet 3.10   Key time question assessment

Key time question assessment is a detailed evaluation of how you performed and how time was used to achieve this performance.

It is preferable that you review *all* your activities over the 3-day time log. Alternatively you may review those activities which are 'A' priority and those which used a large amount of time but were 'B' or 'C' priority.

Refer to the activities on your time logs and for each activity ask the following questions. Please use the note pages overleaf for your working notes.

For each activity:

Questions: *What was the purpose of this activity?* Was it necessary? Could the time used have been better spent? Did this activity have the correct priority rating?

Questions: *Who were the people in this activity?* Were they the right people to achieve its purpose? Was the team well organized and well directed? Was the team spirit good?

Questions: *How was the activity delegated?* Could you have delegated this activity? Was the activity delegated to you? What impact did this delegation (either by you or to you) have on your time management of the day?

Questions: *How was the activity scheduled?* Did this activity arrive at short notice? Why? Was the activity a planned activity arranged in advance? Could you have planned this activity? Was the activity an interruption to the day?

Questions: *How was the activity timed?* Was this activity conducted at the right time of the day? Did this activity break into an 'A' priority activity?

After making your working notes, examine them and see if you can find any consistent patterns that throw light on any problem areas you might have. These are your improvement areas.

My Improvement Areas are:

IMPROVEMENT AREA 1:

IMPROVEMENT AREA 2:

IMPROVEMENT AREA 3:

IMPROVEMENT AREA 4:

IMPROVEMENT AREA 5:

KEY TIME QUESTION ASSESSMENT — Working Notes

Worksheet 3.11   Preferred day assessment

This worksheet is designed to show whether there is a 'match' between your own productivity cycle and the activities of the day. It will also highlight whether you have a structure to your day.
   What are your preferences for your day?

(1) Between what hours of the day are you at your best?

   HOURS: from _____ to _____

(2) Between what hours of the day are you at your worst?

   HOURS: from _____ to _____

(3) Do you have high or low productivity after lunch?
   If it is low, how long does this last for?

   _____ hours

(4) Would you prefer to have a daily job planning meeting with your secretary? If so what time or times would this be best arranged for?

   Best time(s):

(5) Would you prefer to have a daily job planning meeting with YOURSELF? If so what time or times should this be arranged for?

   Best time(s):

(6) Would you prefer to have a 'buffer' in your day so that you can cope with any urgent or emergency activity that arrives on the day? How would you provide this 'buffer' time?

(7) Refer to the example and diagram on pages 26—7 and draw your preferred day. Include in your diagram: secretary time, 'A' priority time, contingency time, job planning time and low priority work time.
   Draw your diagram here:

(leave 16 lines)

(8) Now that you have an insight into your preferred day, refer back to your time logs and assess whether the days in your time log 'matched' your preferred day.

   (i) Did your 'A' priority activities match your 'A' priority time?

   (ii) How about your low priority work. Did it match your low priority time?

(iii) Did you have secretary time, job planning time and contingency time in your time logs? If not, why not? If yes, did they match your preferred day?

(9) Bearing in mind that your preferred day is a PREFERENCE and that you cannot always exercise these preferences, what insights do you now have on the structure of your working day?

Note your insights:

(10) Note your action points for your preferred day:

Action Point 1

2

3

4

Worksheet 3.12   Your performance and time management improvement plan

Review all your improvement areas and action points on the Worksheets 3.7—3.11 and bring these together into an overall plan. Remove any overlaps and consolidate into a single listing of key improvement areas.

MY IMPROVEMENT PLAN IS:

(1)

(2)

(3)

(4)

(5)

(6)

(7)

(8)

(9)

(10)

(11)

(12)

Worksheet 3.13   Your final improvement plan

Study your improvement plans on Worksheets 3.5 and 3.12 and consolidate them into your final plan.

My Improvement Plan is:

(1)

(2)

(3)

(4)

(5)

(6)

(7)

(8)

(9)

(10)

(11)

(12)

Author's request

I am conducting a number of studies in time management and performance improvement for managers. One study is concerned with establishing which are the most common areas of improvement that managers identify for themselves.

I would appreciate it if you would forward to me a copy of your final improvement plan. If it is possible please also send me a copy of your time logs. There is no need to identify yourself so your plan remains fully confidential to you; however, I would appreciate it if you could provide the following information when you send your final plan to me:

Company products or services:

Company size by turnover:

Your seniority in the company: (senior/middle/junior management)

Your function: (e.g. production, marketing, research, etc.)

Your number of *direct* reportees:

Is your job a *line* or *staff* function?

Do you have a secretary?

Please forward to: James Noon
Managing Director
Business Time/System
Knightway House
20 Soho Square
London W1V 6DT

4
Managing people

The last three chapters have been concerned with the evaluation of your performance and time management. From this evaluation you will now have a clearer idea on the areas which are important to you. Remember your IMPROVEMENT PLAN (page 36) is personal to you. On your IMPROVEMENT PLAN it is likely that a number of improvement areas are concerned with people around you in your working situation.

All people you work with have an impact on how you manage your performance and time. For example a good boss, who gives you clear objectives and priorities, helps you to focus your energy and resist the natural bad habit of giving preference to working on low priority tasks. In this example your time is being managed solely for top performance. Good teamwork, well organized meetings, effective delegation and well managed 'A' time are all examples of how other people have an impact on your time. Don't forget also that you are having an impact on how other people are able to manage their time and performance!

How people work together to achieve success is critical to the organization: this is self-evident. However, what is not self-evident is that a 'common performance standard' of how people wish to manage their time is also critical to the success of the organization. A key question for any working team is HOW DO WE HELP OR HINDER THE TEAM'S TIME MANAGEMENT? Addressing this question and establishing a code of practice or method of working is the first step towards a common standard of performance for the team and the individuals in the team. Without a common performance standard it is more difficult for any individual team members to manage their own time and performance at the highest standards. From my experience, when teams establish a common standard of time management, the consistent improvement in time saved is high, approaching 20% on the previous time use, and the output of the team increases accordingly.

In this chapter we will develop the key areas for improving your use of time through and with people, both in terms of how they impact upon you and how you impact upon them. The key areas for consideration are: LEADERSHIP DEVELOPMENT; TEAMWORK; DEVELOPMENT; DELEGATION; PERFORMANCE IMPROVEMENT PLANNING.

Leadership development

Much of what you want to achieve depends upon the cooperation and efforts of others. The ability to lead a team and to manage its efforts and the ability to contribute to the teams of other managers are essential attributes of successful personal performance and time management. In this section we will focus on the key ideas of *leadership*.

Part of the story of leadership, but certainly not the whole story, is the idea that successful leaders have a special sort of personality that separates them from other people. From my knowledge and experience of successful managers and management development, there does appear to be a series of factors that make up the leadership personality. Clearly, not all successful leaders will have high ratings on all factors but, taken as a whole, the factors will form the basis of the person's leadership personality. The factors I believe to be the most relevant are:

(1) *The Planning Factor*: The ability to organize and plan people, resources and time, plus the ability to plan and organize yourself.
(2) *The Doing Factor*: The drive to achieve goals and the drive for action.
(3) *The Visionary Factor*: The ability to create and pursue a vision of the future, and to seek and take opportunities that arise within that vision.
(4) *The Influencing Factor*: The ability to communicate with other people by various means, plus the ability to influence and persuade other people about your ideas and decisions.
(5) *The People Factor*: The sensitivity to understand people and their needs and abilities, and the ability to exercise social skills in many different social situations.
(6) *The Stability Factor*: The ability to maintain emotional stability and resilience, and to show honesty and integrity. Self-awareness of one's own strengths and weaknesses is a key component of this factor.
(7) *The Hard Work Factor*: The natural ability to be enthusiastic about work, and to maintain this enthusiasm over long hours and in different situations.
(8) *The Ideas Factor*: The natural expression of ideas, creativity and imagination, and the ability to bring new light to problems and new ways forward.
(9) *The Risk Taking Factor*: The ability to accept, seek and adapt to change, and to make risk decisions in the face of the uncertainty of change and the future.

Even leaders with very high attributes on all the key factors listed above are not necessarily the best leaders for all situations. Different combinations of leadership factors will make some people more suitable in some situations and less suitable in other situations. Also, to be successful as a leader, you need specialised knowledge or professional knowledge which the situation itself might demand. For example, leadership of an engineering project team requires a professional knowledge of the type of engineering used by the team. It is also probable that the exercise of leadership can be impeded by a lack of authority in the situation. The authority of rank or position will act to reinforce a person's leadership or it will impair it. For example, many younger managers who have high leadership ability and specialised knowledge of the situation, may still be frustrated by their more senior managers who have higher authority and more power.

The factors highlighted above are the factors which form the basis of the leadership personality and which will combine to meet a range of leadership situations, but what are the duties and tasks of the leader? Professor John Adair, an authority on the subject, considers that the leader has eight functions of leadership. He describes these as: defining the task; planning; briefing; controlling; evaluating; motivating; organizing; setting an example. In brief, this is what Professor John Adair means by these functions:

Defining the Task is a vital leadership function that helps to ensure that the group achieves a common goal. Without defining the task and communicating it to the group members, the knowledge and skills of the group as a whole cannot be harnessed effectively.

Planning, a function we stress heavily in this book, is the ability to translate the objectives (derived from defining the task) into action plans for the group to work upon. Planning in a team means allowing the team to contribute to the plan through their ideas and knowledge. Group planning is an essential part of the process of involving everybody in the objective and the activities that will lead to it.

Briefing follows on from planning. When the plans have been fully developed to a stage appropriate to the situation, and the team are fully involved, then it is important to brief the whole team on the various jobs and targets that the members of the team will pursue. Briefing the team helps to create the right atmosphere and continuing teamwork.

Controlling the work of others as the plan unfolds is a key function of the leader. Control does not just mean monitoring what is being done but also working hard to maintain control and leadership in a quiet and restrained manner, combined with firm intentions on achieving the task. The balance between interfering in the work of the group and the need to maintain direction is a critical balance of a leader's control. The most effective control is when the team believes that it has controlled itself.

Evaluating situations and people is a continuous function of the leader. The leader must be constantly thinking forward, while the team is working, in order to assess situations and actions and to think through the consequences that might arise. As the work progresses, the contributions of individuals will vary and these need to be evaluated in terms of their impact upon the objectives.

Motivating the team under all conditions is a vital function. Motivation means ensuring that individuals and the team are maintaining momentum and moving towards the objectives. The ability to provide each team member with a specific motivation is very important, and these must combine for the team as a whole. The motivation can come in many forms: achievement; recognition; job interest; responsibility; advancement; money; status; condition; and good working relationships.

Organizing is another continuous function. Teams need a structure within which they can work; within a large team, there may be smaller groups that need to form sub-teams. Each of these smaller teams will require a team leader. As the organization develops, all the relationships will have to be maintained and kept healthy through good communications and leadership. As teams grow in size, working groups of between five and 15 members will develop. This means that delegation then becomes imperative and the *personal* organization of the leader becomes another key factor in maintaining the whole team organization.

Finally, the function of *Setting An Example* is critical. Sometimes the good example can be unnoticed but the bad example can be immediately detrimental. Leadership from the front is an old and well-established concept, but the basic principle remains the same now — even though this example is now more likely to be symbolic rather than physical. Setting an example means 'doing' or 'being' what you require in others.

LEADERSHIP WORKSHEETS

The two worksheets below are designed to show your strengths and weaknesses on leadership personality and managing the process of leadership.

Worksheet 4.1 Leadership personality

Consider the factors below and circle a number that most closely represents your view of yourself *as your team see you*. Remember that your leadership capability will also depend upon your specific working situation and the authority you have in that situation. Because of these two factors the worksheet can act only as a guide to your basic skills in managing the process of leadership and in developing a more appropriate leadership personality. This guide is for your personal use so be honest with yourself.

(1) I am very conscious of the need to plan the work of my team and to demonstrate to the team my personal skills in planning my work.	1 2 3 4 5	I normally don't think about planning the work of my team and probably my team would agree that I am not a good planner.
(2) My team definitely see me as a manager who drives hard for results by action and quick, considered decisions.	1 2 3 4 5	I normally don't demonstrate to my team that I drive for results and probably they would agree that I am prone to be indecisive.
(3) I firmly believe that I have a vision of the future and I have a strategy to position myself and my team in that future. I have communicated my vision to the team.	1 2 3 4 5	I normally don't spend enough time thinking about the future and I take opportunities as they arise. My team have little awareness of what I think the future will be.
(4) I spend a lot of time ensuring that I communicate well with my team and generally I can influence others to think seriously about my ideas and decisions.	1 2 3 4 5	I think I am particularly weak at communicating with my team and on many occasions I have had to argue strongly for my ideas and decisions.
(5) My top priority is to involve my team in decision making and I am generally seen as being sensitive to other's needs, and confident in social situations.	1 2 3 4 5	My team often state that they are not involved in decisions nor that I take into account their needs.
(6) Even under stress I maintain a level head and even temper. I am seen as very consistent in my behaviour. Whatever the situation I rely heavily upon analysing the facts and remaining fair to people.	1 2 3 4 5	When I am under stress I tend to change my mind and to beome impatient with my team. My team would probably agree that I am not consistent, and prone to moods.
(7) I believe that my stamina for hard and continuous work is very high. I am always enthusiastic about my work even in very difficult situations.	1 2 3 4 5	My stamina for hard and continuous work is probably average. I am fairly consistent in my enthusiasm but it does falter on too many occasions.
(8) I have a strong and natural creative bent. I generate many new ideas and my imagination for new solutions often gets me and the team out of difficulties.	1 2 3 4 5	I am not particularly creative and I rely heavily on ideas from my team.
(9) I believe I am seen as an innovator and with a very positive attitude to change. I believe that managing risk is an essential feature in my job.	1 2 3 4 5	I am definitely not the innovator in the team. I prefer the status quo and I feel uncomfortable when risky decisions have been taken.

Assessment: When you have circled a number for each factor, add the numbers and divide by 9. If you have a number between 1 and 1.4 then you have a unique blend of leadership personality factors giving both good strong direction and the ability to create sound followship in your team. If you have a number between 1.5 and 2.4 then you are very sound in your leadership personality but with slight deficiency in certain factors. If you have a number between 2.5 and 3.5 then you are fairly average in your leadership personality. The balance between LEADERSHIP DIRECTION (factors 1, 2, 3, 8, 9) and FOLLOWSHIP (factors 4, 5, 6, 7) is probably out of balance and needs correcting. If you have a number between 3.6 and 4.5 then you have problems in your leadership personality and you will need to work harder at establishing yourself in the eyes of your team. If you have a number between 4.6 and 5 then you have a strong deficiency in your leadership personality. If you are presently in a position of leadership then you are probably trading very heavily upon the power and authority of your position in the organization and your technical or professional knowledge in the team.

Worksheet 4.2 Leadership process

Consider the factors below and circle a number that most closely represents your view of yourself *as your team sees you*. The worksheet is a guide to how you manage the process of leadership in your team. The guide is for your personal use so be honest with yourself.

(1) At the beginning of a task I spend a great deal of time defining the task at hand and ensuring that the team have a common understanding of the task.

1 2 3 4 5 At the beginning of a task I normally spend little time defining the task and generally the team and I define the task as we proceed in the task.

(2) I firmly believe than any task requires a sound plan of action. I also believe that the team should be wholeheartedly involved in the essential planning process.

1 2 3 4 5 Normally I have a sketchy plan of action for tasks and generally the plan evolves as the team and I proceed.

(3) When a plan of action for a task has been developed I firmly believe that I should spend time on ensuring that all team members are fully aware of everyone else's objectives and activities.

1 2 3 4 5 A common complaint in my team is that the team members are not aware of what the other team members are expected to achieve or what activities are being pursued.

(4) Normally I control the task very effectively by ensuring that each team member is in full control of the objectives and activities.

1 2 3 4 5 Normally I find that I have to check constantly on what is being done and achieved. On many occasions I have to re-direct the team's work.

(5) Once the team is working well on the task I firmly believe that I should then look ahead to spot problems and situations that might arise.

1 2 3 4 5 Probably because I find myself too actively involved in the task I have difficulty or lack the time to spot problems ahead of the team's work.

(6) I firmly believe that I should plan and spend time on motivating the team members.

1 2 3 4 5 I normally rely upon the team members own motivation to achieve the task.

(7) Normally, I keep an eye on the organization of the team. I actively stimulate communication between the teams and team members and I ensure that authority is well delegated throughout the team's organization.

1 2 3 4 5 I very rarely spend time on ensuring that the team is organized. I rely heavily on the team's own ability at communication and in ensuring proper delegated authority throughout the team's organization.

(8) I am always conscious of the need to set the right example. Generally I try and 'be' or 'do' what I expect in others.

1 2 3 4 5 I very rarely think about the impact that my example is having on the team.

Assessment: When you have circled a number for each factor, add the numbers and divide by 8. If you have a number between 1.0 and 1.4, you are always very conscious of the need to manage the process of leadership and probably your team members rely heavily upon your leadership style in achieving the tasks at hand. If you have a number between 1.5 and 2.4 then you have a natural inclination to manage the leadership process. You have probably not given the process much thought and have relied heavily upon what you considered to be your natural leadership ability. You can improve this natural ability by being more specific about improving your process. If you have a number between 3.6 and 4.5 you have a marked overall deficiency. Your team probably suffers from a lack of direction and they have to rely too heavily upon their own strengths to achieve for the team as a whole. If you have a number between 4.6 and 5.0 you are particularly weak at managing the process of leadership and probably all the team achievements are due to their own inherent strengths rather than yours. Your team is definitely achieving in spite of you rather than because of you.

DEVELOPING YOUR ACTION PLAN

Your natural leadership capability will depend upon the power and authority provided by your position in the organization. Normally the more senior you are in the organization the more power and authority you have in your position. A key skill in leadership development is ensuring that your power and authority are well used for the team's benefit. Equally your leadership capability will depend upon the amount of expertise or professional knowledge that is required for the team to work effectively. Here again the more senior you are the more need for technical POLICY as distinct from technical DETAIL. Ensuring the right quantity of technical input and the proper nature of that input, i.e. whether policy or detail, will be a key area for leadership development.

Both the factors of power and authority and technical skill are very specific to your own job circumstances and clearly they will vary from person to person and organization to organization. Nonetheless, these factors will not be utilized well unless the leadership personality and the management of the leadership process is first rate.

Look back at your LEADERSHIP PERSONALITY WORKSHEET (page 57) and list any factor with a score of 3, 4, or 5. The wording of the factor will give you an insight into the basic underlying problems. You can improve on your factors by committing yourself to action. To help this process it is useful to plan your action on three fronts: ATTITUDE, KNOWLEDGE and SKILL. More positive attitudes will create the context for improvement. More knowledge will provide the technical background and improved skill will be the practical implementation of the knowledge. For example if one of your weak factors was factor 4, the INFLUENCE FACTOR, then your action plan could be:

Weak factor: Factor 4 — Influencing

Attitude development	Commit myself to the importance of communicating well and positively seek opportunities where I can influence people and the situation.
Knowledge development	Observe how good influencers and good communicators exercise their skill. Also read about interpersonal communication, persuasion and selling.
Skill development	Plan into a difficult task a specific plan for communication and closely observe when I have success in influencing and when I have failure. Aim to learn by my mistakes. You might also plan to attend a training seminar on influencing skills.

Another level of insight is the combination of strong and weak factors. Factors 1, 2, 3, 8 and 9 are concerned with your ability to create FOLLOWSHIP in your team. The two critical elements in leadership are the ability of the leader to know where to go and what to do, i.e. direction, and the ability to motivate and carry the team in that direction, i.e. the followship. You normally find in leadership development that a manager is strong in one area but weak in the other. For example Type 'A' managers tend to be strong in direction but weak in followship whereas Type 'B' managers tend to be strong in followship but weak in direction. Awareness of your general strength and weakness is an important insight because typically it highlights the need to integrate the factors into a more effective leadership personality.

After you have thought about your leadership personality look back at your LEADERSHIP PROCESS WORKSHEET (page 58) and list any factors with a score of 3, 4 or 5. The wording of the factor will give you an insight into the basic underlying problem. Normally the weakness in managing the leadership process is due to a lack of awareness of the *need* to manage the process. Now that this awareness has been developed by the worksheets and text you need to make a specific commitment to managing your next leadership task more effectively. Think about a task which you are planning to do with your team. Think through the task and think about how you are going to DEFINE, PLAN, BRIEF, CONTROL, EVALUATE AHEAD, MOTIVATE, ORGANIZE and SET AN EXAMPLE. Make notes about your thinking and commit yourself to put your ideas into action when the task is imminent. Remember what makes a good leader is his recognition that active work is required on making leadership work. Without this active work on your part you will continually rely upon both the natural skills of yourself and your team.

Another level of insight is the combination of the factors. Factors 1, 2 and 3 are factors associated with the leader's work to get the task effectively STARTED whereas factors 4, 5, 6, 7 and 8 are factors associated with the CONTINUOUS management of the task. Very typically, good leaders work very hard on getting the task started but then when the team is working well on the task they change into a higher gear of management by *reducing* their 'day-to-day' activity in the task and *increasing* their overall general management of the team and its direction. Basically they change from ground view to helicopter view to ensure that control, communication, delegation, motivation, and direction are managed well. Whereas this is the typical style of the good leader, a less effective leader is normally less integrated in his management of the process. For example, some managers are very good STARTERS with high enthusiasm and concern to get the task off to a good start, but they stay too close to the activities and become too involved in the day-to-day pressures of time. The natural consequence is that their CONTINUOUS management is weak. The ability of a manager to change into the 'helicopter view' of management at the appropriate point is a key factor in how that manager *reduces* the time in task management and improves the quality of output. Good leadership and time management are closely linked to this change in the process of leadership.

Your leadership action plan

Use this worksheet to help you think through your leadership action plan. Remember the key factor between your leadership and your time management is in establishing the right time when you should *reduce* your day-to-day activity in the task and *increase* your overall general management of the task. Apart from ensuring better quality of work and higher performance from your team this will also allow you more time on other tasks.

Do I rely too heavily on the power and authority of my position for my leadership?

Do I rely too heavily on my technical expertise for my leadership?

List the weak factors (i.e. scores of 3, 4 or 5) on the LEADERSHIP PERSONALITY WORKSHEET.

WEAK FACTOR

WEAK FACTOR

WEAK FACTOR

WEAK FACTOR

WEAK FACTOR

WEAK FACTOR

Study the wording of the weak factor and the relevant text and establish action points. Remember to make specific recommendations in terms of ATTITUDE, KNOWLEDGE and SKILLS.

ACTION POINT

ACTION POINT

ACTION POINT

ACTION POINT

ACTION POINT

Highlight any combination of weak factors in terms of DIRECTION or FOLLOWSHIP. Aim to integrate the factors into a more effective personality with greater consistency.

List the weak factors (i.e. scores of 3, 4 or 5) on the LEADERSHIP PROCESS WORKSHEETS.

WEAK FACTOR

WEAK FACTOR

WEAK FACTOR

WEAK FACTOR

Study the wording of the factor and the relevant text and establish action points.

ACTION POINT

ACTION POINT

ACTION POINT

ACTION POINT

Think through your next task with the team and make notes on how you are going to improve on the factors.

DEFINE:

PLAN:

BRIEF:

CONTROL:

EVALUATE:

MOTIVATE:

ORGANIZE:

SET EXAMPLE:

Commit yourself to implementating this plan during the task.

Highlight any combination of factors in terms of Starting Tasks and Continuous Management of Tasks. Plan to change the level of management after the BRIEF STAGE of the process.

Teamwork development

Improving your leadership is the start of improving your performance and time management but your leadership will depend upon the members of your team actively working together to ensure results at the right level of quality. Your ability to change into a higher level of management of the team will depend not only upon your making the change at the appropriate time but also upon the confidence you have in the team working constructively together. Very much part of the leadership issue is your action in stimulating good teamwork development.

Teams of people are like individuals, they have a 'group personality' and character that is unique to that team. The group personality is an important factor in both the short and long term achievement of the team. Although it takes time for the group personality to form, a team leader can influence the formation of that group personality. The successful formation of a group personality is accomplished when a sense of 'commonness' is formed. This is achieved when the values of the team are common and when any individual needs can be accommodated within the value and goals of the team as a whole. Generally we call this commonness the 'team spirit'.

Team spirit is stimulated by both the team leader and the team members. It is normally achieved by paying attention to six very important factors.

(i) Teams need to have a clear statement of objectives in terms of what is to be achieved, at what quality level and by what date.
(ii) Teams need to feel that they have been part of the process of defining the objectives and that they have participated and achieved consensus on the statement of objectives.
(iii) Teams need to feel that they are regularly briefed on progress made towards the objectives.
(iv) Teams need to feel that they can express their feelings about how the team is working and particularly any negative feelings any individual or small part of the team is feeling.
(v) Team work best when harmony between team members is sought and when a conflict is reduced to a minimum.
(vi) Teams need to feel that they are totally involved in making the decisions of the team and that are being well managed by the team leader towards the objectives.

These 6 factors are based on a number of very important observations about team development. The first observation is concerned with the DIRECTION of the team.

Of all the factors that can destroy a team quickly, the chief factor is lack of direction. Teams rely very heavily upon the team leader to establish objectives and the general direction that is to be taken. When this direction is weakly stated or poorly communicated then the team will develop a series of directions each subject to conflict from other team members. The key skills in the team leader are firstly to establish a framework wherein the individuals' directions are discussed and secondly to seek a consensus on the main direction. Having established this participation it is imperative that the team leader ensures that the direction is clearly understood and agreed and that the team is regularly reminded of the objectives. Without clarity of objectives the consensus will fail. Regular reviews of progress towards objectives are a technique to ensure that objectives are restated and that the team is briefed on its successful actions.

The second observation is concerned with the INVOLVEMENT of the team. Teams work well because they produce better decisions than any individual in the team. This is a very important point about team decision making. Both experience and research shows that the quality of the team decision is generally superior to the quality of any individual decision providing the direction of the team is clearly stated and agreed. Many readers may feel that consensus is analogous to compromise at the lowest level but, in fact, if direction of the team is strong then consensus produces better results. However if direction is weak then normally the consensus will produce a low quality decision. Accordingly, ensuring DIRECTION and INVOLVEMENT are two critical factors in team success.

The third observation is that HARMONY is a factor in success for teamwork. Harmony is also a key weakness in the management of a team. There are people who hold the erroneous view that team conflict and dominant coalitions of strong personalities lead to successful team performance. In fact, this performance is generally short-lived and conflict becomes the team norm. However difficult on occasions, the spirit of harmony leads to higher team performance. For some people this is a bitter pill to swallow! Here are a few practical hints on arriving at harmonious conclusions:

(i) Co-operate with your team members — don't compete — you will need them in the future.
(ii) Avoid aggressive arguing of your point — it is stronger if you put it calmly and thoughtfully.
(iii) Avoid at all costs giving the team an ultimatum. Invariably they will reject it and you.
(iv) Never vote to resolve a conflict. It will waste valuable time in the long run. Talk conflict through

however much you might feel that you are wasting time!

(v) Avoid attacking team members at the personal level and don't rise to the attack if you are the victim.

(vi) Listen to other people's point of view and think it through from their side.

The three observations of DIRECTION, INVOLVEMENT and HARMONY are probably the three most critical factors in developing strong and consistent teamwork. With these three factors well established, the team leader will be able to rely confidently on the team working well at its highest level of performance. Here is a practical action plan for developing your team.

(i) Make time to talk through with your team the three critical factors of DIRECTION, INVOLVEMENT and HARMONY.

(ii) Whenever a task team is established, clarify at the outset whether any team member has a special expertise or knowledge about the task at hand.

(iii) Work with the team to establish a clear statement of the objectives, the level of quality and the time for achievement.

(iv) Always ensure that there is agreement on any policy issue that arises. Delay any movement forward in the team until policy has been agreed. If you don't talk policy through then conflict at the detail level of discussions will invariably arise and it will be difficult to maintain good teamwork.

(v) During discussion, always take a 'helicopter view' of the discussion. Ensure that the team's discussion is logical and well managed. Always establish the FACTS first, then move on to the INTERPRETATION of the facts and finally decide and agree on the CONCLUSIONS based upon the facts and their interpretation. Avoid at all costs the very natural tendency to jump from FACTS to CONCLUSIONS without the essential step of INTERPRETATION. Red herrings quickly enter into discussions because this interpretation stage is missing.

(vi) Seek to develop a team atmosphere where feelings can be expressed and where team members feel strongly involved in the decision making process.

(vii) Seek harmony and seek to develop a method of working where conflict can be managed well by team members paying attention to the hints given above.

(viii) Finally, if you are the team leader then manage the team. It is expected of you and the team will respect you for it. Always change into a higher level of management once the team is established on the task and teamwork is developing well.

Worksheet 4.3 Teamwork

This worksheet is designed to provide a guide to the level of teamwork that presently exists in your team or teams. It is based on the key principles highlighted in the text. For each of the factors circle a number that most represents your view of how you normally manage a team. The worksheet is for your personal use so be honest with yourself.

(1) Whenever I bring together a team I always establish any special expertise in the team that might be relevant.　　1　2　3　4　5　Whenever I bring together a team I often forget that a team member may have a special expertise.

(2) I always pay particular attention to allowing the team to participate in the statement of objectives and I ensure that everyone is clear about the objectives.　　1　2　3　4　5　I tend to be weak on deriving a statement of objectives and invariably the objectives tend to be mine rather than the team's.

(3) I pay very great attention to ensuring that everyone is involved in the key decisions of the team.　　1　2　3　4　5　Although I am aware of the need to involve the team I tend to make the main decisions.

(4) I am confident that my team can express any negative feelings about the way the team is working.　　1　2　3　4　5　I am not particularly aware of any negative feeling in the team and whenever they arise I am always uncertain about how I should react.

(5) I am very committed to regular reviews of progress and I always use the review to restate the team's objectives.　　1　2　3　4　5　I tend to review the team's progress on an irregular basis and normally when things are going badly.

(6) There is generally a spirit of harmony in my team and when conflict does arise we normally deal with it there and then.　　1　2　3　4　5　For some reason my team does tend to disagree and develop conflict. Normally I try and move on.

(7) I see team direction as a priority in the management of my team.　　1　2　3　4　5　Normally the direction of my team can falter.

(8) I generally believe that the team makes a better decision than any individual in the team.　　1　2　3　4　5　I generally believe that the individual makes a better decision than the team as a whole.

(9) I always ensure agreement on policy and work hard to resolve conflict on detail by referring to the agreement on policy.　　1　2　3　4　5　I rarely separate the issues of policy and detail and when conflict arises I am sometimes uncertain about the nature of the conflict.

(10) I actively manage the team's discussions to ensure that facts, interpretation and conclusions are taken in a logical sequence.　　1　2　3　4　5　I am not aware of the need to structure a discussion.

Assessment: When you have circled a number on each factor, add your numbers and divide by 10. A number between 1.0 and 1.4 means that you are very actively involved in developing your team and probably you are highly confident that your team will perform well in most situations. A number between 1.5 and 2.4 means that you are strong on team development but with a slight deficiency. More attention to the team will improve your confidence in the team. A number between 2.5 and 3.5 means that you are fairly average in team development. You have a number of strengths but also some weaknesses which need attention. Probably your team members would like a clearer management direction and style from you. A number between 3.6 and 4.5 means that you are weak in team development. Probably your team has significant weaknesses in terms of DIRECTION, INVOLVEMENT and HARMONY. A number between 4.6 and 5.0 means a serious weakness in your team development. It is highly likely that your team is under-performing and that you are constantly aggravated and involved in trying to make things happen for the team. Unfortunately your actions are probably making the team less effective!

DEVELOPING YOUR ACTION PLAN

Good teamwork comes about because you and the team have consciously decide to *improve* your teamwork and team spirit. This doesn't happen of its own accord but happens because positive steps have been taken and have been agreed to be taken. Your first step towards your action plan is to list the factors that are weak, i.e. those with scores of 3, 4 or 5. Normally a study of the wording of these factors will provide an insight into the basic underlying problem.

Another level of insight is to study the combination of weak factors. Factors 1, 2, 5 and 7 are concerned with the DIRECTION of the team. Factors 3, 4, 8 and 10 are concerned with INVOLVEMENT of the team. Factors 6 and 9 are concerned with the HARMONY of the team.

Your teamwork action plan

Use this worksheet to help you think through your teamwork development. Remember the key point about developing good teamwork is that it allows you to use your time with the team more effectively and also it ensures that your team members are using their time more effectively. Lack of direction, poor involvement and team conflict are time bombs which are constantly exploding and destroying the overall team performance and demanding that you have to spend more time on that performance.

List the weak factors (i.e. 3, 4 or 5) on Worksheet 4.4:

WEAK FACTOR

WEAK FACTOR

WEAK FACTOR

WEAK FACTOR

WEAK FACTOR

Study the wording of the factor and the relevant text and establish your action points.

ACTION POINT

ACTION POINT

ACTION POINT

ACTION POINT

ACTION POINT

Highlight any combination of factors and establish whether you have any general weakness in the areas of DIRECTION, INVOLVEMENT and HARMONY.

Study the teamwork action plan on page 65 and based upon this plan develop your own action plan. Always commit yourself to specific action that you know you can take.

PLAN
1.

2.

3.

4.

5.

6.

7.

8.

Effective delegation

Probably the most important technique a manager can use for improving performance and time management is delegation. From my experience managers can improve their output by some 15% by being more effective and 'crisper' in their delegation.

Interestingly, from a great deal of experience working with very successful senior managers, there seem to be a few significant factors which typify the success of these managers in their delegation.

(i) *Delegation Planning*: Successful senior managers plan their own performance and time by *planning* well ahead the tasks which are to be delegated.

(ii) *Delegation Precision*: Successful senior managers spend time on ensuring that tasks are well defined and agree. Normally the actual delegation to a subordinate takes place after a great deal of thought has been given to the task by the senior manager. Consequently when the task is delegated it is quite precise for the subordinate.

(iii) *Delegation Review*: Successful senior managers are almost pedantic over the review and control of their delegated tasks. Delegation review times are well establihed and agreed beforehand and the subordinate is very clear what has to be achieved and by what time. Also, delegation reviews are regular.

(iv) *'Hands Off' Approach*: Successful senior managers are highly committed to allowing their subordinates to get on with the job. Very rarely do they hover and question the subordinate and they are very effective in ensuring that the task or part of he task is not delegated back to them by the subordinate.

(v) *Risk and Time*: Although successful senior managers are committed to a 'hands off' approach they are not oblivious to the risks associated with delegation. Normally the senior manager has evaluated these risks — particularly the risk of low quality or delayed results — and normally the senior manager has established in his or her own mind the last possible time by which he may need to intervene in order to ensure that any risks do not materialize.

It is clear from these points that delegation is a specific skill within effective leadership and within this section we will look at delegation in more detail and establish how you can improve your particular skills.

What exactly do we mean by delegation? Delegation occurs when you temporarily hand to a subordinate some of your authority so that the subordinate can perform work on your behalf. It is important to recognize that responsibility cannot be delegated and that you will bear the responsibility for the results of that subordinate's work.

Even though delegation may appear to be a relatively simple process, it is often the most difficult one for a manager to perform and also the area of conflict that subordinates feel most. Very few managers consider themselves to be good delegators, although they would be the first to admit that they delegate as much as they can. In a similar way, self-assessment of how we delegate is prone to false impressions. However there are many signs of poor delegation and often a critical assessment of these signs in yourself will provide you with a sound indication of your skill. Some of the main signs of poor delegations are:

(1) When you have difficulty in asking a subordinate to perform a task because of that subordinate's dominant personality;

(2) When you have difficulty accepting the ideas and approaches of other people and you generally assess them as less effective than your own approach;

(3) When you have a strong tendency to do things yourself because you feel it is quicker and of a better quality;

(4) When you tend to mistrust the skills and judgements of other people and you fear that mistakes will occur if other people do not perform as well as yourself;

(5) When you tend to have a high leaning towards details, precision and well-defined situations and this leaning affects your attitude towards your view of your job;

(6) When you feel you work harder and longer than your subordinates and, because of this, you have little time to develop and train your subordinates;

(7) When your job has a high proportion of menial tasks or routine matters which could quite easily be done by other people.

Poor delegation comes about mainly because of two factors: negative attitudes and lack of training in delegation. Let us deal with attitudes first. What are these negative attitudes that stand in the way of delegation?

NEGATIVE ATTITUDES TO DELEGATION

A key attitude for delegation is the idea of the 'right to manage'. A manager's job is to plan, organize, control and provide resources for work within their domain; any impediments to this will affect the view managers have of their job and what it can achieve. Constraints within the organization and its systems will act as impediments to job performance, as will a manager's own technical expertise and management ability. Often, in the case of an inexperienced manager, subordinates may represent a threat; so the manager will avoid delegation of any work which may lead to disruption or interpersonal conflict. Part of a manager's job is to work hard at the constraints so that delegation becomes a proper functioning part of the job.

Even though developing your subordinates is a key skill of a manager (and indeed a sound indication of that manager's potential), we find that the development of subordinates has a low priority in the actions of many managers. It is difficult to assess whether this is solely a lack of time and opportunity, or whether it is a sign of a negative attitude towards the subordinate. In any case, a lack of appreciation of the role of delegation when developing subordinates is a negative approach.

The 'do it myself' mentality is another very negative approach. To do work which others are capable of doing shows a strong lack of insight into the role of management, and your own personal performance and time management. It must be made clear that 'doing it myself' equals a 'waste of myself', and it impairs the performance of others within the work team and the overall quantity and quality of work that a team can achieve. You need to check whether your 'do it myself' mentality stems from a feeling of mistrust in the contributions of others, so that you doubt their skills and judgements and approaches; or whether it stems from a fear you have about your own failure and how others may contribute to that fear of failure. You will remember from Chapter 1 that fear of failure or self-doubt was a strong underlying theme to procrastination, and you can see how procrastination and delegation can go hand in hand inasmuch as a fear or mistrust of delegation is a clear mechanism for procrastination.

Another version of the 'do it myself' mentality is that of the person who has the negative attitude of perfectionism. Generally the work of the person is very detailed, such as in engineering, systems and accounting; often the detail of the work can obscure the need to delegate complete batches of work. In many respects the attitude being expressed is that a job is too detailed and meticulous or needs thinking through from concept to final detail and therefore, of course, cannot be performed by a subordinate. In reality the work is often full of menial or routine parts and even the substantial parts could be ideal activities for subordinate development.

Finally, the negative attitude of the 'no time' mentality is very common. Effective delegation takes time in preparation and in monitoring the work; often the manager will consider that it is quicker to perform the work than to delegate the work. This attitude generally supports the complementary attitude that 'subordinates have insufficient skills or judgement'.

LACK OF TRAINING IN DELEGATION

Whereas the above are some of the main attitudes that work against delegation, the second factor which leads to poor delegation is lack of awareness of the process of delegation — or to put it very bluntly — a lack of skill in 'how to' delegate. One of the major errors in this is a lack of definition and thinking through of the work to be delegated so that the task is unclear and the subordinates therefore cannot perform effectively. The second major error is lack of follow-up. Most managers are very poor in this. Without doubt effective and timely follow-up can be the single most effective way of improving a team's overall performance very quickly indeed.

Other important errors are to delegate only parts of a job (generally the worst parts!) rather than the whole, and to delegate a job for which more than one person has responsibility, i.e. the 'multiple bosses' syndrome. The traditional adage of 'only serve one master' is a useful guideline in delegation. Finally, a job can only be performed if the person has authority to perform it: without the proper delegation of authority and the limits to that authority, delegation must be poor.

Thus we can see that, although delegation appears to be a simple enough task, it is in fact quite complicated and prone to error and under-performance. Developing the right attitudes and the right skills for delegation is a prerequisite for effective delegation.

GUIDELINES ON ATTITUDES AND SKILLS OF DELEGATION

The following key points are guidelines for positive attitudes and skills in delegating:

— Delegation is a key skill in my job and one that needs developing fully. Delegation is one of the 'rights' of my job.
— Delegation is an essential method of developing the skill and judgements of my subordinates.
— Delegation requires a trust in other people's ideas and approach and an acceptance that their mistakes will be my responsibility.
— Delegation means I do not 'do it myself', thereby 'wasting myself' and my time.

— Delegation means I have to spend time on delegation in order to produce more time for my work and so improve my performance.
— Delegation means I shall endeavour to follow a sound way of delegating.

The sound way of delegation is:

(1) Always ask yourself if this job could be done better by somebody else: if I were not doing this now, what more important job could I be doing?

(2) Always think through the work to be delegated very carefully. Establish the key goals and standards of performance, the time required and the key skills and resources required.

(3) Consult and select a subordinate who has the skills to perform the work. If these skills are not available, then they will need to be developed or you will have to do the work. This means you need to plan your delegation in advance.

(4) Always check on whether the subordinate will have a number of bosses when the work is undertaken; the preference is for 'one man, one boss'. If multiple bosses are required for the work, then this will need special management.

(5) Determine the limits of the authority that is being delegated: how much money, who is involved, where are the resources, how much authority will the subordinate have to make decisions, and so on. The authority's limit needs to be *clear* before the main job gets underway.

(6) In preference, always delegate a 'whole' job and not a part of a job. Never delegate the bad or boring parts of a job without the good and interesting parts.

(7) Always talk through with the subordinate how the work is to be controlled, how will it be manned, by whom, and when; what results are expected, and how are these to be monitored along the way. When broad controls have been established, then *leave the subordinate to it!* Don't hover and question!

(8) In all delegation establish clear delegation review times and schedule these in your diary. Clearly establish what you expect to have been achieved by the review date.

(9) When a job is under way, then monitor the type of questions and consultation you are getting from the subordinate. When the subordinate raises a problem, ask for the solution; never give the answer to the problem until the subordinate has thought it through. Be very wary of too much consultation, otherwise the job will be delegated back to you by the subordinate.

(10) Whenever the work is completed successfully, then reward and praise. Whenever it goes wrong, then think what you did or did not do to let it go wrong and work through with the subordinate how to correct the errors. Praise in public, but always correct in private.

Worksheet 4.4 Delegation

This worksheet is designed to provide a guide to how effective your present delegation skills are. For each of the factors, circle a number that most represents your view of your own delegation skill. The worksheet is for your personal use so be honest with yourself.

(1) I am confident that I consistently plan *all* my delegation well ahead of when I actually delegate the tasks.
   1 2 3 4 5   I rarely plan my delegation ahead and I tend to delegate quickly and often at the last minute.

(2) Prior to delegation I always think carefully about objectives, authority, how the work is to be done, controls and time required.
   1 2 3 4 5   Normally I work with the subordinate at the time of delegation.

(3) I always agree regular review dates and I keep myself and my subordinates to these.
   1 2 3 4 5   I tend to be irregular and inconsistent with my reviews. Often times are changed because of other priorities.

(4) Wherever possible I try to delegate a 'whole job' which will stretch my subordinate.
   1 2 3 4 5   I tend to delegate parts of my work. Normally the work I delegate is well within the capability of my subordinate.

(5) Once I have delegated I try not to be involved in the work of the subordinate. I rely very heavily on the review periods in order to check progress.
   1 2 3 4 5   I must admit that I tend to hover and question the subordinate. Often I have to handle parts of the work for the subordinate.

(6) At the end of a task I always establish why we have succeeded or failed.
   1 2 3 4 5   At the end of a task I very rarely establish why we succeeded or failed.

(7) I sometimes lack confidence in the skills and judgements of my subordinates but I try to assess the risks of failure rationally.
   1 2 3 4 5   Unfortunately my subordinates don't have the skills and judgement for many of the tasks which I would like to delegate.

(8) Most of the tasks I delegate I know I could do quicker than my subordinate but I try hard to resist the temptation to do the task myself.
   1 2 3 4 5   Most of the tasks I could delegate I know I can do quicker. Often it will take longer to brief the subordinate than to do the task myself so I get on with it.

(9) I believe that my delegation is the most effective means of developing my staff.
   1 2 3 4 5   I would like to develop my staff by better delegation but it seems to take too much time.

(10) I never do detail work or menial tasks which I know others can do.
   1 2 3 4 5   I often find that I tend to have to do detail work and often I do some menial tasks.

Assessment: When you have circled a number for each factor, add the numbers and divide by 10. A number between 1.0 and 1.4 means that you are a very effective delegator with both positive attitudes and a highly developed skill in delegation. Probably your team is well developed and they are always clear about what you require and how you are going to ensure that they deliver to your requirements. A number between 1.5 and 2.4 means that you are effective but with some small areas for improvement. Almost certainly your team are performing well and are clear about your standards of working. A number between 2.5 and 3.5 means that you have a weakness in this area. Probably you haven't spent much time thinking about delegation and if you developed more positive attitudes and spent more time on preparation you would improve considerably. A number between 3.6 and 4.5 means you have many weaknesses in delegation. Unfortunately your team will be critical of your delegation skill and often uncertain about what is required of them. A number between 4.6 and 5.0 means you are very poor at delegation. Almost certainly your team is under-performing and very uncertain about what is expected of them in terms of performance.

DEVELOPING YOUR DELEGATION ACTION PLAN

Good delegation comes from your deciding to take positive steps towards improvement. Even the best delegators need to practise at delegation because practice makes the professional manager. List out the factors with a score of 3, 4 or 5 and study the wording of the factors. This will provide an insight into your underlying problems. Also study the combination of your factors. Factors 1, 2, 3, 5, 6 are concerned with the skill of delegation, whereas factors 4, 7, 8, 9, 10 are concerned with your attitudes towards delegation.

Your delegation action plan

Use this worksheet to help you develop your delegation skills. Remember that delegation improves the overall performance of your team and also releases you to focus upon higher priority work. You can probably improve your output by about 10 to 15% by making your delegation 'crisper' and more effective.

List the factors with scores of 3, 4 or 5 on Worksheet 4.5.

WEAK FACTOR

WEAK FACTOR

WEAK FACTOR

WEAK FACTOR

WEAK FACTOR

Study the wording of the factor and refer to the text. Commit yourself to action points.

ACTION POINT

ACTION POINT

ACTION POINT

ACTION POINT

ACTION POINT

Highlight any combination of factors and establish whether you have a tendency to deficiency in attitudes or skill.

Think about a task which is likely to need delegation. Makes notes on how you are to delegate the task.

- (i) Task objectives?
- (ii) At what standard of achievement?
- (iii) How much authority will the subordinate need?
- (iv) How could the task be done?
- (v) What part of the work will I need to control?
- (vi) What regular review periods will I require?
- (vii) Which subordinate would this task help to develop?
- (viii) Do this subordinate need any special training in order to do the task?

Performance improvement planning

Leadership, teamwork development and delegation have established the ground rules of team management and your personal strengths and weaknesses in these important areas. Building on these areas we can now introduce a very important technique for substantially improving the work output and the team spirit of any work team. The technique is called Performance Improvement Planning or PIP for short.

PIP is based on a very simple concept, namely that a team improves its performance if it is prepared to review what makes it succeed or fail as a working team. Afer this review it then sets objectives about how it can build upon its success factors and dispense with its failure factors. As the team PIP's a series of tasks it eradicates the factors that interfere with success.

Although PIP is a well-tried method for performance improvement in management, the most dramatic and speediest PIP can often be found in teamwork development, in outdoor activity management development such as the OUTWARD BOUND schools. In principle, a group of managers come together to work on physical tasks in order to observe quickly how they work effectively. The first physical task is often a failure and the managers identify those factors, both technically and interpersonally, that contributed to the failure. Factors such as internal competition, lack of definition of the task objectives, personality conflicts, often come to the fore in the analysis of failure. However during the evaluation the team identify some success factors such as enthusiasm, hard work, commitment to succeed. Following the evaluation the team then sets objectives on how it should work. Normally these objectives are concerned with building on the success factors and endeavouring to control the influence of the failure factors. An essential point about the review process is that the evaluation is open and frank and each team member becomes aware of both his or her strengths and weaknesses in the team's achievements.

With these team objectives the team then completes a second task and following the task the team again reviews its performance. During this review it may identify that certain objectives on teamwork are very robust, that is they can be used in any task, whereas certain objectives may be solely dependent upon the nature of the task. The review also establishes whether the team has been successful in managing its failure factors and it may identify additional failure factors as well.

The process of reviewing and setting objectives for performance improvement continues over a series of physical tasks which incidentally are increasing in their difficulty and demands upon effective teamwork. Remarkably, after a very short time, normally over 5 or 6 physical tasks, the team arrives at a very important point in its development. Whatever the difficulty of the next task, the team has to face it confidently, knowing it will succeed. Basically what has happened in this process is that the team has now developed a team spirit of a high degree and has established a robust working formula for its success.

PIP is a very powerful technique for improving performance and clearly any good manager needs to introduce the technique into his working practices with teamwork development. How can this be done?

Firstly, the manager needs to consider whether he or she is prepared to learn the good and the bad about their style of management. If is often the case in the first and second PIP sessions that a manager will expose a number of feelings and technical weaknesses in individuals and the team as a whole. These weaknesses are rarely fundamental and all can be corrected quickly but nonetheless a manager who has not actively and consciously thought about teamwork will be slightly uncertain about the personal risks in letting a team develop frankness and openness on how its performance is developing and managed.

Secondly, the manager needs to establish PIP as a continuous part of management. Normally this involves either a monthly or a bi-monthly PIP session lasting about one hour. An alternative method is to provide a 15-minute session on the end of progress meetings when the team comes together to review technical progress of their work.

A PIP session has four main stages:

Stage 1: Reviewing the tasks which the team has worked on, allow the team to identify those significant factors that have contributed successfully to the task and those significant factors that have impeded the task.

Stage 2: From the success and failure factors select those which are practical to keep and those that the team wishes to dispense with.

Stage 3: Agree with the team its objectives for working on the next task(s). Normally these objectives are concerned with maintaining success factors.

Stage 4: Agree with the team a 'code of practice' or working method based on the objectives and agree with individuals how they are to act or work differently in order to achieve objectives.

Managing a PIP session requires the manager to focus upon three aspects. Firstly the manager will need to focus upon the *process* of teamwork rather than the technical task. For example 'why did the decision take such a long time?'. Secondly, the manager will need to stimulate the team to be frank and open about its performance. Thirdly, the manager will need to focus upon the *future* of the team in terms of constructive actions. Avoid the tendency for the team to over-emphasis the backward-looking criticism of its performance. The manager must quickly acknowledge the failures and equally quickly move on to constructive action to ensure that the failure does not occur again.

As a final point on PIP here are some of the typical areas often discussed in the first PIP sessions. Some of these areas link back into the previous sections on leadership and teamwork development.

(i)   Lack of clarity on the overall direction and strategy of the team to achieve its objectives.
(ii) Lack of understanding on objectives and how the team or individuals are to be measured on their success or failure.
(iii) The need to invest time in developing and agreeing objectives and standards of performance.
(iv) The need to recognize expertise within the work team.
(v)   The need to listen effectively within the group.
(vi) The need to concentrate on priorities of work and the need for the team to manage its time by its priority objectives and tasks.
(vii) The need to manage effectively the processing of work within the team. For example areas such as meetings management, chairmanship, delegation skills, interruptions management, personal organization.
(viii) The need for involvement and harmony within the team.

As you can see from these discussion areas, PIP is very clearly concerned with the overall performance and time management of the team. As a technique PIP is powerful and invariably successful. Often within four or five PIP sessions the team has developed a strong team spirit and has established a method of working which ensures that performance is higher, often by 10% output over that prior to PIP, and that time is a well managed resource.

5
Managing your communications

In the last chapter we discussed how your performance and time are affected by the way you manage people. Working with people means you have to communicate well. In fact, about 70% of a manager's time is spent in some form of communication with other people so it represents a very large part of your work. This 70% breaks down into four main topics — speaking, listening, reading and writing — and it is these topics that we will cover in this chapter.

Effective speaking

From my own experience and from observing managers over many years I now believe that the gift of speaking well is a natural gift for some managers. Although some do have a natural gift and they gain the benefits of higher communication and higher productivity through their speaking, it is also clear that speaking is a skill that can be developed for all managers.

In this section we look at how speaking can be developed more effectively. It is important to state that managerial speaking is completely different from any other form of public speaking. The reasons for this as quite straightforward. Managers speak mainly to individuals or small groups of less than 20 people and in the main the contents of their speech are technical or professional. The main purpose of managerial speaking is to work more effectively and to gain greater return or productivity for the organization. In essence, managerial speaking is solely concerned with managerial tasks on an every day basis. Managerial speaking is about speaking with

authority and confidence in the many, day-to-day, small groups that managers find themselves in. In this section we highlight the golden rules of speaking effectively and then apply these rules to the specific situation of a management presentation.

THE GOLDEN RULES OF SPEAKING

The first golden rule is that, *for a manager, speaking is very important.* Many managers underestimate the importance of speech and suffer the consequences. There are many facets to this problem. Speaking with authority and confidence is always an indication of managers' ability to perform well in their job. There is no mystique in this, it is just a matter of common sense. The daily activities of a manager are mainly concerned with planning for the future, solving the problems of today and ensuring that the daily decisions and work flow are well organized and running smoothly. These are the 'technicalities' of the manager's work and all depend upon communicating ideas and solutions to other members of the work team. To add to this there is the truism that 'it's not what you say but the way that you say it', so not only is the content of speech important but that content can be enhanced or reduced in impact solely by the manner and technique of its delivery. The WHAT and HOW of speaking are normally a good guide to a manager's clarity of understanding of the job and to the degree of enthusiasm and commitment that he shows in the job. Certainly in my own experience of management development I have invariably observed that very senior managers often use the ability to speak well as an indication of the younger and middle manager's ability to move upwards in the organization into bigger and more responsible jobs. I have also oberved the opposite phenomenon, namely that a manager's potential has been stunted in its growth solely by the inability to speak well. Without doubt, reputations are made and lost by speaking. Probably the most telling situation in which a reputation can be lost very quickly is when a middle manager makes his or her first board presentation or presentation in public. For good or bad, first impressions are important and a first time, poor presentation to the board can live with a manager for a long time.

The second golden rule is that *speaking is about the strength of your enthusiasm.* Speaking is only effective when you let your enthusiasm and commitment *DRIVE* your ideas, spoken words, gestures and actions. Speaking starts deep inside the mind and the body and effective communication comes when the whole body talks with authority and confidence. Observe good speakers around you and you will see that they are committed to their words, however provocative, and they always show a strong enthusiasm for *what* they say and *how* they want to say it.

The third golden rule is that *speaking is about your right to assert yourself.* Many managers often break this rule. Some are uncertain about the contents of their speech or are nervous or cautious about speaking their mind. Consequently they either make an inadequate contribution or a very passive and weak one. Other managers go to the other extreme. They are so convinced that they are right and keen to express their dominant personality that their contents and delivery are both dogmatic and aggressive. Both extremes are poor in communication. The alliance between the passive and the aggressive is your assertion. You are committed to expressing yourself but you maintain the essential pragmatism of managerial communication and resist the strong aggression that all managers feel on occasions. Your assertion is your strongest ally in persuasion — you neither sell yourself too weakly nor too strongly.

The fourth golden rule is probably the most important. *Speaking is about the simplicity of your ideas.* Far too many managers over-complicate their speech. They fill their speech with long words, technical jargon, long sentences and sophisticated ideas. All of these stop communication between you and the audience. One golden rule I never break in my own professional life is that the more senior the manager you are talking to the more simple the words and the ideas. Senior managers expect and demand simplicity, not because they are incapable of dealing with complicated ideas, but because the essence

of communication is to lodge simple ideas in the senior manager's mind and then to let the senior manager transform and modify the simple idea into a meaningful and pragmatic concept. Communication occurs when your audience *own* your ideas and they only *own* them when they have worked on them and made them workable. Keep it simple!

The fifth golden rule is that *speaking is brief.* No manager gains by speaking too much and for too long. Only talk when you have something important to say. Never 'wrap up ideas in fancy paper' and always keep your speech short and to the point. Even in the managerial presentation lasting (say) 20 minutes, you only have sufficient time to communicate three to five main points because if you go above this, you will lose your audience. The knack in speaking well is to think clearly about your main points before you open your mouth, then talk briefly and shut up! If your main points are logical, spoken with authority and enthusiasm, then you have communicated and thus achieved your objective. Any more talk will probably begin to confuse your audience.

The sixth golden rule is that *your audience is important.* I am always surprised at how many managers are prepared to disregard their audience completely. They prepare their knowledge about the audience inadequately in terms of the audience's seniority, expertise and personality. They also pay scant attention to the need to 'read an audience' and to 'work with an audience'. Audiences are very responsive and they tell you about themselves very quickly. The key thing an audience tells you is their level of interest in your words and ideas and they do this by their eyes and facial expressions. 'Lively' eyes and smiles or 'serious' eyes and 'serious' facial expressions tell you that you are communicating well. If you can balance your speech between 'lightness' and 'seriousness' then you are communicating very well indeed. 'Dull' eyes tell you about how 'dull' your words and ideas are. Whenever you see 'dull' eyes it is time for you to sparkle and recapture your audience. If you don't sparkle, either by your ideas or delivery, then you may as well stop talking because communication is poor. Never, never say to yourself 'this audience will listen to what I have to say whether they like it or not'. And don't forget . . . never take your eyes off your audience's eyes!!

The seventh golden rule is to *manage your speech by rhythm, stress and interest.* The essential structure of speech is a balance between WHAT you have to say and HOW you need to say it. 'What' you have to say follows a simple structure:

Concept — Example — Opinion — Key communication point

Concept is a brief opening statement about the central ideas or ideas you are going to talk about. The concept is essential to the introduction of your ideas.

Example is a practical example showing how the concept is being implemented presently. You normally choose an example that fits the audience's interest and experience.

Opinion is your view of the example and what it means in a more general sense. Always be committed to your opinion.

Key Communication Point is the essential message that comes from the concept, example and your opinion. The key communication point is what you want to leave in the audience's mind. Key communication points are always about ACTION you want the audience to take.

Here is an illustration:

Concept	Delegation is a key skill in improving the productivity of managers.
Example	How often have you observed poor delegation? I recently came across a Managing Director who was so quick with his delegation that all his senior managers were confused. The MD was so quick that when he was walking down the corridor to the loo, he used to delegate one and the same task to four senior managers he happened to meet along the way.
Opinion	I am sure you will agree with me that the effect of this was that the four senior managers were uncertain about who was to progress the task. In fact, over a period of time, the senior managers had now agreed amongst themselves that much of what the MD wanted to be done would not be done until they received a more specific instruction.
Key communication point	What have we learnt from this example? Delegation is an important skill but you must take time to think about your delegation if you want it to be effective and lead to higher productivity.

What about the 'HOW' or the DELIVERY in this example? How can we tie rhythm and stress into the example above? Normally rhythm is a sequence of *pauses, slow speech* and *quick speech*, and normally stress is a sequence of *speech volume* and *facial* and *body gestures*. How would we deliver the example above?

	[*Pause*]
Concept	[*Slow*] Delegation is a key skill in improving the productivity of managers.
	[*Pause*]
Example	[*Slow*] How often have you observed poor delegation?
	[*Quick*] I recently came across a Managing Director who [STRESS] who was *so quick with his delegation* that all his senior managers were confused . . .
	[*Pause*]
	[*Slow*] The MD was so quick that when he was walking down the corridor to the loo . . .
	[*Quick*] [STRESS] *he used to delegate one and the same task to the four senior managers he happened to meet along the way.*
	[*Pause*]
Opinion	[*Slow*] I am sure you will agree with me that the effect of this was that the four senior managers were uncertain about who was to progress the task. In fact, over a period of time, the senior managers had now agreed amongst themselves . . .
	[*Quick*] that much of what the MD wanted to be done would not be done [STRESS] *until they received a more specific instruction.*
	[*Pause*]
Key communication point	[*Slow*] What have we learnt from this example?
	[*Quick*] Delegation is an important skill [*STRESS*] *but you must take time to think about your delegation* if you want it to be effective and lead to higher productivity.
	[*Pause*]

When you STRESS in the above example, you need to raise the VOLUME of your speech, speak every stress word very clearly, and let your face 'light up' with enthusiasm.

The above example provides a general model for building up your speech.

Content	**Delivery**
	Pause
Concept →	Slow Speech, no Stress
	Pause

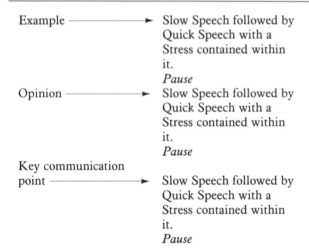

Example ——————▶	Slow Speech followed by Quick Speech with a Stress contained within it. *Pause*
Opinion ——————▶	Slow Speech followed by Quick Speech with a Stress contained within it. *Pause*
Key communication point ——————▶	Slow Speech followed by Quick Speech with a Stress contained within it. *Pause*

And when you STRESS, always raise the VOLUME OF SPEECH SLIGHTLY and speak with noticeable ENTHUSIASM.

The eighth golden rule about speaking is *wherever possible use visual aids*. The greatest aid a manager has for communicating is the flip chart. Every manager should have one in his office. Visuals are the 'pictures of your speech'. Be bold, draw your ideas as you speak them. Use the flip chart to think and talk and your communication will improve quite dramatically.

The nineth golden rule is a *never* rule. There are certain emotions that should never show in your speech. Never be passive or submissive. Never show aggression to your audience. Never show impatience with questions or other people's ideas. Never show a fear of your audience. Never hide an error on your part — admit it immediately and move on. Never apologise for speaking and never say 'I won't keep you too long' or 'this is a dull subject'. Never hide your hands in your pockets and never cross your arms over your chest. Never look at the floor — always look at the eyes of your audience. All of these NEVER rules show one emotion to your audience — that you are uneasy talking to them and that you are not committed and enthusiastic about what you have to say.

The tenth, and final, golden rule is *always know your subject*. No manager has made a reputation by talking about something he or she does not know about. If you are not fully familiar with a topic keep quiet! It takes a special skill in presentation or speaking to talk about a topic you are not fully familiar with and unless you have the special skill you are risking your position as a manager and possibly your career. If you have to give a presentation on a topic, prepare it very well indeed. You must aim for a minimum standard of knowing your subject *better than any person* in the audience.

MANAGEMENT PRESENTATIONS

In my own career to date I have sat through and given many thousands of presentations and I believe that there are nine basic failings in management presentations. These basic failings are all covered by the 10 golden rules highlighted previously but it is useful to put these rules into the specific context of a management presentation to show how they operate.

Here are the nine failings of a manager giving his presentation:

(1) The manager is not BOLD enough.
(2) The manager rejects the audience.
(3) The manager suffers and shows nerves.
(4) The manager doesn't use visual aids effectively.
(5) The manager speaks for too long.
(6) The manager tries to be clever rather than simple.
(7) The manager is poorly prepared.
(8) The manager doesn't demonstrate a logic in the presentation.
(9) The manager tends to waffle.

Remember that speaking is a skill. It doesn't matter whether you are speaking to one person or 20 people, the golden rules all apply. It is only when the audience becomes large, i.e. over 20 people, that more emphasis needs to be given to certain golden rules. For the everyday activities of a manager making presentations to small audiences, he needs to stay close to the golden rules. Let us look at the nine failings in terms of key action points using the golden rules as a guide:

(1) *The manager is not bold enough*. Too many managers concentrate on the 'WHAT' of a presentation and not on the 'HOW' of the presentation. Although the presentation is sound, the enthusiasm and commitment doesn't show through. Remember speaking is very important to you, give it GUSTO, speak with enthusiasm, with authority and confidence and assert your right to speak. Always engage a higher gear when you are making a presentation. Speak louder, speak with more facial gesture and body movement, use gesture and movement to emphasize and stress.

(2) *The manager rejects the audience*. Managers reject the audience because they believe the audience has rejected them. This is normally untrue. If the manager doesn't build rapport at the start by talking about common experience and expertise then the audience will reject the manager. Also there are certain signs which make an audience reject a speaker. Many of these signs will be covered below, but the key signs are: lack of clarity and

logic, lack of enthusiasm and assertion, lack of subject knowledge, and nerves in the speaker. All of these are under the control of the speaker. The key discipline in keeping an audience is to *ensure* eye contact at all times. Be bold, sweep your eyes across your audience then rest on an individual and speak to him individually for a moment, then sweep your eyes across your audience. SWEEPING and RESTING is the essential rhythm of keeping the audience with you.

(3) *The manager suffers and shows nerves.* Nerves are the most *positive* reaction you can have for a presentation. Nerves make the adrenalin flow and ensure that you engage top gear. All the most professional speakers rely very heavily upon having nerves prior to the start of a presentation, because without nerves the presentation starts slowly and possibly will never engage top gear. You must use nerves very positively. Here are some of the key signs of *bad* nerves, particularly at the start of a presentation.

    (i) The manager makes a nervous smile.
    (ii) The manager puts his hands in his pockets and jingles money or keys.
    (iii) The manager tells a joke that falls flat.
    (iv) The manager crosses his legs at the ankles.
    (v) The manager crosses his arms across his chest.
    (vi) The manager has a dry mouth and lips and has difficulty speaking clearly.
    (vii) The manager speaks too slowly or too quickly.
    (viii) The manager looks at the floor rather than the audience.
    (ix) The manager makes a comment about how dull or uninteresting the presentation will be.
    (x) The manager noticeably rushes to the first visual aid and then talks with his back to the audience or talks to the visual aid.

Interestingly, all of these key signs of bad nerves can be overcome very simply and quickly by the following technique. Always remember that the first three or four minutes of your presentation are the most important as far as your nerves are concerned and if you manage these few minutes well then you are off into high gear quickly and effectively. Follow these steps for the first few minutes of your next presentation:

Step One   Always STAND UP smartly. PAUSE for about 10 seconds, look at the audience and sweep your eyes across the audience. Never SMILE (leave smiling till later!).

Step Two   Take a drink of water (always ensure a full glass of water before you stand).

Step Three   CHECK that your hands are free and loosely hanging at your sides. CHECK that your ankles are not crossed and stand firmly with slightly open legs. Always empty your pockets before you speak so that if you do put your hands in your pockets then you won't fidget.

Step Four   Look at *one* person in the audience, preferably on the front row, and begin your presentation to that person. Then move off the person and sweep your eyes across the audience. Never look at the floor.

Step Five   NEVER tell a joke at the beginning of a presentation. Preferably you should give a strong example of your key theme. The example should relate to the audience and contain the key communication point of your presentation. The beginning of your presentation is very important. Don't waste it on jokes and stories. You have plenty of time to relate stories later in your presentation once the ice is broken. Speak at your natural speech rate — not too quickly or too slowly and speak loudly and with enthusiasm.

Step Six   Take your time getting to your first visual aid. Always try and use the first visual aid to show the contents or the key points of your talk. Never forget the rule of presentation: TELL YOUR AUDIENCE WHAT YOU WILL TELL THEM, TELL THEM, AND THEN TELL THEM WHAT YOU HAVE TOLD THEM. Audiences like to know where you will lead them because this gives the structure and logic of your presentation.

Step Seven   Never turn your back on the audience, if you need to turn then turn sideways on and keep eye contact as much as possible.

(4) *The manager doesn't use visual aids.* Remember, management presentations are not like after dinner speeches. Use slides or a flip chart to get your points across. If you use flip charts then build up your picture in colour and explain what each part of the diagram represents. Don't expect the audience to know. Simple diagrams are best, don't crowd them with numbers and always explain

numbers to your audience. Draw your diagram large and write words large. Diagrams on flip charts can be informal so work the diagram with enthusiasm. However, if you use overhead slides or 35 mm slides then ensure that they are formal and very well produced. Try to design your slides so you don't have to mask any lists or written words. The dark shadow across the slide is always distracting.

(5) *The manager speaks for too long*. The longest management presentation you should ever make is 20 minutes. Over this length and your audience will begin to lose interest. Never be afraid of the 10-minute presentation; if you do it well you will gain the respect of your audience. Even in the most professional 20-minute presentation you can make will contain no more than five main points. Allowing time for introduction and summary then you probably have about 3 minutes per main point. Finally, never overrun your time.

(6) *The manager tries to be clever rather than simple*. If you want to lose your audience immediately, talk over their heads. Audiences respect the speaker who can deal with substantial matters in simple and pragmatic ideas. You are standing on your feet to communicate, not to impress your superior knowledge.

(7) *The manager is poorly prepared*. The absolute minimum you need to prepare for a management presentation is five times your speaking time and this assumes you know your subject very well. If you are to give a 20-minute presentation then allow a minimum of 100 minutes to organize the structure and logic of your talk. Your presentation is mainly concerned with identifying the five main communication points and developing these in terms of interest, stress and rhythm. You will need extra time for research, making slides and a rehearsal. The overall objective of management presentations is PROFESSIONAL INFORMALITY which means an easy, relaxed but thoroughly well presented talk. Don't write your talk and try not to use note cards. Certainly NEVER read from a typed script unless you are very skilled at a lecture. Rehearse carefully thinking about and making certain that you have the logic firmly placed in your mind. Your natural knowledge and enthusiasm will give the flesh to your talk.

(8) *The manager doesn't demonstrate a logic in the presentation*. The path you are to take during your presentation is the LOGIC. Ensure that you know this logic very well by adequate preparation and always ensure that the logic is stated, both verbally and diagramatically at the start of your presentation. When you come to the end of your presentation, summarize the logic again and summarize the key communication points of the presentation. Invariably the last few minutes of your presentation should consolidate your ideas in the audience's mind.

(9) *The manager tends to waffle*. If you haven't given sufficient time to preparation on the logic of your presentation or you have insufficient knowledge about your topic then you will waffle! The responsibility for the presentation rests solely on your shoulders and there can be no excuse for your waffling.

In summary, speaking is not an art for managers, it is a skill. Of course, there are managers who have a natural gift of speaking but for any manager he or she has the potential to develop their skill to a higher level. Work through the worksheets and action plan on the following pages and gain some insight into your skills and improvement.

Worksheet 5.1 Effective speaking worksheet

This worksheet is designed to highlight how effective you are in your *management* speaking. Think about the factors below and circle a number that most represents your view of yourself. The worksheet is for your personal use so be honest with yourself.

(1)	I believe that speaking is one of the most important skills of management.	1 2 3 4 5	I believe that speaking is important but no more important than any other management skill.
(2)	Whenever I make an important speech I always think very carefully about its delivery as well as the contents.	1 2 3 4 5	Normally when I make an important speech I tend to rely more on the content than the delivery.
(3)	Speaking shows the strength of my enthusiasm.	1 2 3 4 5	I tend to be cautious when I speak.
(4)	I believe I have the right to speak my mind.	1 2 3 4 5	I tend to be passive or too aggressive when I speak.
(5)	Speaking is about expressing substantial ideas in a very simple way.	1 2 3 4 5	When I speak I rarely ask myself if I have expressed myself in the simplest way possible.
(6)	I never speak for too long and I try as far as possible to say only important things.	1 2 3 4 5	I tend to speak for too long and I do tend to say whatever is in my mind at the time.
(7)	I always look for signs of interest or disinterest in the eyes of my audience.	1 2 3 4 5	I tend not to be conscious of my audience's level of interest in what I am saying.
(8)	I am always conscious of the need to give my speech a rhythm and stress.	1 2 3 4 5	I have never thought consciously about rhythm and stress in my speech.
(9)	Wherever possible I will always use visual aids when I am talking.	1 2 3 4 5	I tend to rely solely upon my spoken word rather than visual aids.
(10)	Although I am sometimes uneasy when I am speaking I do try to ensure that nerves don't interfere with my talking.	1 2 3 4 5	I tend to suffer from nerves when I talk, particularly if the audience is five or more people.
(11)	If I don't know my subject well then I keep quiet.	1 2 3 4 5	I normally give an opinion even when I am not certain about the subject.
(12)	I rarely show aggression or impatience with my audience.	1 2 3 4 5	I tend to become irritated with the audience and sometimes I do show aggression.

Assessment: When you have circled a number for each factor, add the numbers and divide by 12. If you have a score between 1.0 and 1.4 then you are probably a very effective speaker in managerial situations. Whatever the size or seniority of the audience you are confident and well ordered and you fully recognize that effective speaking is a key factor in your performance as a manager and a key skill that is recognized by your senior managers. If you have a score between 1.5 and 2.4 then you are effective in your speaking. Probably you tend to be slightly nervous when you speak, particularly to larger audiences, but you also tend to keep your nerves to yourself. If you have a score between 2.5 and 3.5 then you have an average ability in managerial speaking. You do have some deficiency, probably in the areas of simplicity, enthusiasm and nerves. Your progress up the organization ladder will be quicker if you gain the 'extra' skill that makes the average speaker a good speaker. If you have a score between 3.6 and 4.5 then you do have an overall deficiency in the effectiveness of your managerial speaking. If you have a score between 4.6 and 5.0 then you are particularly weak. Almost certainly you are being suffered rather than enjoyed and your overall style of communication is substantially interfering with your work and your team.

DEVELOPING YOUR ACTION PLAN

Your style and effectiveness in speaking does affect very substantially how you communicate and how effective you are in persuading other managers about your ideas and solutions. Poor communication leads to wasted time and poor performance. Examine the factors where you have a number of 3, 4 or 5. The factor will give you some insight into your basic underlying problem.

Your effective speaking action plan

Use this worksheet to develop your personal action plan. Remember you are trying to increase your performance by better communication.

(1) List the factors where you have a score of 3, 4 or 5.

WEAK FACTOR

WEAK FACTOR

WEAK FACTOR

WEAK FACTOR

WEAK FACTOR

(2) Study your weak factors and the text and identify your key action points for improvement.

ACTION POINT

ACTION POINT

ACTION POINT

ACTION POINT

ACTION POINT

(3) Think about your next important speech or management presentation and work through your preparation by making notes below.

(i) Why is this presentation important to me?

(ii) What are the key points I need to communicate?

(iii) How can I express these key points in the simplest manner possible?

(iv) Am I enthusiastic about these points and do I really believe that they make a contribution to people's thinking?

(v) How long shall I talk for
and what is the essential
logic I want to
demonstrate to my
audience?

(vi) What about rhythm and
stress?

(vii) How shall I start the
presentation? What shall
I say to start? How
shall I behave to start?
How shall I manage my
nerves?

(viii) What visual aids will I
need?

(ix) What techniques shall I
use to 'read' the
audience and ensure that
interest is high?

Effective listening

In the previous section we looked at how we may develop more effective speaking. How about developing more effective listening? The skill of listening is an important one. Apart from the actual technical skill in listening which by itself improves understanding and communication, listening also has a symbolic value. Your managerial style and how it communicates itself to your subordinates is very much conditioned by your ability to DEMONSTRATE to your subordinates that you are listening and listening effectively. Listening therefore is an important skill for managers and the essential 'partner' skill to effective speaking.

What do we mean by listening? Listening is when we hear *and understand* the meaning of the person speaking to us. Many managers hear but few managers actually understand the meaning behind the words. What are the facts behind this observation? Managers tend to spend about 70% of their time in some form of communication. This communication time is made up approximately as follows: 45% listening, 30% speaking, 15% reading and 10% writing. Even though a substantial amount of time is spent listening, most managers have a poor ability to listen. About 75% of all oral communication is ignored, misunderstood or forgotten quickly. Only about 25% of what you say is received by the listener and of the 25% that is heard only a small proportion is actually understood completely.

Thus, although listening is an important skill, it is also a much under-used skill. What are the consequences of this? Well apart from the obvious consequences of poor communication, misused resources and wasted time, there is also a symbolic consequence.

From working with managers and making observations about how they listen I have come to a general conclusion. Managers tend to listen UP the organization rather than DOWN the organization. Simply stated a manager will listen more effectively to his or her boss than he listens to his subordinates. This is not surprising, inasmuch as a boss makes a heavy demand upon·a manager and also the boss has the ability to sanction the manager if instructions are not carried out effectively. Building on this observation I have carried out a number of experiments with managerial audiences on what qualities they recognize in a good boss and what qualities they recognize in a bad boss. Invariably subordinates recognize a few key qualities in their good and bad bosses. Six key factors tend to emerge:

Good Boss Factor

(1) Ability to give a clear direction.
(2) Ability to involve managers in the decision making.
(3) Ability to give the manager freedom to achieve in the way the manager wants to achieve.
(4) High technical or professional expertise in the area.
(5) Firmness and fairness in their dealing with subordinates.
(6) Ability to listen well and give time to listening to subordinates.

Bad Boss Factor

(1) Lack of direction for the subordinates.
(2) Autocratic decision making.
(3) Too close a control of the subordinates actions and decisions.
(4) Low technical or professional expertise in the area.
(5) Lack of consistency in their dealing with subordinates.
(6) Inability to listen and always too busy to listen to subordinates.

The first five factors above are dealt with more fully in the chapters on managing people. The sixth factor is concerned with the effective listening of the boss. It is clear that subordinates associate listening skills with the senior manager's style of managing. When the senior manager listens DOWN the organization as well as UP then he or she demonstrates to the subordinate a style of management that is highly associated with good leadership and sound teamwork. Without effective listening both leadership and teamwork development cannot work well.

Although we need to improve our listening skill generally, there are certain situations where listening is imperative. These situations are:

(1) When you are contemplating some action or making a decision, always listen very carefully to the ideas and words of others.
(2) When you are about to argue or criticize, make absolutely certain you have listened fully.
(3) Whenever anybody wishes to talk over a sensitive or personal issue, always listen well and hard. Often the person wishes to sort out their ideas and feelings: a good listener is essential to this.
(4) Whenever a new idea, direction or concept is raised, you should listen well at that stage.
(5) Whenever you are approached by a subordinate, pay particular attention to listening.

There is another situation where you are strongly advised to listen well because it is this situation where the greatest indiscipline of listening occurs. The greatest indiscipline of listening is GAP SEARCHING and this occurs, very frequently indeed, in meetings between managers. The phenomenon of gap searching is both interesting and dramatic. How does it operate?

Imagine two managers talking and listening in a meeting. Manager A starts to talk and manager B starts to listen. However manager A mentions an idea which sparks off the gap searching phenomenon. At the time, manager B hears the idea he stops listening and his mind remains with the idea put into his mind by manager A. Manager B might want to disagree or seek clarification or the idea has sparked off a chain of thought which he wants to talk about. From the time the idea enters manager B's mind he no longer listens effectively but seeks to interrupt manager A. For all intents and purposes it looks as though manager B is listening but in actual fact, manager B is seeking a GAP within which he can jump. When he finds a GAP he enters and starts his speech. For a short time manager A will listen to manager B but shortly he will have an idea and begin to seek a GAP whereby he can jump into the speech of manager B. Figure 5.1 illustrates gap searching.

Gap searching is a serious indiscipline for two main reasons. Firstly, it means that the time spent on effective listening in a meeting is very low. Most of the time is spent in gap searching. Secondly, gap searching always has the effect of dragging a meeting back to its beginning. The arrows marked DRAG EFFECT in the diagram show the natural drag backwards of gap searching as managers endeavour to clarify missed points due to ineffective listening.

Can managers improve their listening skills? Listening is a natural skill that can be improved. There are a few general guidelines that are important and there is also a specific skill for demonstrating more effective listening. Firstly here are the general guidelines:

(1) Be prepared to listen. Being interested and attentive are key factors in your listening. Listening requires you to *work* at listening by stimulating the speaker with your attention and trying hard to understand what is being said.

(2) Speech is *transmitting* ideas through words. Listen to the ideas that are being spoken. Work hard on the ideas and listen critically to them.

(3) Don't allow *distractions* to interfere with your listening. Don't distract the speaker by your gestures and don't respond to distractions if they occur. Concentrate on the speaker solely. Arrange your office or workspace so that distractions do not occur, e.g. close the door and redirect telephone calls.

(4) Be wary of your *prejudices*. Much of what you listen to you may not agree with; unless you can control this disagreement, it will build into a substantial barrier to all the ideas of the speaker.

(5) *Stimulate* the speaker by your listening. Use the ideas of attending, following and responding to keep your speaker active by your interest.

(6) Don't *search for 'gaps'* so that you can interject. Let people finish what they want to say, think about what you want to say, then say it. Always bear in mind that a good listener understands the need for silence.

In point 5 above I mentioned the idea of attending, following and responding. What do I mean by this? This idea is based on the work of Robert Bolton who has written widely about listening and developing assertion.

The skill of listening can be demonstrated to the speaker by following a three step process. ATTENDING — FOLLOWING — RESPONDING.

Attending Skills are basically those which heighten your attention and show that your attention to the speaker is high. Many of our attending skills depend upon body communication. When we are relaxed and alert, we show the speaker that we are ready to listen. When we incline our body towards the speaker or when we sit forward in our chair, we signal to the speaker that

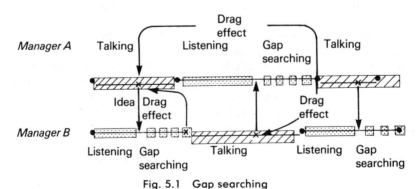

Fig. 5.1 Gap searching

we are interested. Facing the speaker squarely, with eyes at the same level, indicates that attention is high; when we sit with arms and legs open, we signal our interest and attention. Being too close or too far tends to indicate that we are not interested, whereas a comfortable distance of about 3–5 feet can signal our attention and sole interest.

Slight, rhythmic body motions also signal our attention, whereas a lack of motion, or rapid motion, signals coldness and distraction. Many gestures, such as drumming fingers, or playing with coins in pockets, signal lack of attention. Eye contact which is continuous and warm will signal attention, whereas a blank stare or avoiding direct eye contact will signal both lack of ease and attention. Clearly the specific circumstances affecting how we listen will change, but there are some general positive factors which will show attention. The negative factors tend to indicate coldness, reserved character or distraction. *Showing* that you are attending is the first basic skill of listening.

After attending, the second skill in listening is *following*. Most people do not follow a person's words or thoughts totally. In the main, the listener will interrupt the speaker and attempt to divert them. In many respects listeners seek 'gaps' within which they can interject a question or make a statement; of course, while searching for the gap and thinking about their interjection, they are not following the words and trend of thought of the other person.

A number of things help to show that we are following. Encouragements to carry on speaking are essential to show you are following. Brief responses such as: 'Oh!', 'I see', 'Right', 'Yes', 'And . . .?', 'Go on', all indicate that you are following the speaker. They all signify 'Please continue, I'm listening and I understand you'. Asking questions shows that we are interested and following the line of thought. Open-ended questions, which allow the speaker to continue and develop their replies, often show the level of understanding of the listener. However only ask one question at a time and *do not* ask too many questions.

Apart from encouragements and open-ended questions, the right sort of silence can be a powerful way of showing that you are following every word. Most listeners talk too much; the showing of responsive silence is an art. Silence itself can be a gentle nudge to conversation and it allows the speaker and the listener to communicate well. People need room to think and talk through their ideas; a silent listener is a good person for this. Being uncomfortable with silence is a sign of a poor listener! The good listener attends to the other person, observes the speaker's eyes and expressions, and thinks about what the other has said and wishes to say. All of these silent activities indicate a good listener, even in silence. Good listeners are silent and speak only when appropriate. In this way they can follow the person's words, ideas and thoughts. They avoid 'gap searching' and interjecting in the identified 'gaps' within another's speech.

Showing you are attending and following the other person are the first two skills of listening. The third skill is to show you are reflecting upon the ideas and words of the speaker. This skill, known as *response* comes from restating the speaker's ideas and feelings in such a way that they know that the ideas, etc. have been understood and accepted. These responses are made by paraphrasing the essential ideas of the speaker in a concise and factual way. Paraphrasing often shows you understand the speaker fully and that you have empathy with the speaker. It also shows that you have accurately interpreted what has been spoken. Paraphrasing concentrates on the *facts* but often the *feelings* of the speaker need to be accounted for as well.

Interpreting the feelings behind the speaker's words can be critical to good communication and the listener needs to pay attention to the feelings and emotions that are being expressed or indicated. Just as facts can be paraphrased, feelings can be summarized by the listener and this shows a truer appreciation of the situation which the speaker faces. Very often facts and feelings can be combined in a response that shows you have fully understood the whole situation. For example, simple restatements such as; 'You're disappointed because of the increase in your workload . . .', 'You're very happy about the promotion . . .', can stimulate the speaker and provide a very effective discipline for the listener to seek the core of the speech.

As a final point on listening it is worthwhile accepting that you cannot listen well at the time. One of the skills of listening is the skill of knowing which situations require more effective listening than others. In effect one is engaging a higher level of listening than is the normal everyday level. No manager can listen well if he or she feels pressured or is stressed and it is often more acceptable to accept this and state to the speaker that you cannot listen well at this time. To pretend to listen, whilst your own mind is distracted by your own problems is a guarantee of poor communication and the increased likelihood of error.

Use the following worksheet and action plans to gain insight into your own listening skills and areas for improvement.

Worksheet 5.2   Effective listening

This worksheet is designed to provide an insight into your listening skill. For each of the factors, circle a number that represents your view of your listening. The worksheet is for your personal use so be honest with yourself.

(1) To my knowledge I am rarely accused of poor listening.   1 2 3 4 5   On many occasions I have been conscious of not listening to speakers.

(2) To my knowledge no errors have occurred in my work due to poor listening.   1 2 3 4 5   On a number of occasions I have made errors in my work due to poor listening on my part.

(3) I tend to listen well to my boss, peers and subordinates.   1 2 3 4 .5   I believe I listen more intently to my boss than I do to my subordinates or peers.

(4) When I am making an important decision I always listen hard to the views of others.   1 2 3 4 5   When I am making an important decision I tend to rely on my own ideas rather than listen to others.

(5) When I have to discipline a subordinate I listen hard to their point of view.   1 2 3 4 5   When I have to discipline a subordinate I do tend to close my mind to their point of view.

(6) When I am approached on a personal matter I always give it my full attention and I listen hard.   1 2 3 4 5   When I am approached on a personal matter I am often conscious of not given the matter my full attention.

(7) I rarely search for gaps and I tend to let the other person finish their speech fully before I begin to talk.   1 2 3 4 5   I do search for gaps and I am conscious of interrupting the speaker before they have fully finished their speech.

(8) Whenever it is important to listen hard I make a conscious effort to avoid any distractions.   1 2 3 4 5   There are so many distractions in my office that I find it difficult to listen hard to other people.

(9) Whenever possible I keep an open mind about the ideas of speakers.   1 2 3 4 5   I am often accused of fixed ideas and not listening to people.

(10) I can honestly say that I am a very good listener.   1 2 3 4 5   I can honestly say that I am a very poor listener.

Assessment: When you have circled a number for each factor, add your numbers and divide by 10. If you have a score between 1.0 and 1.4 then you are a very effective listener with the ability to demonstrate that you are listening well to the speaker's words. You have made a conscious effort to improve your communications and errors or delay due to listening are at a minimum. If you have a score between 1.5 and 2.4 then you are a good listener. You could probably improve by giving more time to listening and trying to control any potential indiscipline such as 'gap searching'. Your communications are good and your performance is not impaired by poor listening. If you have a score between 2.5 and 3.5 then you are a sound, average listener. You are probably not fully conscious of the need to listen more effectively and some deficiency is due to your lack of effort in this area. Probably some error or delay has occurred because of your listening skill and your performance is slightly impaired. If you have a score between 3.6 and 4.5 then you are a poor listener. You have a general weakness across many of the factors and almost certainly you have never given listening any priority nor have you considered its effect upon your performance. Your general deficiency is probably more due to lack of awareness of the importance of listening rather than any major or fundamental weakness on your part. If you have a score between 4.6 and 5.0 then you are a very poor listener indeed. You probably hear a great deal but understand very little. You have a very closed mind about the thoughts and ideas of others and probably speaking to you is marked by many distractions and interruptions. Your performance is substantially impaired by your poor listening and it is likely that your subordinates are critical of your ability to listen. This is affecting your overall style of management.

DEVELOPING YOUR ACTION PLAN

Poor listening has many consequences. It leads to error in your work and the need to correct errors. It leads to delay and time wasting. It leads to frustration and impatience and it seriously affects your ability to lead a team and to develop a team to its full potential. In essence, poor listening can lead to very low performance. List the factors in the worksheet with scores of 3, 4 or 5 and study the factors. These will give you some insight into any underlying problems.

Your effective listening action plan

(1) List the factors with scores of 3, 4 or 5.

WEAK FACTOR

WEAK FACTOR

WEAK FACTOR

WEAK FACTOR

WEAK FACTOR

(2) Study the weak factors and the text and identify your action points.

ACTION POINT

ACTION POINT

ACTION POINT

ACTION POINT

ACTION POINT

(3) Think about your next major meeting and also any meetings you have with your subordinates. Develop some key areas for your observation in order to check on your listening skill and the skills of others.

(i) Is there any potential for error or delay due to poor listening?

(ii) Are people listening with open minds or closed minds?

(iii) What is the level of gap searching?

(iv) How much distraction or interruption is occurring?

(v) Are people listening hard?

Effective reading

One of the most frequent requests one hears in self management seminars is the request for more effective ways of handling the printed word. Business reading is now so demanding of time and concentration that even the most seasoned of businessmen can find it a chore. Often the request is not just for the time saved but for the lost pleasures of reading. Many businessmen now read a 'good novel' only during their summer holidays and the days of reading the newspapers from front to back cover are a luxury. Unfortunately, the pure pleasure of reading is now quickly being replaced by the pressure to process more and more business reading.

As with other aspects of self management, the 80/20 rule applies again. The plan fact of the matter is that we read too much because we don't select what we need to read, because we try to read all of what we have selected and, surprisingly, because we try to read everything we read many times over just to make sure we have read it! In this section, we shall look at the key skills of business reading and develop way in which business reading should be handled so that the content of reading is useful but the time spent is minimal.

The average reading speed of adults is about 200 to 300 words per minute. This reading rate will fall substantially if the material being read is very complex, monotonous, unfamiliar or written in an awkward style. On the positive side, the reading rate can be improved by about two or three times by the use of a few simple techniques, practice and a proper sense of management of your reading matter.

INCREASING READING SPEED

The simple techniques of reading effectively are of two types: correcting eye regression and sub-vocalization. *Correcting eye regression* can have a quick and substantial impact upon your reading speed. When you read, your eyes do not run smoothly across the page from left to right. In fact they stop, read a word or a few words, then move on once again, and so on. Your eyes are continually stopping and starting so that they can focus on the words. These stopping points are called 'fixation points' and at these points your eyes will read as many words as they can on either side of the fixation point. Some people can read many words at these points while others can read only one or a few. The more stopping and starting your eyes are required to do, the slower your reading speed. Associated with these rapid eye movements is the regression of the eye. Essentially this means that when

you have read a word and moved on, your eyes will return (regress) to the original word to remember what it is and to put it in the context of other words around it. So not only are your eyes stopping and starting, but also you are continually forgetting and remembering as you build up an idea of what is actually being written. We can illustrate these ideas by some diagrams of words (see Figs 5.2 and 5.3).

Eye movements for this paragraph will vary from person to person but it is likely that they will be similar to the pattern shown in Fig. 5.3. From this word diagram you can see that the eye spends considerable time moving *backwards* rather than forwards and it spends time at *rest*. To gain immediate benefit in reading speed, you need to correct this regression and develop the habit of driving your reading forward without stopping to understand every word. When the regression is corrected, you will read 'thought patterns' and not words. Then the same word diagram is likely to look like Fig. 5.4.

The other major factor which reduces reading speed is *sub-vocalization*. This is a habit we acquire as children learning to read, when we are required to read aloud and later we are required to read aloud to ourselves. Most people never break this habit and as they read, they mouth the words and mentally try to register each word.

After another appeal the council's decision was upheld by the Department of the Environment but the directors took the matter to the High Court where the appeal decision was quashed.

Fig. 5.2   Text

After another appeal the   council's decision

was upheld by the Department of the Environment

but the Directors   took the   matter to the High

Court where the   appeal decision was   quashed.

Fig. 5.3   Reading pattern before exercises

The average reading aloud speed and the reading aloud habit act as brakes on reading. As you correct regression of eye movements, it will become difficult to register each word or to read aloud to yourself effectively. Correcting regression acts as a method of correcting subvocalization.

As an aid to practising correcting regression, use a pointer (such as a pen) to run under the lines of words. Make certain you move the pointer quickly and try to concentrate on following the words as the pointer moves underneath them. As you become more proficient, then increase the speed of the pointer. After a little practice at correcting regression and reading 'thought patterns' you will be able to improve your reading speed by about two or three times. Generally it only takes a couple of hours of practice to improve your reading speed substantially. After you have practised a little, try and read everything very fast to establish the habit. Once the technique is established, you can drop back into your normal speed and only put yourself into top gear when you need to do so.

REDUCING READING LOAD

After you have increased your reading speed, you should endeavour to read *less* and not more. When faced with a heavy pile of reading, the first decision you should make is that only a small part of the pile is essential to you and, of this essential reading, only a small part of each piece will be essential reading. The first decision you should make therefore is to *reduce* substantially the volume of reading you feel required to do. On this much-reduced volume, you can then use your new reading speeds. To

After another appeal   the council's decision

was upheld   by the Department of the Environment

but the Directors took the matter to the High

Court   where the appeal decision was quashed.

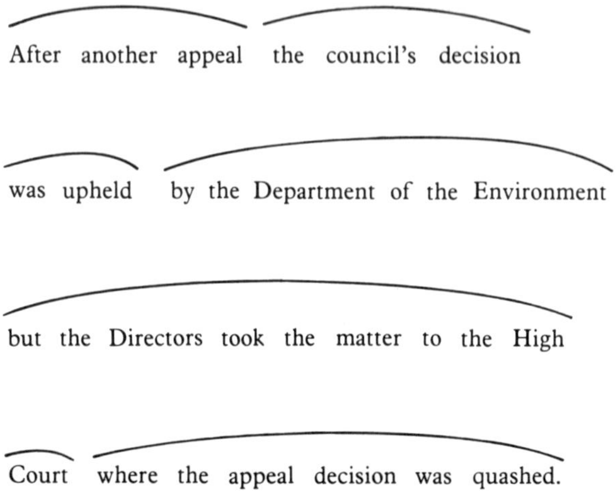

Fig. 5.4   Reading pattern after exercises

achieve this quantity reduction, rely upon the ideas of A/B/C priorities of reading and on the techniques of scanning and skimming of the reading matter.

SCANNING

The purpose of scanning is to establish the priority of the reading. 'A' priority reading relates closely to 'A' priority objectives. As a general rule, the majority of your reading should be 'A' priority reading: 'B' priority reading can be delegated for comment and 'C' priority reading matter should be screened out of your system. Scanning is probably the most natural of reading techniques. Everybody scans and generally people are effective at it.

Scanning amounts to ranging your eyes quickly over the reading matter; looking at contents pages, summaries, opening and closing paragraphs, first and last lines of paragraphs; and focusing on important words which are 'keyed' in your mind and which 'spring' from the page. The purpose of scanning is to assess what is contained in the reading so that a priority can be established for it and to gain an insight into the framework of the reading. When used effectively, scanning can reduce a pile of journals, etc. to a few pieces of essential reading in a very short time.

SKIMMING

When the essential reading is identified, the technique of skimming can be used. Skimming is essentially reading at your top speed. After you have corrected your regression, this is likely to be of the order of 600–700 words per minute. There are about 450 words on this page. When effectively skimming, you should be able to process the words on the page in less than one minute.

Effective skimming depends upon knowing and identifying the *main sentences* in a paragraph. Each paragraph will generally contain a sentence that gives the topic of the paragraph. Generally the main topic is given either in the *opening* or the *closing* sentence. Only very occasionally is a main idea expressed in the middle of a paragraph.

Another aspect of effective skimming is that signposts are generally used externally. The main signposts are *headings* and *sub-headings*. Other signposts in the body of the text are generally listings of ideas such as the use of the sequence: firstly, secondly, thirdly, and so on. Also, certain words and phrases will signal a start of an idea, e.g. 'If we look at this more closely . . .' Other words will signal a change in ideas: e.g. '. . . nevertheless it is likely that . . .' And, of course, some words and phrases will signal that the end of an idea is now in sight, e.g. '. . . therefore we can conclude that . . .'. This technique of skimming has a number of elements to it. In brief these elements are:

(1) Read at your most rapid rate.
(2) Read the title, contents page and summary.
(3) Scan the headings and sub-headings of the material.
(4) Read the first and last paragraph of each major section.
(5) Read the first and last sentence of any major paragraph.
(6) Read the final conclusion or final paragraph of reading material fairly carefully.

Taken together, the correction of regression, scanning to separate reading into levels of priority, and effective skimming, will all lead to a substantial gain in your ability to process reading material. These techniques do not have to be used on all occasions, but they represent your 'top gear' when you require to use it. As a matter of habit these techniques will give you significant control over your business reading and lead to large potential time savings. For example, in the case of a manager who may spend some 10% of his time reading, he should expect to cut this down to about 2 or 3%.

Finally in this section let us look at concentration and memory. Both these factors affect your efficiency in reading. Concentration will substantially affect your ability to comprehend and understand the reading matter and memory will affect your ability to recall the information when you need to do so. Both concentration and memory are skills that can be developed.

Concentration means that you have 'focused your attention' and are prepared to ensure that this attention remains focused on the reading matter. Lack of concentration is probably the most widely acknowledged failing in human beings. It ranges from daydreaming through to distractions but whatever the reason, the attention is drawn from the reading matter to other thoughts or ideas in your mind, or attention to other matters in your office environment.

There are a number of ways of assisting our concentration when we need to read more effectively. Here are some guidelines:

(i) It is always a good idea to schedule your reading time. As a daily discipline, set aside 15-minutes to read any pending reading or reports. Clearly on some days you will need to read for longer periods and on many occasions you will need to read continuously, in small bursts, throughout the day.

However, get into the habit of scheduling a 15-minute period for reading and this will have a cumulative effect in ensuring that your reading load is managed consistently and kept at a reasonable level.

(ii) Clear your desk of any working projects or materials. If you are following a 'clear desk' policy this will be a natural discipline after you have finished a task and before you start your reading task.

(iii) Place on your desk *all* the material that you wish to read in this reading session. Ensure that any physical distractions are under control for the 15-minute period. For example, divert your telephone and close your office door.

(iv) Sort your reading matter into priority piles. Don't worry too much about the amount of reading for your 15-minute session. If you have a great deal then only *scan* the material. If you have a little reading then you can *skim* or *study* the reading in more detail. Let the amount of reading dictate your method of processing it and your reading speed.

(v) Now you are ready to start. Mentally say to yourself '*now I must concentrate*' on this reading and '*I must finish it within the reading session*'. Make a strong effort to keep your attention on the reading.

Concentration is actually improved by providing the discipline of time and by providing a set objective to be achieved within the time.

Your level of concentration will affect your ability to recall what you have read. Invariably low concentration means low recall or memory, and high concentration means high recall or memory. Why is this the case?

Basically, your memory has two stages. You have a short-term memory which lasts for about 24 hours after your reading. However your short-term memory falls off very dramatically over the 24 hours. 80% of what you read will be completely lost within the 24-hour period. Your long-term memory is very much conditioned by the effectiveness of your short-term memory. Normally by improving your short-term memory you are increasing your chances of a better long-term memory, providing you are prepared to review your reading material at regular intervals.

However, we are more concerned with the short-term memory and concentration is a key factor in ensuring that information is lodged in your memory's filing system. Your ability to recall is determined in the first place by your ability to register the information.

When we discussed concentration we advised that you should concentrate hard and read with an objective in mind. Basically this ensures that your mind is focused upon finding the most important ideas in the author's writing. The knack in improving your short-term memory is to discard a substantial amount of what you are reading and focus *only* upon the important points. The important points create an overall picture of the author's theme and it is this theme that you should commit to your memory. When you have identified the theme put it into your own words and experience, and draw a picture of your theme and the key points.

The most useful picture you can draw is a STAR DIA-GRAM. The centre of the star has the main theme in your own words and the points of the star contain the main points. Figure 5.5 shows an example based on this section. Put a HEADING in the star diagram to assist your recall.

It is often useful to draw the star diagram on the reading material itself. If this is not practical then attach your star diagram to the reading material. Try to get into the habit of NOT re-reading material but use the star diagram for your review.

As a summary of concentration and memory, here is a list of the key action points for the improvement technique.

(1) Schedule a reading period.
(2) Keep a clear desk with only your reading material on it.

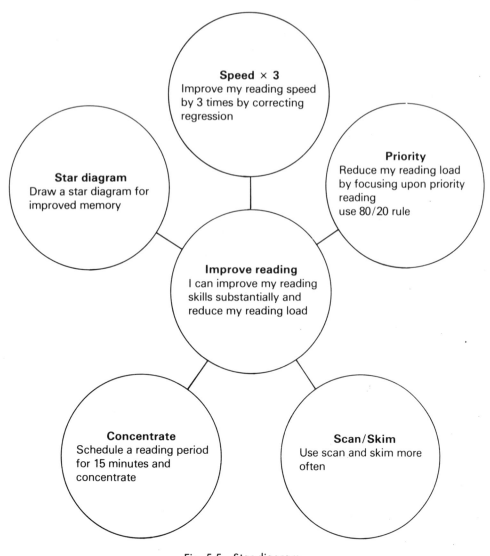

Fig. 5.5   Star diagram

(3) Control distractions.

(4) Sort your reading material into priority piles by SKIMMING.

(5) Take your important reading, focus your attention and SCAN with the objective of identifying the key points and the theme.

(6) Draw a STAR DIAGRAM of the theme and key points. [The activity of drawing the diagram tends to reinforce the learning of the key information and commits it to short-term memory.]

(7) Use your star diagram for reviewing the reading material.

Use the following worksheet and action plan to gain insight into your reading skill and any improvements which might be possible.

Worksheet 5.3   Effective reading

This worksheet is designed to provide an insight into your present level of reading skill. For each of the factors below, circle a number that represents your view of yourself. The worksheet is for your personal use so be honest with yourself.

(1) I change my reading speed to suit the reading material.　　1 2 3 4 5　I keep a constant reading speed. My reading speed is probably average.

(2) I always sort my reading into priority piles. I try to read only the important material.　　1 2 3 4 5　I don't give any priorities to my reading and I normally read all material.

(3) Whenever possible I delegate lower priority reading for comment from my subordinates.　　1 2 3 4 5　I read all my material and I very rarely delegate for comment.

(4) I use scanning and skimming techniques.　　1 2 3 4 5　I do not use scanning and skimming techniques.

(5) I never read every word but try to search for the important points.　　1 2 3 4 5　Normally I read every word.

(6) I have a regular and consistent approach to my reading. I normally schedule a reading session each day.　　1 2 3 4 5　I tend to read at any time during the day.

(7) I try always to remind myself that I need to concentrate when I am reading.　　1 2 3 4 5　I give reading my normal concentration, however I must admit that my concentration does wander.

(8) I try to set an objective to read a certain amount in a specific period.　　1 2 3 4 5　I don't set any objectives for managing the volume of my reading.

(9) I read purposely to establish the key theme and the important points.　　1 2 3 4 5　I don't necessarily set the objective to identify key themes and points.

(10) I tend to draw a picture or diagram of the key themes and points.　　1 2 3 4 5　I never draw a picture or diagram of the key theme and points.

Assessment: When you have circled a number for each factor, add the numbers and divide by 10. If you have a score of 1.0 to 1.4, you are managing your reading load very well. You have organized your reading into priorities and you process it efficiently using the minimum of time. Your recall is probably very high and overall you read very effectively. If you have a score of 1.5 to 2.4 then you read very effectively. Probably you could improve your concentration and memory but overall you are well organized with a clear understanding of priority. If you have a score between 2.5 and 3.5 you are an average reader. Probably you have not developed any system for managing your business reading. If you have a high reading load in your job you have the potential to process this reading more effectively and quickly. If you have a score between 3.6 and 4.5, you have an overall deficiency in your business reading skill. You are definitely in need of a system for managing your business reading and if your reading load is high in your job then you have a substantial opportunity for gaining more performance. If you have a score between 4.6 and 5.0, you have a very low business reading skill. Your reading priorities are haphazard and you are reading far too much for your job. You probably have difficulty in concentrating and recall because you have overloaded your interest and memory with too much low priority reading.

DEVELOPING YOUR ACTION PLAN

Business reading is a skill. It is different from any other reading you might undertake because business reading is managed by your job priorities. Many managers fall into the trap of reading everything in great detail but this is a very wasteful use of your valuable work time. Probably at least 80% of what you read is not important to your job. You must be ruthless with your business reading and give yourself a discipline for handling it effectively. List the factors with a score of 3, 4 or 5 and this will provide an insight into your basic problem.

Your effective reading action plan

Use this worksheet to develop your action plan for better organized and effective reading.

(1) List the factors with a score of 3, 4 or 5.

WEAK FACTOR

WEAK FACTOR

WEAK FACTOR

WEAK FACTOR

WEAK FACTOR

(2) Study the factors and the text and identify your key action points.

ACTION POINT

ACTION POINT

ACTION POINT

ACTION POINT

(3) Think about your present reading load at work and identify a system for handling it.

   (i) Shall I schedule a
       reading time?

   (ii) How can I sort it into
        priorities?

   (iii) Could I delegate more of
         my reading for comment?

   (iv) Shall I experiment with
        scan and skim?

   (v) Shall I experiment with a
       star diagram?

   (vi) Shall I set objectives to
        read a certain amount in
        a specified time?

Effective writing

Business writing needs a disciplined system just as business reading does. The sole purpose of business writing is to communicate well and in essence we communicate well when we are BRIEF and SIMPLE.

It is not the purpose of this section to restate the basic rules of sentence construction and the use of language; that task lies firmly in the hands of the school teacher. However, I do want to restate firmly a number of guiding principles that should not be far from the manager's mind whenever he puts pen to paper or mouth to dictation microphone.

The first observation about business writing is that the average manager writes far more than his or her job demands: fresh, newly typed memos when an internal telephone call would suffice; letters when a telex would suffice; discussion papers when key points would suffice; and reports when report summaries would be perfectly adequate. The two basic reasons for writing are when information is to be RECORDED and/or when information is to be CIRCULATED. If neither of these reasons can be identified then the manager SHOULD NOT WRITE but seek an alternative means of communication.

The second observation about writing is that many managers write for themselves rather than the reader. It is quite common in business organization to observe that written communication moving UP the organization is fully detailed and explained to the point of boredom whereas written communication moving DOWN the organization is brief and clear. Probably the reason for this is that managers writing UP the organization feel a need to justify their work fully and to demonstrate the great depth and quality of their thinking whereas managers writing DOWN the organization are more relaxed without the need to demonstrate their management skill in the practice of business writing. The plain fact of the matter is that *all* senior managers prefer the SHORT, CLEAR and ACTIONABLE document and moan with frustration when yet another 40-page report lands in their in-tray for comment.

It is worth summarizing these key principles at this early stage in the section:

(i) Write for your reader's ACTION.
(ii) Keep your writing SHORT.
(iii) Keep it SIMPLE.
(iv) Only write when you want to RECORD or CIRCULATE.

Let us take the point about READER'S ACTION and develop it more fully. The vast majority of business writing is connected with ACTION. It may be action you have taken or wish to take or it may be recommendations concerning another person's actions. If this is the case then the first step in business writing is to identify very clearly what these actions are or should be. The action must form the focal point of your writing so that supporting points are clearly connected with the action. Actions themselves must form the basis of the layout and presentation in a form that allows them to be clearly identified as such. If a reader of your written communication is unclear about what you have done, wish to do, or expect the reader to do, then much of what you have written has missed the essential point about writing for the reader from an action point of view.

How can we keep our writing SHORT and SIMPLE? The guiding principle is to write as you speak. Apart from making our business writing more human and informal, the discipline of writing as you speak corrects four basic failings:

(i) it acts as a check against long words.
(ii) it acts as a check against long sentences.
(iii) it acts as a check against long paragraphs.
(iv) it ensures that our words are concerned with action.

Words of two syllables or less are easier to read and understand. They are very familiar to readers and they communicate more powerfully. Short words are also more precise. Try to aim at 80 or 90% of your written work containing words of one or two syllables.

A sentence is a unit of thought, an idea or a concept. Each sentence should be as long as the thought requires. However, if we have the guiding principle of short sentences then we impose a stricter discipline for clear thinking. As many professional writers and journalists know, it is harder to write short sentences than it is a long one. Try to keep a sentence below 20 words.

A paragraph is a collection of sentences, or units of thought that develop a theme. Short paragraphs help the reader to read and improve the overall presentation of the written document. Normally when we want to INFORM or INSTRUCT a reader we use the *first* sentence to put across the total message. Further sentences are then used to develop any supporting points or issues. When we wish to PERSUADE or SELL to a reader then we put the main message in the *last* paragraph and we use the preceding sentences to develop our supporting points. The discipline of *first* and *last* sentences is an important one because it assists the readers when they are scanning and skimming your document.

There is a simple rule of thumb that can be used to ensure that your written work is CLEAR and expressed in the simplest form. That rule of thumb is called the

CLARITY INDEX and it is commonly used by journalists and writers to ensure that their writing is effective. This is how you work out the CLARITY INDEX:

(i) Choose a sample of 100 words.
(ii) Count the number of major punctuation marks. These are full stops, colons, semi-colons, exclamation marks and question marks.
(iii) Divide the number of words (i.e. 100) by the number of major punctuation marks. This gives you the average length of a sentence.
(iv) Record the average length of sentence.
(v) Underline all words in your sample of 100 which have three or more syllables.
(vi) Work out the percentage of long words in the sample of 100.
(vii) Record this percentage.
(viii) Add the average length of sentence to the percentage of long words (disregard the percentage sign).
(ix) This gives the CLARITY INDEX.

People in conversation normally use an index of about 30 and professional journalists aim to write their articles and pieces to the same conversational index. As a general guide each form of business writing has an index range:

business memos	— 20 to 25
business letters	— 23 to 28
business reports	— 30 to 35
business articles and books	— 35 to 40

As a general guide don't go below an index of 20 nor above 40. Aim as much as possible for the 30 index. Only go above 30 if you are dealing with anything of a technical or a descriptive nature.

Very rarely in my own professional life do I come across poorly written letters and memos. I receive too many, like other managers, and of course they could be improved by more attention being paid to the guiding principles above, but broadly speaking they are normally short and clear and written in a friendly but matter-of-fact style. However, I do complain about reports because it is this area that managers spend a great deal of time and unfortunately much of this time is wasted, certainly as far as the reader is concerned. How can we improve a manager's report writing?

The guiding principles for *all* report writing are to write your report for the purpose of being SKIM READ, or such that only the report *summary* is circulated. These are two very important writing disciplines.

In the previous section, on reading, we established how to SKIM READ. This follows a set pattern:

(1) Read title, contents page and summary.

(2) Scan the headings and sub-headings.
(3) Read the first and last paragraphs of each major section.
(4) Read the first and last sentence of each paragraph.
(5) Read the conclusions or final paragraph carefully.

If reports are written as they should be read then they have a very distinct structure and style of writing.

(1) All reports should have CLEARLY DEFINED titles, contents pages, summary and section headings.
(2) The first and last paragraph of a major section should contain the important points.
(3) Every report should have detailed conclusions, recommendations and actions.

In principle all the important points should be contained within about 20% of the report and a reader should know how to find this important 20%. More often than not, the summary and the conclusion should do the major part of this work for the reader.

I don't want to labour the point about report writing but it is an irritating aspect of a manager's life. I remember an occasion when discussing report writing with a senior manager in a large organization, he was very frustrated at the volume and density of reports that he had to respond to. He quoted the example of a 70-page report that came to his desk. He opened it and there was no clear summary or conclusion and he immediately placed the report on his reading pile. During the conversation he mentioned that he received the report about 9 weeks previously so I asked him what the report contained. I was not surprised at his answer 'I don't know, I haven't read it yet'. One could imagine the report writer — a middle manager in this case — still awaiting a reply but cautious about reminding his boss. More importantly, I thought of the vast amount of effort and time which had been devoted to the report and the possible importance of some of the actions and recommendations buried deep within it. The whole thing was yet another example of desperately poor communication and misuse of time and performance for all concerned.

This leads me to the final guiding principle on report writing. The art of report writing lies in writing effective summaries and circulating them. There are very few occasions in business when a properly constructed summary cannot do the work of the report. It need contain only the title, an indication of the contents list, the key points or issues in the report laid out in a clearly headed sequence and a full listing of the recommendations or actions. Even that lengthy report of 70 pages can be condensed into 2 or 3 pages and the chances of reading and action increase very dramatically.

Let me now finally summarize the key action points for effective business writing:

(i) Think before you write and think about ACTION.

(ii) Write only if it is absolutely necessary to RECORD or CIRCULATE.

(iii) Write about ACTION.

(iv) Always write for the reader and assume that the reader will only SKIM READ.

(v) Keep your writing SHORT.

(vi) Keep it SIMPLE. Aim for a clarity index of 30 or below. This means short words, short sentences and short paragraphs.

(vii) Discard old fashioned phraseology and write as you speak. Aim for a friendly, matter-of-fact style.

(viii) When you write a report, write it for SKIM READING. Always ensure that the important points of action are in the summary and conclusions.

(ix) Never assume that your report will be read fully. If it is not read then it is your fault and not the reader's.

(x) Get into the habit of writing good summaries and circulate these. You'll do more for your own reputation and you will lead the organization towards a better use of its time as well as improving communications and action.

Use the following worksheet and action plan to gain insights into your own effectiveness in business writing and to identify areas for improvement.

Worksheet 5.4   Effect writing

This worksheet is designed to show your present level of effectiveness in managing your business writing. Study the factors and circle the numbers that represent your view of yourself. The worksheet is for your personal use so be honest with yourself.

(1) I believe I write the minimum possible for my type of job.	1	2	3	4	5	I believe I could reduce my writing quite substantially in my type of job.
(2) Wherever possible I concentrate upon ACTION.	1	2	3	4	5	I tend to be too descriptive in my style and unfortunately ACTION tends to be hidden.
(3) I would describe my writing as SHORT and to the point.	1	2	3	4	5	I would describe my writing as probably too long and descriptive.
(4) 'Keep it simple' is one of my principles when I write.	1	2	3	4	5	I tend to be complicated and detailed in my business writing.
(5) I write as I speak.	1	2	3	4	5	I tend to have a different style for writing and for speaking.
(6) I don't generate paperwork.	1	2	3	4	5	I do have a reputation for generating paperwork.
(7) I never assume that a reader will read all my words, so I plan to get the main points across quickly.	1	2	3	4	5	I have always assumed that readers will read all I have written.
(8) I write reports for SKIM READING and I concentrate on the summary and conclusion.	1	2	3	4	5	I don't particularly write for SKIM READING and I assume that the reader will read all the report.
(9) I never circulate a report but I always circulate the summary.	1	2	3	4	5	I circulate all my reports in their entirety.
(10) I believe I have developed a good skill in business writing.	1	2	3	4	5	I believe I have substantial improvements to make in my business writing.

Assessment: When you have circled a number for each of the factors, add the numbers and divide by 10. A score between 1.0 and 1.4 means that you have mastered the skill of effective business writing. You use your time well by ensuring effective communication in the minimum amount of words. If you have a score between 1.5 and 2.4 then you are well on the way to being very effective in your writing. If you have a score between 2.5 and 3.5, you are an average business writer. You probably have an overall deficiency in terms of CLARITY and BREVITY and you could improve your performance and time usage be being more succinct. If you have a score between 3.6 and 4.5 then you are a poor business writer. Your are not writing for action nor for the reader and you are probably far too descriptive in your style. If you have a score between 4.6 and 5.0 then you need to improve quite considerably. Your performance, communication and time usage is being affected and a fair proportion of what you produce is clogging up the system.

DEVELOPING YOUR ACTION PLAN

Business writing is about speed of response and action. It is about clarity and simple communication in the briefest possible manner. All of these features affect your performance and the performance of others around you. List the factors with a score of 3, 4 or 5 and this will give you some insight into your underlying problem.

Your effective writing action plan

Use this worksheet to develop your personal action plan.

(1) List the factors with a score of 3, 4 or 5.

WEAK FACTOR

WEAK FACTOR

WEAK FACTOR

WEAK FACTOR

WEAK FACTOR

(2) Study the factors and the text and identify your key action points.

ACTION POINT

ACTION POINT

ACTION POINT

ACTION POINT

ACTION POINT

(3) Think about your business writing for next week. What strategy are you going to pursue to make sure you move it quickly without reducing the quality of its communication.

My strategy is:

6
Managing your work flow

So far in this book we have looked at how you can assess your performance and time management and how you can develop an improvement plan. Part of your improvement plan would cover how you effectively manage people around you and your subordinates, and how you effectively communicate.

Your improvement plan would also have covered various areas which are all involved with how you process your work or how you ensure that work under your control flows smoothly. It is in the area of work processing that many managers have developed bad habits. Often these bad habits have existed for many years and undoubtedly the impact that these bad habits have had upon their performance is very high. In this chapter we will cover a number of key areas. Each area itself will provide substantial gains in personal productivity but when taken together and effectively managed there can be no doubt that a manager's performance would improve very substantially. The topics we will cover are: meetings management; working with your secretary; and personal organization. This latter topic of Personal Organization will cover the essential ideas behind how you organize your desk, control interruptions and how you handle your telephone work.

Meetings management

Meetings between people at work are the largest users of time at work. Many people will spend about 40% of their time in meetings, while people in senior positions in an organization are likely to spend about 60–70% per cent of their time in meetings of one sort or another. With all this time devoted to meetings, how can we assure that the time is well used?

Because so much time is spent in meetings, you can rest assured that people have strong views about them. A review of their views shows that there are 'Seven Deadly Sin' of meetings:

(1) Meetings do not have a purpose or are unnecessary.
(2) Too many people at the meeting.
(3) Meetings do not have agendas or have bad agendas.
(4) People do not prepare for meetings.
(5) Time keeping is poor in meetings.
(6) Chairman (if any) exercises poor control of the discussion.
(7) Action of the meeting is unclear.

The 'seven deadly sins' are not the total picture of people's complaints about meetings. There are many other points of complaint which all tend to underline the basic problem with meetings: namely that meetings are the worst managed aspect of organizational life. Bearing in mind their importance to the health of the organization and the amount of time spent in meetings, meetings management must be one of the prime areas for improvement.

Let us review the main points of weakness in meetings management and establish some golden rules of good practice. A weakness in their management is the lack of purpose for a meeting. This manifests itself in a lack of objectives, priorities and resources, a lack of awareness of what decisions are required or what problems are to be solved and so on. The main reason why meetings appear to have no purpose is because the person calling the meeting is unclear of the purpose. Therefore the proper management of the meeting fails from the very early stages. Frequently the meeting is called with the purpose of finding the purpose, or the often quoted 'meeting about a meeting'. Thinking through their purpose at an early stage is a prerequisite to good meetings.

If you have difficulty with thinking about the purpose, then it is often useful to consider that meetings tend to fall into one of eight main categories:

(1) Meetings to progress and co-ordinate projects, activities and people.
(2) Meetings to brief people and exchange information.
(3) Meetings to build team morale and involvement or to reinforce personal relationships.
(4) Meetings to solve problems.
(5) Meetings to make decisions.
(6) Meetings to share risks and sensitive or difficult decisions.
(7) Meetings to plan developments and direction.
(8) Meetings to generate ideas.

Although a meeting can have a number of identifiable purposes, it is often preferable to concentrate on one or two of them only. In this way the meeting is clear from the outset and the contribution of the participants can be directed and effective. The difficulty comes when different purposes are combined and different participants are required for these different purposes; consequently the meeting grows in people, time use and content. The first golden rule in meetings management is *concentrate the meeting on a concise and easily understood purpose*. Always ask the question: 'What is the purpose of this meeting?' State the answer in about six words: 'To brief managers on developments'; 'To generate new product ideas'; 'To make a decision on Project X'; 'To develop rapport with our main customer'.

Another aspect is the calling of unnecessary meetings. We have seen the substantial amount of time many managers spend in meetings and we must accept that many of the meetings attended are, in fact, unnecessary or unjustifiable in terms of the time and people devoted to them. More often than not the unnecessary meeting comes about from *habit*; people just get into the habit of regular meetings and the purpose of these meetings becomes weak over time.

The other main reason for unnecessary meetings is the lack of design and thinking through of the purposes as stated in the previous section. It is a very good practice to think about the *costs* of a meeting and then assess whether your estimates of the cost actually justify the meeting being called or your attendance. Not only will you have the direct costs of salaries, over-heads, travel, accommodation or whatever, but also the opportunity costs of working on more important matters. Without doubt, meetings are extremely expensive and the costs of meetings should be a strong guiding principle in your management of meetings. The second golden rule is *only attend a meeting if it is absolutely necessary and important*.

A weak area of meetings management is the lack of thinking that goes into the participant list. The purpose of the meeting will clearly define the participant listing. For example, if the meeting is to make a decision, then the key decision makers are the participants. If the purpose is to solve a problem, then only those affected by the problem and who can make a contribution to a possible solution, should participate. One of the major difficulties in this area is the erroneous idea that every meeting should involve everybody who might be associated with the purpose of the meeting. It is useful to remember that a *briefing meeting* is often the best mechanism of keeping people informed and involved. If the briefing meetings can be staged at appropriate times, then the need to involve everybody in working meetings is substantially reduced. As a general rule, the fewer the people at a meeting and the higher their relevancy to the purpose of the meeting, then the more effective the meeting will be in outcome and use of time. The third golden rule is *limit meetings to as few people as are relevant*.

A further weakness in meetings management is the misuse of agendas. Agendas are very much conditioned by the purpose of the meeting and any meetings that have been held previously. Often the action points of previous meetings are agenda points for the present meeting. Agendas tend to be either non-existent, poorly structured, or too long and incapable of control. Many people forget that one of the purposes of the agenda is to inform people who will be attending the meeting, of which subjects they need to prepare themselves on. If this is the case, then *all* agendas should be circulated prior to a meeting with a note on preparation by the participants. The fourth golden rule is *always ensure that your meeting has an agenda that describes the purpose, what is to be discussed, what is to be achieved and what is to be prepared by the participants*.

Another weakness is the lack of preparation by participants. Preparation for a meeting is an absolute *must* if the meeting is to be short, effective and enjoyable. In the structure of an agenda, it is often useful to place a 'unifying' or 'consensus' topic at the beginning of the agenda in order to generate the harmony of the team and to set the climate for the meeting. Any topic that could lead to conflict is best handled in the middle of the meeting and a meeting should always end on a 'unifying' topic.

A very desirable aim is always to ensure that the IMPORTANT agenda items come first in the meeting and the UNIMPORTANT come last. Always state on the agenda those items which participants must prepare for. The fifth golden rule of meetings is *ensure preparation by identifying the IMPORTANT items*.

Meetings management can also be weak on time keeping. The agenda must always stipulate the START and FINISH TIME of the meeting. It is always a good rule for the chairman to establish in his or her own mind how much time is to be spent on each item. This ensures that the meeting is both well structured and follows the priority of the items rather than the whims of the participants. The chairman should always start on time and resist any pressure to re-start the meeting for late arrivals. It is always a good idea to keep items on the agenda to a minimum and ideally you should aim for a 20% time saving on your present time use unless there are exceptional circumstances. The sixth golden rule of meetings is *always ensure good time management*.

The chairman's failure to control the meeting properly is another weakness in meetings management. Let it be stated at the outset that meetings with an effective chairman are superior to meetings which have no chairman or weak chairmanship. The essential purpose of the chairman is to control *how* the meeting goes about its business rather than the content of the meeting. Clearly the chairman will have a contribution to make to the purpose of the meeting but, over and above this, he is responsible for the overall effectiveness of how the meeting is conducted. Some of the key mistakes in chairmanship are:

(1) Failure to state the purpose of the meeting at the outset of the meeting.
(2) Failure to start and finish on time.
(3) Failure to ensure agreement on policy before the discussion of details.
(4) Failure to manage conflict between individuals.
(5) Failure to control the proportion of time spent on agenda items (often the least important item takes the majority of time).
(6) Failure to lead a discussion effectively by establishing FACTS, followed by INTERPRETATION OF THE FACTS, followed by CONCLUSIONS.
(7) Failure to control 'Red Herrings' or discussions that are off the point.
(8) Failure to stop 'meetings within meetings' by groups of participants.

(9) Failure to control interruptions.
(10) Failure to ensure that all participants are involved and contributing to the discussion.
(11) Failure to ensure that participants are listening to the meeting effectively and that 'gap searching' is minimized.
(12) Failure to summarize agreements and actions and which participants are accountable for actions.

The seventh golden rule of meetings is that *good chairmanship of the meeting is critical to the success of the meeting*.

It is often a weakness in meetings that the participants are not clear on who is accountable for what actions. This clearly is the responsibility of the chairman, however it is so important that it is worth repeating the point more directly. The function of a meeting is to achieve action, and actions must be very clearly stated and made accountable. Actions must describe: WHAT, WHO and WHEN. Ideally, participants at meetings should leave the meeting with their ACTION MINUTES. The eighth golden rule of meetings is that ALL ACTIONS SHOULD BE CLEARLY STATED AND AGREED.

Action points on good practice

The following action points will summarize the text:

— The amount of time you spend in meetings is high. Aim to make your meetings substantially more effective by being CRISPER and better PLANNED.
— Always clearly define the purpose and state times at the outset of the meeting.
— Aim to plan meetings that have a single purpose and a minimum agenda.
— Never hold a meeting where the purpose does not justify the costs incurred and always be very selective about attending meetings which are unclear or badly managed.
— Aim to have only those people at the meeting who are relevant to the purpose.
— Plan an agenda in advance and circulate it in advance. Each agenda item needs a full description of the item, which is to be achieved by discussing it, what preparation is required, and the importance of the agenda items. Always know in your own mind how much time you will allocate to each item and ensure that important items and those establishing rapport come first.

— Publish both start and finish times for the meeting. Always start on time and always try to finish on time. Try to plan your meetings for a 20% time saving.
— If you are the chairman then manage the HOW of the meeting as well as making a technical contribution. Re-read the failure points of chairmanship above and establish your own strengths and weaknesses. Remember chairmanship is a skilled job.
— Never finish a meeting without clearly establishing ACTION and ACCOUNTABILITY.
— Remember that probably about one half of all the meetings you attend are under your chairmanship. In this case you can only blame yourself for low performance and time wasting. For the other half you need to suggest gently that meetings management is improved and it is always a good idea to establish a 'code of good practice' with your peers on how meetings should be managed. Also remember that the action points stated above apply to small 'one to one' meetings as well as to larger more formal meetings.

Worksheet 6.1 Effective meetings

This worksheet is designed to provide a guide to how effectively you presently manage *your* meetings. For each factor, circle a number that most represents your view of your own management of the meetings that you chair. The worksheet is for your own personal use so be honest with yourself.

(1) I spend the minimum amount of time in meetings and they are effective and well planned.   1   2   3   4   5   I spend far too much time in meetings and mainly they could be more effective.

(2) I always plan ahead and clearly define the purpose of my meetings.   1   2   3   4   5   I rarely plan my meetings in advance and the purpose is probably unclear.

(3) I always establish in my own mind that the meeting is cost effective.   1   2   3   4   5   I very rarely attempt to establish whether my meetings are most effective.

(4) I always try to keep my meetings to the minimum number of relevant people.   1   2   3   4   5   Probably my meetings have too many people and not all those people are necessarily relevant.

(5) I always publish an agenda in advance and I spend time thinking carefully about my agenda.   1   2   3   4   5   I rarely publish an agenda and probably my agendas are weak and sketchy.

(6) Normally people are well prepared for my meetings.   1   2   3   4   5   I always have the common complaint that people are not well prepared for my meetings.

(7) I always publish the FINISH time and allocate time properly to each agenda item.   1   2   3   4   5   I rarely publish a FINISH time and probably my time management could be improved fairly substantially.

(8) I am very conscious of the need for good chairmanship and I actively try to improve my skills.   1   2   3   4   5   I am afraid that my chairmanship is haphazard.

(9) At the end of each meeting I allocate time to summarizing, and ensure that all actions are accountable.   1   2   3   4   5   I often end a meeting without ensuring that actions are clearly accountable.

(10) I always try to ensure that meetings where I am not chairman are properly managed.   1   2   3   4   5   Other people's meetings are their responsibility.

Assessment: When you have circled a number for each factor, add the numbers together and divided by 10. A number between 1.0 and 1.4 means that you have very firmly grasped that meetings need to be effectively managed and you are always conscious of the need to ensure good performance. A number between 1.5 and 2.4 means that you are a strong meetings manager but with a few weaknesses. A number between 2.5 and 3.5 means you are average in your meetings management. Bearing in mind the importance of meetings and the amount of time you spend in them, you need to improve very actively. A number between 3.6 and 4.5 means that you are very weak in this area. Almost certainly your meetings are low in effectiveness and not particularly productive for you or the participants. A number between 4.6 and 5.0 means that you are wasting your time and everybody else's time in your meetings. Almost certainly the output of your meetings is very erratic.

DEVELOPING YOUR MEETINGS ACTION PLAN

Good meetings are good because you have decided to manage them rather than just hold them. Remember you can improve your performance very substantially by managing your meetings and save a lot of time in the bargain. List the factors with scores of 3, 4 or 5 and study the wording of the factors to highlight your underlying problem areas. Also study the combination of factors. Factors 1, 2, 3, 4, 5 are concerned with your PLANNING of your meeting and factors 6, 7, 8, 9 and 10 are concerned with your performance WITHIN THE MEETING itself.

Your meetings action plan

Use this worksheet to help you to develop your meeting management skills.

List the factors with scores of 3, 4 or 5 on the Meeting Worksheet

WEAK FACTOR

WEAK FACTOR

WEAK FACTOR

WEAK FACTOR

WEAK FACTOR

Study the wordings of the factor and refer to the text. Commit yourself to action points.

ACTION POINT

ACTION POINT

ACTION POINT

ACTION POINT

ACTION POINT

Study the combination of weak factors and highlight whether you are weak in PLANNING or WITHIN THE MEETING itself.

Think about a meeting that is imminent. Make notes on how you are to manage this meeting.

(i) What is the purpose?
(ii) Is this purpose cost effective?
(iii) Who will attend?
(iv) What is the agenda in terms of description, action, preparation, importance and time allocation?
(v) How can I ensure good preparation for the meeting?
(vi) What time should I FINISH the meeting?
(vii) What are my main weaknesses in chairmanship and what will I do in this meeting to improve my skills?
(viii) Have I allocated time to summarize and ensure that ACTIONS are ACCOUNTABLE?

Working with your secretary

One of the most valuable resources you have is probably the resource you use least and use the least effectively. For many managers, secretaries represent a great potential which is rarely tapped to the full. On one hand, we have managers who under-use their secretaries while on the other hand, we have secretaries who consider their jobs as busy but not necessarily stretching their potential or as rich as they could be. There can be no doubt that the relationship between manager and secretary is one which needs attention if greater personal performance is to be achieved.

There appear to be a number of features that impede the proper working relationship between manager and secretary. Firstly, very few managers actually consider that they may or can use their secretary to *achieve important performance goals*. Just as managers have some difficulties in delegating important work, they experience the same difficulties (and probably more so) when it comes to delegating work to secretaries. Not using a secretary for important performance goals is an under-utilization of the secretary and the manager's time. Much of the resistance in this area rests not upon facts but upon prejudice, traditional social values and a lack of willingness to experiment with or develop secretaries to work on important goals with the delegated authority of the manager himself.

Secondly, managers tend not to involve secretaries in the *planning* of their work, in the work itself and how this work relates to the overall goals of the organization. Managers tend to have a very restricted view of their secretaries. They tend to take a short-term outlook on how a secretary can work with the manager and consequently the need to plan work together is low. Another aspect of this restricted outlook is that secretaries are not properly inducted into or briefed on the policies, markets, customers, technologies and so on of the company. Very rarely will the secretary's abilities be developed to the extent that they will have a broad overview of the company and only on the odd occasion, will a secretary receive business or management training so that she may perform her duties and, within defined limits, those of the manager more effectively.

The third factor is that managers receive *no training* whatsoever on how they should or may work with their secretaries and how they can work effectively as a team. Secretaries, on the other hand, if they have been trained well, will have some skills. However, because managers are not trained in good habits, even the most effective

and brightest secretary will have difficulty in working with the manager as well as her potential would allow. There can be no doubt that *the main responsibility lies with the manager* to improve the working relationship.

Are there any guiding principles that will improve the productivity between secretary and manager? If we look at this from the secretary's point of view for a moment, then we might gain an insight. Probably the first principle is that the secretary should be stretched more in terms of performance. This does not necessarily mean that she should work longer or harder, but that the *nature of the job* and the *importance of the activities* should be stretching and demanding. This job enrichment necessarily means that the secretary may perform, within defined limits, the important performance objectives of the manager. Often the best first step in this direction is to choose one of the performance objectives of the manager and consult the secretary on the objective and how it may be performed. In the early stages, establish a development and training plan whereby the secretary acquires the necessary skills or techniques to perform the activities of the objective. When this has been completed then, just as we advised in the section on delegation, delegate the whole objective and coach the secretary through it as and when required.

The second guiding principle is that secretaries should be treated with greater consideration and warmth. A key factor in the potential productivity between manager and secretary is the *personal relationship* between them. Without a mutual respect based upon a consideration for each other and personal warmth and confidence, the relationship cannot grow past the basic thresholds of work achievement and productivity. There can be no doubt that a sound personal relationship will stretch the performance of both the manager and the secretary. Consideration shows in many ways, for example, preparing for dictation in advance, praising when appropriate and supporting more.

The third guiding principle is that a secretary should be closely involved in your job and informed on all its aspects. Probably the greatest criticism from secretaries is the *lack of involvement* in and information about the manager's job. This can be contrasted with the reasons a secretary rates a boss highly, because they feel involved and continually informed. Managers should plan their jobs with their secretaries and brief their secretaries on all aspects of the company and business. Monthly, weekly and daily schedules should be planned together; in many respects, your secretary should be seen as a 'personal' manager helping to plan and organize your work. Through this closer relationship with your job, involvement is developed and consolidated as indeed is personal warmth and confidence.

The fourth guiding principle is to *consult together* on how effectively you are working together and how improvements can be gained. Often the secretary will have many ideas — either from her training or previous experiences with different managers — on how to gain improvements through better organization. Because the issue has never been raised and you have become set in your own ways, these ideas have never been expressed. Probably the most significant single task you can undertake to improve your productivity is to sit down with your secretary and decide on how you can both work best together to attain higher output. Have a go! Set aside one hour as soon as you can and you will be very surprised at the outcome.

Bearing in mind these guiding principles, can we translate them into a plan of action for you and your secretary? Clearly the individual personalities and characters of the manager and secretary will dictate their individual plans as indeed will the job environment. However there are a number of pointers to more effective practice:

— Brief your secretary on your business, its organization, its personnel and its customers. Go through the corporate plan, its key policies, its key strengths and weaknesses as a business and the major aspects of its business environment. Work through the major trends in the sales and markets of the business and identify the key competitive factors that make your business different from and better than the competitors. Brief your secretary on how the parts of the business fit together into a whole and the major performance objectives of your job. Highlight your plans for your job over the next year and identify the key areas where your secretary can be of most help.

— Brief your secreary on the key objectives, activities and priorities of your job as you presently see them. Concentrate on the immediate term. Concentrate particularly on the priorities of your job, the priority activities, your priority times, key deadlines, priority people affecting your job. Work out a broad plan on how these priorities can best be managed between you.

— Work through with your secretary how your 'A' priority time is spent and managed. Discuss your work and time preferences and establish guidelines on how your secretary can protect your 'A' priority time and how she can organize your meetings and appointments in order to create continuous working time. Brief your secretary on how people are to

be dealt with if they seek to use your 'A' priority time.

— Establish weekly planning sessions whereby you and your secretary can review the work of the week ahead, update the work approaching over the next few weeks and the work which is presently in hand. Always have a daily planning session early in the day so that you can both confirm the priorities of the day and any special matters to be dealt with. Never confuse job planning time with handling correspondence or dictation. Keep planning time separate.

— After consultation with your secretary, review the requirements of one of your 'A' priority performance objectives. Work through the goal with your secretary and identify how she may help or manage certain aspects of the objective. Based upon this consultation, set up a specific training and development programme to provide your secretary with the necessary skills and techniques to perform the work. When appropriate, delegate the objective (within the limits defined) and monitor the progress. Involve your secretary as much as you can on your 'A' priority work.

— Consider delegating 'B' priority work to your secretary in its entirety. Minor projects can be handled from start to finish. Create a climate of ideas and initiative so that projects relating to improvements can be self-initiated and implemented. Let your secretary deal with all 'C' priority work, once you have established whether it should be delegated, deferred, scrapped or screened. A well-briefed secretary should be able to handle, probably more efficiently, all the 'C' priority work which you refuse to let go of, but which interferes considerably with your working performance.

— Work through with your secretary how you would like routine work handled; how visitors and telephone calls that interrupt your 'A' priority work should be handled. You should also work through her duties and authority when you are absent from the office. In your absence, your secretary should be able to handle a substantial part of your 'B' and 'C' priority work and she should be able to handle, with sensitivity, any demands for 'A' priority work. At the very least, she should be briefed on a 'holding position' for your important work.

— Work through with your secretary how people should best be handled. Apart from the need for courtesy with visitors, how can both of you impress your energy and performance on the visitor? What sort of image do you both project? Work through your telephone reception of callers and ensure that calls are handled immediately or returned as promised. In the case of visitors establish a gentle reminder system for removal of visitors who overstay their welcome.

— Work with your secretary on how best to organize your desk workspace. Develop a system that your secretary can manage for you. The basic system could be: *Urgent, To Do, File, Abeyance, Mail.* Once the basic system is established, let your secretary push the work through the system. This will mean that she will arrange incoming work in order of A, B, C, X priority and provide all the necessary background information or files to support the work. 'A' priority work will mainly be handled by the manager but a substantial proportion of 'B' and 'C' priority work will be handled by the secretary.

— Establish a *Quality Standard* for outgoing work such as mail, memos and any typewritten work. Once the standard has been agreed, don't re-read the secretary's work. Checking on typed work is an indication of a lack of trust and will hamper the development of your relationship with your secretary. Clearly the standard should be that no typed work will leave the office with errors or badly presented, but this standard should be your secretary's for checking, not yours. Overcontrol of the technical skills of the secretary stunts the proper development of the proper performance role.

— Wherever possible, develop a personal relationship with your secretary. As we have stated previously the proper basis of the relationship should be consideration. This means that trust, confidence, warmth and good temper are essential to the relationship between you. If appropriate, let your secretary handle personal matters and confidential matters.

— Work through with your secretary how best she can be developed. Secretaries perform better at their work when they are develped as a 'manager'. A development plan should include the basic skills of management: communication, interpersonal skills, leading and planning, etc. Depending on the technical or professional nature of your work, your secretary should attend familiarization training courses on your basic professional and technical matters. Whenever appropriate your secretary should attend your business seminars, exhibitions and sales conferences, etc., so that she acquires the experience, knowledge and skills of your business environment. Just as you would appraise subordinate managers and subordinate supervisors, always appraise your secretary and develop the necessary training programme to suit.

— Work through with your secretary the bad habits you have acquired over time. Removing these will improve the consideration and confidence between you. Almost certainly the bad habits will include:

(1) Not preparing for correspondence in advance.
(2) Not keeping your workspace and desk tidy.
(3) Not advising when you are leaving your office.
(4) Not praising enough and not supporting enough.
(5) Not keeping appointments or making wrong appointments.
(6) Asking your secretary to tell white lies.
(7) Not keeping work flowing across your desk.
(8) Avoiding return of telephone calls, or returning calls late.
(9) Lack of planning affecting your secretary workload and schedule.

— Discuss thoroughly how your travel arrangements should be best handled, what standards of travelling and accommodation are required, and when the best timings are for you to plan your trips. Establish how best you should be prepared for your trips and what information and work preplanning is essential for a successful trip. Let your secretary handle all the de-briefing and follow-up arrangements. Wherever possible, let your secretary remind you and handle all your expenses for business purposes.

— Work through with your secretary how your meetings are to be managed. This means which meetings are to be attended and all the necessary preparation for effective meetings. Your secretary should manage the meeting arrangements, the agenda and its distribution, and any necessary work preparation for the meeting. After the meeting, minutes should be distributed within 24 hours.

— Building on the meetings management, go through with your secretary how work that has been delegated by you can best be monitored for time. Generally the secretary can manage an abeyance file, and at the appropriate time, the action points and the necessary reference file can be placed in front of the manager.

— Brief your secretary on the information and reading needs of your job. Establish how best to train your secretary in information searching and retrieval. Concentrate on the priority information needs of your job. Work through your reading requirements and, if appropriate, delegate reading and commenting back to your secretary or other assistants. When used effectively your secretary should be an additional pair of 'eyes and ears' for your job.

You can see from the points raised above that the working relationship between yourself and your secretary covers many aspects. It is interesting to note that, whereas, in the past, the principal tasks of the secretary were of a technical secretarial nature, this is not now the case. The secretary of today is very much a manager of work and time and is much more involved in the work of the business and better management of the decision-making process. The secretary has a greater role in your productivity than you probably acknowledge; this potential could be released by better consultation between you about how you may work together.

Worksheet 6.2 Secretary

This worksheet is designed to show whether you are using your secretary to her full potential. Study the factors and circle a number that most represents your view of how you are using your secretary. The worksheet is for your personal use so be honest with yourself.

(1) I am very confident that my secretary is fully aware of the business, its plans, its policies and its market place. 1 2 3 4 5 It is likely that my secretary is not fully aware of the business, its plans, its policies and its market place.

(2) My secretary is fully aware of my job objectives, my job priorities and the key activities and their deadlines. 1 2 3 4 5 My secretary is only partially aware of my job objectives, my job priorities and the key activities and their deadlines.

(3) My secretary is fully briefed on how I should spend my time on job priorities and she ensures that my 'A' time is well protected by effective diary control. 1 2 3 4 5 My secretary is not aware of my job priorities and there are many examples of where diary control could be improved.

(4) My secretary and I always have a job planning session each day. 1 2 3 4 5 We have irregular job planning sessions.

(5) I have trained my secretary to handle important work and much of my low priority work is handled completely and very effectively by my secretary. 1 2 3 4 5 I am not confident that my secretary could handle important work. Much of my low priority work could be handled but we have not discussed how this should be done.

(6) My secretary and I have discussed how we handle people and improve our overall image to visitors and callers. 1 2 3 4 5 To be frank, my secretary and I have not discussed our overall image to the visitors and callers.

(7) My secretary and I have now established a first class office and desk system to streamline work. 1 2 3 4 5 Our desk and office system are in need of improvement.

(8) I rely on my secretary to ensure good quality typing work. Unless it's important I rarely check for error. 1 2 3 4 5 I insist on checking all typed work. I believe I am responsible for the work that leaves my office.

(9) My personal relationship with my secretary is very good. We rely on our strengths and are good tempered about our weaknesses. 1 2 3 4 5 My personal relationship with my secretary could be improved.

(10) I always appraise the performance of my secretary and we plan how to build experience and gain training for the secretary. 1 2 3 4 5 To be frank, I have never considered a formal appraisal of my secretary.

(11) My secretary feels free to remind me about my bad habits as a manager and I try to eradicate them. 1 2 3 4 5 I don't have any bad habits, certainly as far as my secretary is concerned!

(12) My secretary is fully involved in helping me to manage my meetings and she has established a first class system for reminding me on preparation and follow-up. 1 2 3 4 5 To be frank I think my secretary could be more involved in managing my meetings and ensuring better preparation and follow-up.

Assessment: When you have circled a number for each factor, add the numbers and divide by 12. If you have a score between 1.0 and 1.4 you have a superb working relationship with your secretary and your performance as a manager is greatly enhanced by the level of management support your secretary is providing. A score between 1.5 and 2.4 means that you have a very good working relationship and you probably rely heavily on your secretary to support your own performance as a manager. A score between 2.5 and 3.5 means you have an average working relationship with your secretary and there are a number of areas that could be improved. Almost certainly any improvements you make will lead to better organization and greater control over your time and self management. A score between 3.6 and 4.5 means that you are weak in your working relationship. Probably you have never *constructively* thought through how you should work together and without doubt you are treating your secretary solely as a typist rather than a part of your management team. A score between 4.6 and 5.0 means that you are using your secretary very ineffectively. You are probably oblivious to the strengths of your secretary and she is greatly under-used. Your own performance would improve substantially if you improved the working relationship.

DEVELOPING YOUR ACTION PLAN

List the factors where you have circled 3, 4 or 5. When you study these factors you will highlight the general areas of improvement. Also study the combination of factors. Factors 1 and 2 are concerned with BRIEFING your secretary on the wider context of your job. Factors 3, 4 and 5 are concerned with your secretary's role in PLANNING your job. Factors 6, 7, 8, 10 and 12 are concerned with how INVOLVED you and your secretary are in ensuring higher performance and Factors 9 and 11 are concerned with the quality of the PERSONAL RELATIONSHIP you have.

Your action plan

Use this worksheet to develop your action plan. Remember your own performance as a manager depends upon your working relationship with your secretary. You have probably never *constructively* appraised this relationship and whatever the strengths, they have probably come about solely as a result of experience and habit. Secretaries are not solely typists and are more properly used when they are part of your management team. A well trained secretary allows you to have more time on your top priority work and also a better control of all your time at work.

List out the factors with a score of 3, 4 or 5.

WEAK FACTOR

WEAK FACTOR

WEAK FACTOR

WEAK FACTOR

WEAK FACTOR

Think through ideas on how these weak factors could be improved. Develop action points.

ACTION POINT

ACTION POINT

ACTION POINT

ACTION POINT

ACTION POINT

Study any combination of factors to highlight areas of BRIEFING, PLANNING, INVOLVEMENT and PERSONAL RELATIONSHIPS.

Now, put in your diary a one-hour session for a CONSTRUCTIVE APPRAISAL of your secretary. Inform your secretary of this appraisal session. In order to prepare for this appraisal session work through the agenda points below.

Agenda Points	Your Notes

(1) What are the main strengths of my secretary?

(2) What are the main weaknesses of my secretary?

(3) In my secretary's eyes what are my main strengths and weaknesses?

(4) What recent incidents have indicated that our relationship may need review and improvement?

(5) How well informed is my secretary about the business, its plans, its strengths and weaknesses, etc.?

(6) How well informed is my secretary on my job, its performance objectives activities and priorities?

(7) How may my secretary help me to manage my priorities and time better?

(8) How can I involve my secretary in my work more? In particular, how can we plan our work together?

(9) Could my secretary manage any important work?

(10) How best can my secretary handle my 'B' and 'C' priority work? Could these be handled as a matter of routine?

(11) Do we have the proper image for visitors and callers?

(12) Can we establish a desk and workspace system that will improve our workflow?

(13) What quality standards are acceptable for the various types of work that leave the office?

(14) How may confidence, consideration, warmth and good temper be developed?

(15) What are my secretary's training needs?

(16) What are my bad habits? What are my secretary's bad habits?

(17) Can my travel arrangements be improved?

(18) Could my secretary be more involved in my meetings management through assistance with better preparation and follow-up?

(19) How best can my secretary help me with information and reading?

Personal organization

Apart from meetings management and working more effectively with your secretary, your third most important aspect of managing your workflow is your own personal organization. Personal organization refers to three components: your desk organization; your control over interruptions and your handling of the telephone. All these three will either enhance or impede your workflow as you sit at your desk working. Let us look at these three elements in more detail.

DESK ORGANIZATION

As you walk around your office, factory or work place, you will find that every person has a different style of working and a different style of arranging and managing their workspace. Some people will work in a complete shambles where everything is stacked badly and haphazardly; their desks are generally piled high with work and papers and their filing cabinets are bursting at the seams. In contrast, some people will have very few papers and what is being stored is kept in neat manilla files, or well organized filing systems. On their desks you will find one or two projects (but no more!) and generally the office and workspace gives the impression of neatness and effectiveness.

Clearly it is very dangerous to make value judgements about the way people organize themselves and how this may reflect upon their general performance. Being excessively neat may be a feature of high work flow and effectiveness; on the other hand, it may be a sign of low work volume and procrastination on the basis of precision and detail while major performance objectives are slipping by. However, apart from value judgements, are there any guidelines to better desk organization which are appropriate to your style of working?

Let us create a very simple model of desk organization styles. From general observation of people at work, we can acknowledge that they organize themselves somewhere between the two extremes of excessively messy and excessively neat. Most people will have a bias towards one of the two extremes, although very few people will, in fact, be at the extreme points. It is not necessary, or indeed practical, to measure how messy or neat you are; on the other hand, you will certainly have an opinion about your own personal habits and desk organization.

Another important aspect of a person's work is the amount of *paperwork* which has to be processed through the job. Paperwork can be anything from correspondence to reports or magazines to computer printouts. The volme of paperwork will very often dictate your storage facility, desk organization, information search and retrieval needs and the rate of work processing. Very high paperwork volume will require well-organized storage and retrieval, very high organization and generally very rapid processing. Very low paperwork volume may suggest a more informal system of storage and organization, although the work processing rate may still be high because of the type of job.

If we continue the factors of neat/messy and high volume/low volume of paperwork we can create a simple description of work styles as shown in Fig. 6.1. Using this diagram as a basic idea, some general guidelines appear for improving your desk organization and, through better organization, your personal performance. The general direction of improvement in Fig. 6.1 is from the top left-hand box to the bottom right-hand box. Although this movement may not be fully

	Messy worker	Neat worker
High volume of paperwork	Disorganized storage Full desk of work in progress	Neat, highly formal and effective storage Clear desk as a matter of discipline
Low volume of paperwork	Informal storage Desk tends to be used as storage of work in progress	Neat, informal storage Very clear desk

Fig. 6.1 Desk organization styles

practical within the context of your job, it is useful to highlight the direction so that it can act as a basic description. This basic direction suggests two key ideas from which many other ideas on desk organization stem:

Idea 1 — REDUCE PAPERWORK
Idea 2 — KEEP A CLEAR DESK

REDUCE PAPERWORK

Any organization will create paperwork and unfortunately there is very little that can be done to reduce it at the present moment. Eventually, electronic paperwork will supersede the paperwork but, until this has a major impact, the reduction will need to come by organizational and personal change.

Paperwork has an A/B/C priority rating. You should only create new paperwork for your 'A' priority work. 'B' priority work should preferably use re-cycled, handwritten, speed memos on other people's original paperwork; 'C' priority paperwork should be curtailed in its creation. Paperwork also includes reports by yourself and other people. Most business reports are too long and badly structured. As a guiding principle, try to circulate effective summaries of reports rather than the report itself. If you receive large, badly structured reports, return them for an effective summary. If you receive excessive amounts of computer printouts, ask for summaries of your relevant information.

Reading of magazines and journals is now a major and important activity of many managers. As managers strive to keep abreast of developments, they submerge below an in-tray of magazines, newspapers, journals and papers. Only the very disciplined will ever read or even skim the contents. Much of what is received to read for current awareness can, in fact, be delegated for comment to members of your staff. Not only does this mean you receive a summary of relevant contents to your job, but you can also develop a more widely informed and more involved staff.

Try to establish a system of screening, managed by your secretary, which only allows the important paperwork through to your desk. This means only the 'A' priority paperwork. Finally, don't be afraid to throw paperwork away. If you start from the 80/20 rule, then only about 20% of the paperwork you receive is relevant to your work. Probably the greater part could be screened, delegated, deferred, scrapped or returned! Be ruthless on paperwork because it clogs up the system and impedes the *action* of the organization.

CLEAR DESK

Keeping a clear desk comes from discipline. Many people will use their desk to *store* work rather than *process* work. Your desk is really a machine you use when you have to work on a specific project or activity. If you reserve your desk solely for this work, then you will lay the foundation for a very sound discipline. Work which is awaiting your action should be stored away from the desk or filed in an appropriate place.

A very sound discipline that comes from keeping a clear desk is the 'handling once' philosophy. Basically this suggests that, after you have established priorities for your work and sorted your work into these priorities, then when you handle any work you *do it once*! The aim must always be to complete the work; if this is not possible you must aim for substantial progress. Building on the *do it once* philosophy is the idea of moving work on as rapidly as you can. Work that awaits attention is work that has not been done.

A very basic system for organizing your workspace has a number of main components. These components can be modified to suit your personal circumstance and style:

(1) 'URGENT': This is for 'A' priority work and some 'B' priority work that may arise during the day. We have stated previously that work that demands urgent attention is 'AX' and 'BX' priority and clearly provision in both time and organization will have to be made for this type of work. By its very nature an URGENT file is only used for a short period of time; ideally it should contain only a couple of projects or activities.

(2) 'TO DO': Again this is for 'A' priority work and some 'B' priority work. The TO DO file should be the progress file for all your current goals and activities; by its very nature it is the 'workhouse' of your personal organization. Your secretary should keep a tight control on the file ensuring that work completed is moved into *File* and work to be followed-up is moved into *Abeyance*. Work that is coming along will enter the TO DO file for action. The common mistake with the TO DO file is that it acts as a temporary storage file; the TO DO file is for working, not storing!

(3) 'FILE': This is your desk's out try. Work here is taken away and filed or actioned elsewhere.

(4) 'ABEYANCE': Probably one of the most important files you can have but generally not a feature of a manager's desk. The ABEYANCE file is your Follow-Up File. Any projects or activities which need to be followed up at a later date are placed in

the ABEYANCE file. At the appropriate time, your secretary takes them out of the ABEYANCE file and places them in your TO DO file. The simplest ABEYANCE file is a concertina wallet or a filing cabinet drawer which has 31 sections. If you wish to follow up in 10 days, then this work is placed in the section equivalent to the day's date plus 10. For example, if the day of filing was the 5th and you wish to follow up in 10 days, then the work would be placed in the 15th section (the months of the year are not relevant). When the 15th arrives, the 15th section is sorted into relevant work for that day.

(5) 'MAIL': This is a pending file for correspondence or work action by your secretary. It is always a good idea to let your secretary have charge of the IN and OUT trays. This means that any incoming work can be stored into priority of A/B/C and some 'B' and 'C' work can be handled independently of your work.

Many managers do get into trouble on their desk organization. Certainly from my experience the common complaint is the amount of paperwork that has to be handled. In fact, this complaint is completely unfounded. It is clear that two managers in roughly equivalent jobs in the same organization will have completely different styles of organizing their desks — one will be well organized while the other will be a shambles. The fact of the matter is that desk organization is mainly a function of the manager's discipline rather than the volume of paperwork.

Your desk organization does affect your performance. You find that managers with good desk discipline tend to process their work quicker and with more efficiency. They tend also to have a clear view of job priorities and are able to organize themselves so that the priorities of the day are managed *on that day* and not in three days' time. You also find that they retrieve information quicker and with less mental hardship. On the other hand poor desk organizers develop many problems. They tend to work slower and hold on to work longer. They are often unclear about the priorities of the day and often they handle their work three to five days later than an equivalent, well organized manager. Certainly they have more difficulty in retrieving information and often they lose essential work quickly. You also find that, over time, they suffer more mental hardship over their desk organization and on occasions they will become stressed about their workload and their lack of efficiency in managing its flow.

What action can managers take to improve their desk organization? Here are some very practical action points

which will lead to immediate and consistent improvement:

(1) Accept once and for all that the volume of paperwork you have to process is not the root of your problem. The root of your problem is your lack of commitment to better desk organization.

(2) When you have made this commitment to improve, allocate half a day to review your paperwork. Be very ruthless, go through your work-in-progress and your files and THROW AWAY most of it! Keep only important papers and put these into manilla folders which are *clearly* titled. Wherever possible try to use *One* folder per project. To do this you may have to summarize notes, reports and correspondence in order to reduce the bulk of paperwork.

(3) Set up your system. As a guide use the URGENT, TO DO, FILE, ABEYANCE and MAIL system. If you have a secretary, then let her handle the IN and OUT trays. Brief her on how to handle low priority paperwork.

(4) If you have a secretary, let her handle the STORAGE of work. You can rely on your single work file (point 2 above) and the secretary can retrieve the files when you need the information in her files.

(5) Never use your desk to STORE work. Keep on your desk *ONLY* the work of the day. When a piece of work is finished then place it in the file.

(6) If you use your manilla folder system well you will develop the important attitude of SINGLE HANDLING. You pick up a work folder to DO THE WORK and DO THE WORK ONCE!

(7) Allocate ahead in your diary a series of one-hour sessions on a monthly basis. Use these sessions to go through your manilla folder system to re-organize and to throw away unwanted paperwork.

Controlling interruptions

Probably the most frequent complaint of people at work is that they have to deal with interruptions to their work. People will start an important piece of work and may be five minutes into the task when a staff member will enter the office and ask for advice or comment on a project or another piece of work. Courtesy demands that the person is dealt with straight away and this takes (say) eight minutes. This pattern will continue and, when time is assessed later, about 30% of the time has been spent on the important work and the other 70% on lower priority work which has interrupted (either by a visitor or by the telephone) the 'A' priority work. Interruptions drain away time very quickly and that is one of the reasons why so little of your time is spent on 'A' priority work.

Although interruptions do interfere with performance and people will complain about them, it is still surprising to see how often interruptions are considered important and indeed regarded with affection by the people who complain the most. Although an interruption may break concentration, it also provides a temporary relief from a single task; thus it is likely that many people will have an ambivalent attitude towards interruptions. This ambivalence certainly accounts for some of the non-management of interruptions.

Another reason to permit interruptions is the common courtesy we extend to those who penetrate our domain. Visitors are always greeted and their needs are catered for; telephone calls are generally received unless they represent a discourtesy to other people, such as in a meeting. It is very surprising how certain signals will stimulate a reaction, even though it is not warranted. Take, for example, a situation where you are being served in a shop. You have examined a consumer durable, your salesman has taken you through the selling stages and you are very close to deciding in favour of the product. Just at that point, the telephone rings and both you and the salesman react to it. The salesman will probably excuse himself while he answers the telephone and you will expect his request and accept it. Meanwhile, the person on the telephone has been transferred to the wrong department! Common courtesy requires you to act as you do. Whenever your attention is demanded, which is what interruptions do, you give it freely. Generally it is only after you have responded freely that you consider that your time is being misused.

Interruptions come about because we give prior right to the interrupter. We may do this for relief from a single task, from procrastination, from common courtesy or because of an automatic response, but whatever the reasons, they penetrate your work time and space because you have allowed them to do so. Generally you cannot avoid interruptions at the actual time of the interruption itself. At that time your only strategy is to minimize the time that is being used. If you want to control interruptions effectively, apart from minimizing them when they occur, you must screen or stop them *before* they occur.

If you operate an 'open door' philosophy, then operate it properly. The 'open door' philosophy is based on the idea of *consultation* between managers and staff and between colleagues. Its primary purpose is to improve communications between people and to establish a climate of participation. When badly managed, the 'open door' philosophy leads to excessive consultation on minor issues at a time demanded by the interrupter. The original 'open door' philosophy, as we now understand it, has many disadvantages; rightly it should be replaced by a better system, of 'open consultation'. For better performance, open doors should be closed whenever you are engaged on 'A' priority work. The philosophy of the business organization should be *performance*; this means that everybody should be free to do 'A' priority work *without interruptions*.

There are two guiding strategies on interruptions. The first strategy must be to establish your 'A' priority time and then commit yourself to managing it well. Telephone calls which attempt to interrupt your 'A' priority time should be screened by your secretary. She can handle them tactfully by suggesting that you will ring back at a pre-arranged time at the end of your 'A' priority time. Probably the only exceptions you should make to this rule are when the interruption itself is an 'AX' priority — i.e. an important emergency or when the person interrupting is senior to yourself, or when a customer or client is requesting your attention. If the interruption to your 'A' priority time is an internal visitor, then a closed door must mean you are engaged on important work.

The alternative guiding strategy on interruptions is to try to accumulate them until you want to action them. Basically this system can be operated by your secretary or yourself but, in both cases, interruptions are allowed to penetrate your time. However, as soon as you have established its priority, you then defer it until the time which you have set aside to handle it. The immediate decision rule is: *Should I handle this now?* If 'yes', then handle it; but if 'no' (which will be the answer for the vast majority of your interruptions!), then defer the action until a later time. Generally this means you, tactfully, state that you are working on an important task and that you will deal with the person's request at a set time after this task is completed. Probably the most effective and acceptable way of making this point is to say 'Look, I'm a bit tied up at the moment, would you mind if I ring you back at 11 o'clock?' If this is acceptable, then make certain you do ring at 11. Generally, your interruptions can be accumulated by this technique into a time period you have set aside.

Often managers have difficulty in handling the interruption of a visitor to their office or workspace. The most effective way of handling a visitor who is interrupting your 'A' time is to STAND UP IMMEDIATELY THEY ENTER. The effect of you standing up is quite remarkable. It is a clear signal to the interrupter that the visit is to be short and generally within two minutes the interrupter will leave. Even if it is your boss, remain standing even if he sits down. Very shortly your boss will stand up and again with two minutes he will leave. Basically what is happening in this situation is that your body, by standing up, communicates with the interrupter. On the other hand if you remain seated this signals to the interrupter to sit down and this lengthens the interruption. On no account if you are being interrupted in your 'A' priority work should you *offer* a seat.

Generally the tactics on handling interruptions are quite straightforward. Clearly your tactics will not work all the time but they will work for the majority of the interruptions. Here is a summary of the main action points:

(1) Establish your 'A' time and publish to your boss, peers and subordinates when that 'A' time is to operate. If you have a secretary then brief her and allow her to protect 'A' time from calls and visitors.

(2) If you are working on 'A' priority work *never* give prior right to the interruptions. If it is an 'A' priority interruption then handle it now but keep your time on the interruption SHORT. If it is a 'B' priority interruption then defer it until later and if it is a 'C' priority interruption, have it handled by somebody else. Always endeavour to have low priority interruptions SCREENED OUT by your secretary.

(3) In 'A' time, always stand up when a visitor (even your boss!) enters your workspace.

(4) Establish with your work team a 'code of practice' on how to handle interruption. If you have 'A' time for the team then this will substantially reduce the impact that interruptions will have on your top priority work.

Handling your telephone

Your telephone is probably the most practical tool you have for improving your work flow. Could you imagine your job without a phone? Work would take longer and of course the cost of doing it would be substantially higher. In principle your telephone is your best friend but, like all good friends, it can be misused on occasions. Can we establish a few good disciplines for making better use of the telephone?

When I telephone business colleagues I have noticed a number of irritants which stand in the way of my work flow:

(i) The person you are ringing is not available. They are away on business or engaged in a meeting with their work colleagues.

(ii) When you leave a message to be rung back the return call is never prompt but is delayed, sometimes by days.

(iii) The person you ring doesn't have the relevant information at their fingertips and consequently needs to ring you back.

(iv) The person you are ringing is engaged on the telephone and the telephone receptionist puts you on hold or asks you if you would like to hold.

(v) When you get through to the person there is always a tendency to talk for too long on low priority matters.

(vi) When you want to have a long conservation, in preference to a meeting with the person, they are unwilling to spend the time on the telephone then, and unwilling to make a time appointment for a long telephone conversation.

(vii) The secretary to the manager is generally not briefed to handle the call and deal with the matter even though she is perfectly capable of doing so.

How can we handle these irritants in an effective way? When you are making a call you can follow a few well tried disciplines.

The key to the telephone lies in your management of 'A' time. Top priority telephone calls are made in the morning, preferably at the beginning of your 'A' time. Prepare your calls into a batch and make them all consecutively. For each call make a note of the purpose and the actions you require from the call. Make certain that you have prepared any information that may be required for your side of the call.

Make your first call; if the person is engaged then never hold on. Put this call at the end of your list. If the person is engaged or unavailable, establish when the person will be available and make an appointment to ring at the time available. Always make your appointment for a 15-minute period. For example, if you are advised that the manager will be available at 11 o'clock then make an appointment to ring between 11 and 11.15 a.m. When you are making the appointment to ring back state to the manager's secretary what the purpose of the call will be and what actions are sought. Always ring the manager back at the end of the period you agreed, i.e. 11.15 in this example.

If the manager is available when you first ring then state your name and purpose in your opening line. As the discussion develops, if it becomes clear that the information is not available then make an appointment to ring back when the information is available. Again, always endeavour to obtain a 15-minute period and ring back at the end of the period.

The process described above has a number of golden rules within it. Remember you are making 'A' priority calls.

(i) Prepare your 'A' priority calls in advance and batch them at the beginning of your 'A' time.

(ii) Never go on hold but put these calls to the end of your list.

(iii) Never rely on being called back. Only about one in ten returned calls come back promptly. Always state your name and purpose and actions and ring back yourself at the appointed time.

(iv) Never rely on being called back by the manager. For 'A' priority calls you must always control the time when you will ring. Persist until you have the information.

However, if you are making low priority calls the procedure changes quite radically. These are made towards the end of the day in your low priority time. Again batch your calls into a call listing and rotate the list until completed. Never go on hold and if the manager is not available then suggest to the secretary that she handle the matter. If she is not forthcoming then ask the manager to ring you back the following afternoon in low priority time. For low priority calls always state your name, purpose and action but limit the call to five minutes in total. Here is a summary of the golden rules for low priority calls.

(i) Prepare your low priority calls and ring at the end of the day.

(ii) Never go on hold but put these calls to the end of the list.

(iii) Always suggest to the secretary that she handles the matter. If not then ask the manager to ring you back the following afternoon.

(iv) Again, always state your name, purpose and action to the secretary or the manager but limit all low priority calls to five minutes duration.

(v) Never persist with low priority calls.

A very useful way of handling long conversations for 'A' priority work is to book the conversation ahead. Many managers don't use the telephone enough for high priority work. Often they prefer a meeting to a telephone conversation but always remember that meetings are more expensive of your time. For a long conversation ring the manager at the beginning of your 'A' time and suggest that you hold a meeting over the phone. Normally they agree quickly to this request. Agree the purpose and the key points to be discussed and fix a telephone appointment for later. Always agree a commitment that the time needed will be set aside.

How about telephone calls coming in to you? Here the rules work generally in reverse.

Brief your secretary on your 'A' priority time. Handle all incoming 'A' priority calls at the time. Defer all low priority calls by having your secretary screen them or by suggesting you will ring back in the afternoon. Always be willing to let your calls be actioned by your secretary as she is briefed to do so. If you have agreed to ring back then do so at the time agreed.

Finally, two points that often are overlooked. Always keep a telephone directory so that numbers are close at hand and always ensure that the calls you are handling are, in fact, part of your job. Don't handle calls for your subordinates because this is often a sign that people are not clear on who they should be speaking to. If you have delegated authority to a subordinate, make sure that it remains with the subordinate and not you.

Worksheet 6.3   Personal organization

This worksheet is designed to provide a guide to how well organized you are in controlling your workflow. For the factors below circle a number that most represents your view of your organization. This worksheet is for your personal use so be honest with yourself.

(1) I am ruthless with paperwork. I only keep top priority paperwork for the time it is needed.	1 2 3 4 5	I have never thought about paperwork. I tend to keep all of it for too long.
(2) I have now developed a desk organization system based upon my top priority work.	1 2 3 4 5	My desk organization system is haphazard; often it is non-existent.
(3) Normally I can retrieve information quickly from my system.	1 2 3 4 5	I normally have to search a great deal for my information. Sometimes I lose essential pieces of information.
(4) I use my desk for WORKING on and I operate a CLEAR DESK policy.	1 2 3 4 5	I use my desk to STORE work on. I don't operate a CLEAR DESK policy.
(5) When I am working on top priority work I make sure that I will not be interrupted unless it is a top priority interruption.	1 2 3 4 5	When I am working on top priority work I am often interrupted. I have difficulty in dealing with these interruptions.
(6) I very rarely give PRIOR RIGHT to an interruption.	1 2 3 4 5	Normally interruptions do take PRIOR RIGHT over the work I am doing at the time.
(7) In my work team we have established a 'code of practice' on interruptions.	1 2 3 4 5	We have no 'code of practice' for interruptions in my work team.
(8) I always batch my telephone calls into top and low priority.	1 2 3 4 5	I have no priority system for telephone calls and I do them at any time during the day.
(9) For top priority work I never rely on being rung back. I make appointments to ring back again until I have the information.	1 2 3 4 5	For top priority work I always ask the manager to ring me back if not available or if information is not available.
(10) My opening line in a telephone call is my name, purpose and action.	1 2 3 4 5	My opening line in a telephone call is my name.
(11) I often hold long telephone conversations on top priority work in preference to a meeting.	1 2 3 4 5	I very rarely hold long telephone conversations on top priority work. Meetings are preferable.
(12) For much of my lower priority work my secretary or subordinate will handle directly.	1 2 3 4 5	I have not briefed my secretary or subordinates on handling lower priority work.

Assessment: When you have circled a number for each of the factors, add the numbers and divided by 12. A score between 1.0 and 1.4 means that you have established a very efficient and constructive way of handling your personal organization. It is always focused on top priority work and you reduce to a minimum the time lost from disorganization. A score between 1.5 and 2.4 means that you are very well organized but with some room for improvement. Probably you have organized yourself in some areas but have not followed through in all of them. Your workflow is probably down and you could improve your time saving by better organization. A score between 2.5 and 3.5 means you are average in your personal organization. You probably haven't thought about your organization in a constructive way and you rely upon your habits, both good and bad, as the basis for organization. Your workflow could improve and you will save time by better organization. A score between 3.6 and 4.5 means that your organization is patchy and in need of improvement. It is likely that you have never constructively thought about your organization and without doubt your workflow and time management have been affected by this lack of constructive thought. A score between 4.6 and 5.0 means that you are probably totally disorganized. You are submerged under your paperwork and have difficulty finding your desk and top priority work. Interruptions are a kind relief for you!

List the factors where you have circled numbers 3, 4 or 5. The wording of these factors will highlight the basic problem areas you face. Also the combination of factors will indicate your key problem areas. Factors 1, 2, 3 and 4 are concerned with DESK ORGANIZATION. Factors 5, 6, 7 and 8 are concerned with HANDLING INTERRUPTIONS and factors 9, 10, 11 and 12 are concerned with HANDLING THE TELEPHONE.

Your personal organization action plan

Personal organization is a key factor in ensuring that work flows both smoothly and quickly. Your organization will never be able to handle all the inconveniences and problems of the working day but good organization can keep you more effective for longer periods. Your personal organization is an essential barrier against the lack of it in others. Better workflow and better time management are the essential fruits of your personal organization and your disciplines.

List the factors with a number 3, 4 or 5 on the Personal Organization Worksheet.

WEAK FACTOR

WEAK FACTOR

WEAK FACTOR

WEAK FACTOR

WEAK FACTOR

Study the words of the factors and the appropriate text and identify action points.

ACTION POINT

ACTION POINT

ACTION POINT

ACTION POINT

ACTION POINT

Study the combination of factors and identify any weak areas in desk organization, handling interruptions and handling the telephone.

Think constructively about your DESK ORGANIZATION. Allocate half a day next week to sorting out your system.

Make a note card about your tactics in handling interruptions. Place the card on your desk for a few days.

Make a note card about your telephone calls tactics. Place the card on your desk for a few days.

7
Developing objectives and year plan

A very common failing in self management is the lack of planning application. Although lack of personal planning is a common failing, the techniques and practice of planning are in fact very simple and practical. In this chapter we will introduce you to a very flexible system of personal planning that will provide you with a framework for managing your time effectively and achieving your performance objectives in a well managed and reliable manner. The first step in your planning is to develop your job performance objectives in a way that will improve your overall job effectiveness and achievement.

Developing performance areas

Throughout this book we have stressed very heavily the need to plan in order to achieve objectives. The ultimate test of self management is whether it will achieve higher performance with more effective use of time. There are many reasons why people at work under-achieve; but more often than not the main reason is that they are not clear as to what is expected of them and which parts of their job they should concentrate upon. I believe that a clear view of a job and what is expected of a person in it is essential to the achievements of that person and ultimately to the achievements of the organization. Building on this view, we believe that jobs should be defined in terms of their performance objectives because only in this way can a person direct his energies and manage his resources and time in an effective way.

The basic principle of establishing better performance objectives is that a person needs to review his present job in terms of *Performance Areas* before defining the performance objective itself. A performance area relates to the output of a person's job in the general area of results for which he is responsible. Generally a performance area statement is very general and brief. The purpose of performance areas is to focus where your energy and time can be used most productively. A list of performance areas for a production manager could be:

(1) Production Levels and Schedules.
(2) Production Costs and Controls.
(3) Quality Level and Methods.
(4) Stock Level and Costs.
(5) Delivery Times.
(6) Machine Utilization.
(7) Staff Development.

In essence this production manager needs to achieve a throughput of products using his staff and machines to the best advantage and the lowest cost, at the quality level demanded by the customer at the time the customer needs the products. If the production manager managed his job on this basis then the company would achieve 'the right product in the right place at the right time' and he would have performed well.

You will notice from this statement that we have not given the production manager a job description. We have not, for example, described his responsibilities for ensuring that machines are well-maintained, or that they are of the right type and technology. Job descriptions tend to be concerned with controlling inputs to a job. For example 'a manager is responsible for ensuring that all employees will conform to the safety regulation' is a typical component of a job description which controls inputs. In our discussion on performance areas, we see this same statement as a sub-component of staff development (performance area 7). So, whereas job descriptions are mainly concerned with controlling inputs, performance areas and objectives are primarily concerned with stimulating outputs.

It is important to recognize that each job will have its own performance areas. Two people with the same job title in two separate companies may have different performance areas. There are many reasons for this. One person's performance areas may be broader than another's because one has more delegated authority. Also just as resources are a prerequisite of achieving objectives, different availability of resources will affect the definition of performance areas. The important feature about performance areas is that each individual job will have its own set of these areas. Generally the higher you are within an organization, the more unique and flexible your performance areas will be.

To define performance areas a person needs to ask a number of questions. The central question must, of course, be 'What am I expected to achieve in my job?' However to help with this question there are a further series of probing questions that need to be asked. The first of these is concerned with the unique and valuable contribution that each person makes. Even though you may liaise and work closely with others, you are still making a unique contribution in that particular job. To help clarify performance areas, ask the question:

'What unique contribution does my job make to the organization?'

If you have difficulty with this probing question, think about your job in another way — what would the organization lose, in terms of its effectiveness, if your job wasn't performed? Often this issue tends to throw some light on a job's contribution. Ask the probing question:

'What would the organization not achieve if my job was not performed?

A person's performance areas have an impact upon other people. Your bosses, for example, will depend upon you achieving your performance objectives in order that they may achieve theirs. The same principles apply to your colleagues, your subordinates and your external relationships such as with customers. In many respects, people with whom you have a job relationship will have expectations as to which are the areas where they believe you should perform well. Satisfying people's expectations is an important part of your overall performance. Ask the probing question:

'What am I expected to achieve in my job, by my boss, my subordinates, my working colleagues, my external relationships?'

It is important to recognize that your performance areas do not have to include all aspects of your job. We have seen in the previous chapters that higher performance comes from concentration on important performance objectives; the Pareto principle or 80/20 rule applies. The central question is what 20% of your performance areas are responsible for 80% of your overall job performance? Ask yourself the probing question:

'From all the area of my job, which are the key areas that will account for the major part of my performance?'

After these probing questions you should be able to develop your performance areas and have a clear idea of how they are important to you. After proper development you are likely to find that you have between four and eight performance areas in your job. With these four to eight areas you are almost certain to have a performance area concerned with people, as in staff development, and your personal development.

A performance area can normally be defined in a maximum of 5–6 words and it should not include any statements of quantity or direction. For example, in the case of the production manager mentioned earlier, the performance area of 'delivery time' did not include a measure of time or whether this should be improved, maintained or slackened. Measures and direction are reserved for developing performance objectives which we will cover later. The four Golden Rules about developing performance areas are worth emphasizing:

(1) Concentrate your questioning on the most unique and important achievements of your job. Concentrate on output, not input. You are likely to have about four to eight areas, including a people area.
(2) State your performance areas in about 5–6 words; do not mentioned measures or directions. Concentrate on describing the performance areas succinctly and precisely within the 5–6 words.
(3) Concentrate solely on your job. If part of your job is delegated then this is still part of your job. If you have part of your job delegated to you, but you do not have power and authority to perform in this delegated area, then this belongs to somebody else. Question the boundary of your job carefully.

(4) Don't think that your performance areas can be developed by considering how your time is presently used in your job. Areas where you spend most time are not necessarily performance areas.

To reinforce the idea of performance areas, let us look at the Case Examples of Barry Catwell and Robert Ashworth.

CASE EXAMPLE: BARRY CATWELL

Barry is the Managing Director of a large manufacturing company specializing in high technology instrumentation. Barry considered that his main mission in the company was to 'make the future happen'. Although he spent a fair amount of his day working on short-term problems, he considered this to be bad use of his time if it was excessive. He thought very hard about the unique contribution he made to the company and gradually came to the conclusion that what he was really responsible for was the state of the company tomorrow. He thought that if his position was scrapped, then all the day-to-day activities would continue but there would not be one person in the company who had an overview of all the company and its position and where its strength and resource could take it. He was convinced that his performance areas must therefore be related to areas within the company that had a future orientation and that this was expected of him.

After thinking about where he should concentrate his efforts in his job, he was able to refine his listing of performance areas down to eight. He was now very happy that, if he performed well in these eight areas, then he would be an effective senior manager, managing his time and effort well. Barry's eight performance areas were:

(1) Corporate Direction and Leadership.
(2) Market Standing and Strategy.
(3) Organizational and Management Development.
(4) Corporate Image and External Relations.
(5) Return on Investment.
(6) Product Innovation and Technological Position.
(7) Availability of the Right Resources.
(8) Staff Development and Personal Development.

CASE EXAMPLE: ROBERT ASHWORTH

Robert's job title was given as Personnel and Administration Manager for a large design engineering consultancy partnership. He thought about his unique contribution to the design partnership and he thought hard about his relationship with his boss, John Podmore. Although John was his boss, Robert considered himself to be the most senior personnel manager in the organization. John was a senior partner and, in many respects, John acted as an adviser and advocate for the personnel function with the rest of the partnership. Robert considered that his unique contribution must be related to a 'smooth-running personnel function'. He was realistic enough to recognize that personnel policy was, in reality, the jealously guarded terrain of the senior partners and there was no way that this could be a key performance area for him. He was an implementer rather than a policy-maker and he considered that if his position was scrapped, then the personnel function would continue but it would not be as smooth or as professional as it was under his authority. In many respects this smooth-running personnel function was expected of him and after considering which areas he should concentrate upon, he finally decided that the following performance areas would suffice:

(1) Staff Availability and Planning.
(2) Personnel Administration and Systems.
(3) Pay Policy Advice.
(4) Corporate Staff Development and Training.
(5) Office Administration and Systems.
(6) Staff Development and Personal Development.

Defining performance areas is a very important part of improving performance. As you can see from the reasoning and the examples above, the process of thinking about performance areas helps you to concentrate upon which areas of your job are indeed the most important to you and your organization. Performance areas provide a very useful way of separating the 'wood from the trees' and the method described is probably the most valuable and quickest way of establishing selective performance objectives that are meaningful to your overall job effectiveness.

Key factors in your performance areas

The performance areas we established in the last section are the focus for your efforts to achieve high performance. The next step towards developing your performance objective is to consider what are the *key* factors that will affect your job over the planning horizon of one year.

Key factors need to be considered in your job because they affect your performance objectives. In essence, key factors give an added focus and direction to your performance areas. Whereas a performance area can remain the same from one planning period to the next, the performance *objectives* themselves, within that performance area, will be modified because of the key factors within the planning periods. For example, if we take a performance objective of 'sales volume' for a marketing director of a manufacturing company, then 'sales volume' is likely to be a performance objective within the performance area of 'profitable sales'. This performance area will remain the same from one planning period to the next but the actual specification of the performance objective will be changed subject to a number of key factors within the period. In this case they key factors could be: change in competition, change in technolgy, increase in selling effort, introduction of a new product, and so on.

Key factors help to define the performance objective for the relevant planning period. Clearly each particular job and organization will have its own key factors for a particular period. Sometimes key factors will be described as opportunity for the organization, for example:

New sales trends forecast,
New research concepts coming to fruition,
Change of company ownership, or
Change of government or policies.

Some key factors may be threats to the organization, for example:

Political unrest in overseas markets,
Unfavourable exchange rates,
Loss of clients, or
Change in legislation affecting company.

Some key factors may be resource constraints, for example:

Lack of investment capital,
Loss of skilled personnel,
Lack of training facilities, or
Shortage of raw materials.

Some key factors may be organizational difficulties, for example:

Lack of skill in new technology areas,
Weak management,
Lack of success in launching new product, or
Too few clients of sufficient size.

Key factors can clearly come in many forms and with different impacts on performance objective development, but in all cases a key factor will help to define the most appropriate performance objectives to suit the circumstances. You will probably find that key factors have themes that permeate a number of key factors. For example an organization experiencing rapid growth or decline will find many of its key factors will be permeated with this growth or decline theme. Bearing in mind the 80/20 rule, the number of key factors affecting your particular job may be few in number: possibly between four and eight factors will have a significant impact on your performance objectives.

If we return to our example of Barry Catwell, Managing Director, we could find that Barry is expecting to have to deal with a number of key factors over his planning period of one year. For example he may have to face any or all of the following:

The need for higher returns for shareholders,
The threat of Japanese technology imports,
The retirement of his R&D Director,
The need for re-structure the organization,
Competition for technology expertise, and
The need for innovating products.

As Barry works these factors through his performance areas, he is likely to find that each performance area will have a performance objective that in some way is created or modified by these key factors. The case study of *Mary Mathews*, at the end of this chapter, shows another example of factors affecting performance objectives.

Developing performance objectives

A performance objective is a statement about what is to be achieved. You cannot 'do' an objective because objectives are the result of doing activities. Objectives are end results whereas activities are the means to achieve the end. The purpose of stating the performance objective is to develop its description so that it is focused and clear. A clear statement of your performance objectives will help you to develop activities to achieve the objective and to assist in the communication of that objective to other people.

To give an example of a performance objective we may bring forward a few performance objectives from the Case Study at the end of this chapter. The case study *Mary Mathews* (an R & D Manager), has the performance area of 'New Product Innovation'. Within this performance area, she has the following performance objectives:

(1) Ensure all tests and development work on product 'Y' are completed for market launch by August 1985.
(2) All product safety tests on product 'Z' to be completed and accepted by the Product Safety Committee by October 1985.

By setting down these performance objectives, Mary is making a statement of what she wants to achieve within the performance area of 'new product innovation'. Her statements are fairly specific and they are not activities in themselves, they are the results of activities.

There are a number of general points which help us to develop performance objectives in a consistent and practical manner. Performance objectives *must* have a *time frame*. Generally a performance objective has to be achieved by a specific date or time period. Setting the completion time for a performance objective is important because activities which will lead to this objective will be positioned in time by the deadline for the objective. Time must always be specific in performance planning. It is a sound general rule to set your performance objectives for a period of about one year. Although the planning horizon of you job may be longer than a year — for example you may be working on a 5-year capital investments project — it is still preferable that you concentrate your planning on the one year period. Your job will determine your planning period but it should never be less than three months and rarely more than one year. Major projects lasting longer than a year should be co-ordinated back to the personal planning horizon.

A performance objective also needs a *description* of what is to be achieved. Generally a performance objective is described in terms of 'how well' or 'how much' is to be achieved. In this book we advocate description of performance objectives that are not rigid or overly detailed. We believe that to overspecify a performance objective is to lose its essential nature as a direction and output from your job. The purpose of stating the performance objective in a general and flexible manner is so that planning can be directed well, but at the same time, performance objectives and monthly planning remain flexible. The other important consideration is that, as a general rule, people will work in general directions and towards general objectives that are motivating. Very specific and overly-detailed statements of objectives do not enhance this motivation. Indeed there is a commonly held view that excessive specification is detrimental to a person's performance because of its lack of flexibility and its over-emphasis upon control. Clearly in some cases a performance objective can be specified in a precise way if it is a quantitative objective but it must always remain motivating and directional.

Generally all people at work have qualitative goals in their jobs. Whatever the occupation you are likely to find qualitative objectives which are key performance objectives for you. As you rise in the organization, you tend to find that the more senior a person is the more likely their performance objectives will be mainly qualitative. For example, one performance objective for a company Chairman could be:

'Achieve better community relationships with the key community organizations by November 1985'.

Apart from time frame and objective descriptions, performance objectives need to be set at levels which are realistic but *stretching*. Bearing in mind that the fundamental objective of time management is to assist a person to achieve more in less time, then the performance objective must stretch a person to their full potential without over-reaching or jeopardizing other performance objectives. To set a stretching performance objective it is often useful to consider a number of facts:

(1) Special opportunities or threats that may give rise to higher or lower performance objectives.
(2) Performance objectives in the past. Have these been easily achieved or achieved with difficulty?
(3) Will I have the skills and resources to achieve the performance objectives?
(4) Do I want to achieve this level of performance and how will it affect my other performance objectives?

How many performance objectives should you have? This is a very difficult question to answer. If you have too many performance objectives, then time and effort is spread too thinly and a quiet, relaxed but effective work style cannot be developed. A performance objective or set of objectives always runs the risk of non-achievement. If you have too few performance objectives then your time is excessive, and may become filled with trivia. Alternatively you will continue to under-achieve across all aspects of your job front. Clearly the number of performance objectives will depend upon job circumstances, the climate of the organization, the stage of growth of the organization and many other factors. As a general rule, for each performance area identified, it should be possible to identify between one and two key performance objectives. Generally, if a person is pursuing a range of 8–16 well-defined performance objectives, then after accounting for the different phasing of individual activities within each of the performance objectives, the time management will be effective and a person will be stretched. After field experience with your number of performance objectives you will be better able to assess the most appropriate stretching and manageable number.

Performance objectives need to be achieved but how do we know when we have achieved them? If we have quantitative objectives and the appropriate measurement and control systems, knowledge of achieving the objective should be straightforward. In the case of qualitative objectives this is clearly more difficult. Often with a qualitative objective, there is a criterion that indicates achievement or a series of impressions or events that indicate achievement. When the question of 'how well' is asked of a qualitative objective, then this question tends to indicate surrogate measures of performance and often these criteria can be used as knowledge of achievement. A final point with regard to objective development is to think about the benefits of the objective to you and the organization. Often benefits will help to develop the objective into a workable and consistent form as well as providing strong motivational factors while the performance objectives are being implemented.

Finally, it is often a good idea to develop the performance objective in two stages. The first stage is a general statement of what is to be achieved so that a 'ball park' objective is given. Then by taking into account time frame, level of performance, benefits and measurements of achievement, a more concise statement can be finally developed.

Objectives and priorities

The process for developing your performance objectives is systematic, beginning with your performance areas, identifying your key factors and finally, making a specification of the objective. However, how do objectives affect priorities?

Managing priorities is often a difficult task for managers. The primary purpose of clarifying objectives is in fact to assess the priorities between the objectives. For example a manager with five performance areas may have (say) eight key performance objectives which need to be achieved over the one-year period. Each of these eight objectives will, in fact, have a priority rating from 1 to 8. You will also find that as you examine objectives in more detail, they tend to be of two types: CONTIN-

UOUS and PROJECT OBJECTIVES. Continuous objectives are those which are permanent parts of your job extending through time without beginning or end, for example sales development. Project objectives are those which have a distinct start and finish time in the planning year, for example introducing a new system.

Many managers will manage their priorities on a day-to-day basis. For many reasons this approach can be very damaging. Often a manager who takes a short-term view of his or her priorities also runs the risk of not achieving all he or she sets out to achieve. The main reason for this is that priority conflicts develop AHEAD of the manager, normally about 2–3 months AHEAD. If the manager takes too short a view then the priority conflict arrives almost without warning and all he can do is respond at best.

Why do priority conflicts develop AHEAD of the manager? There are two main reasons for this. Firstly, managers don't plan their work ahead so they are oblivious to conflicts that are in-build into the planning year and, secondly, they have a tendency to delay work into the future. The impact of delaying work only heightens the priority conflict which is looming ahead. Interestingly, the manager who manages his priority conflicts as they occur is always under pressure to trade off one objective against another. For example a project that started on low priority at the beginning of the planning becomes a high priority project as the deadline approaches. Because this project is now higher in priority the other parts of the manager's job will suffer.

Let us look at an example of how priority conflicts can be spotted. Imagine a manager with eight objectives, three continuous and five project. The manager's yearly plan may look like Fig. 7.1.

The first task of the manager will be to assign priorities 1–8 for his objectives over the year period. It is

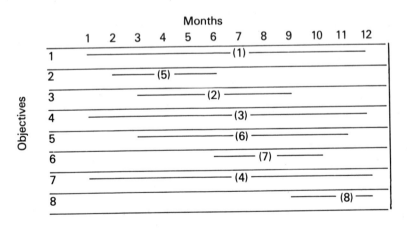

Fig. 7.1 Manager's year plan

clear from an examination of the plan that month periods 6 and 7 are quite critical. During this period the manager has most of his high priority work operating. I mentioned earlier that managers have a tendency to delay work. This delay can be for very recognizable reasons such as procrasination and lack of commitment to manage high priority work. For the manager in this example let us assume that delay is a feature. What are the consequences of delay? It is likely that objective 2 with a lower priority will slip, putting pressure on objective 3 with a higher priority. It is also likely that objective 5 with low priority will slip, putting more pressure on the critical month periods of 6 and 7. Of course as lower priority work slips then ultimately it will gain a higher priority as deadlines approach and in this example it is likely that months 10 and 11 will become critical months. In fact, what is happening in this example is very typical of how managers manage their priorities. The plain truth of the matter is that very few managers will assign any priority to their objectives and this makes it difficult to spot priority conflicts that lie ahead. When delay becomes a feature then priority conflicts are heightened or indeed created and low priority work gains in status which in turn reduces the quality of high priority work. Another important feature is that if quality of high priority work is to be maintained, then normally this will be at the expense of dropping or curtailing low priority work. Basically what this often means is that a manager sets out at the beginning of the year with the enthusiasm to meet eight objectives but because of his or her inability to manage the priorities, they end up at the end of the year achieving five objectives and suffering extended delays or possibly worse consequences of three low priority objectives. In other words they under-perform because of the conflict of priorities.

The knack in managing priorities actually lies in BRINGING FORWARD objectives. This is probably the most misunderstood feature of priorities. In the example above, if the manager BROUGHT FORWARD objectives 2, 3 and 6 then the priority conflict of months 10 and 11 would not be created.

Clearly examining priority conflicts is a very important part of managing performance and time. It is useful to summarize this chapter by setting out the sequence of developing objectives and priorities.

Stage 1: Develop your performance areas.
Stage 2: Identify the key factors affecting your performance over the year period.
Stage 3: Develop one or two objectives for each performance area. Ensure that each objective is described and allocated a time frame.

Stage 4: Examine which objectives are continuous and which are project.
Stage 5: Draw up a rough plan of the year showing your objectives in terms of lines on the plan.
Stage 6: Assign to each objective a priority ranking. Try to be specific on this and to avoid equal priority objectives.
Stage 7: Examine the year plan and identify any priority conflicts AHEAD. Normally these are indicated when many deadlines are close in time and when low priority objectives may interfere with the quality of high priority ones.
Stage 8: Assume a factor of delay and examine how these priority conflicts can be heightened or whether any new priority conflicts may be created.
Stage 9: Examine which objectives can be brought forward in order to reduce or remove any priority conflict area.
Stage 10: Examine which objectives can be delegated as WHOLE or PART jobs and make plans to delegate.
Stage 11: Ensure that brought forward objectives and delegations are planned for START in the appropriate MONTHLY PLAN.

To consolidate this chapter please read the case study of Mary Mathews (page 00). Mary goes through the whole process of creating her objectives and her year plan. Following the case study are a set of WORKSHEETS which you may use for your own planning purposes.

CASE EXAMPLE: MARY MATHEWS

Mary Mathews was Research and Development Manager for a medium sized pharmaceutical company. She had many strong positive features but her general weakness was that in certain areas of her work she performed well, while in others she under-achieved. In many respects she thought that the under-achievement was due to lack of thought on her part about her job and lack of personal organization.

Mary had difficulty at first with clarifying her performance areas. She had always considered that she was employed for her ability to generate 'new ideas'. While at university studying chemistry and biology she had been recognized as a bright and able study with a strong creative bent. These qualities had carried her forward into her commercial career and she was widely regarded as an 'ideas' person. This was her greatest strength and clearly it had to be the basis of her efforts. The central question Mary had to address in order to clarify her performance areas was:

'What am I expected to achieve in my job?'.

When faced with this broad question Mary was a little confused. However the probing questions: 'What unique contribution does my job make to the organization?' and 'What would the organization not achieve if my job was not performed?' did help to clarify the job performance areas. She was still certain that her unique contribution was in new ideas but that these new ideas had to be channelled into certain areas. She considered, for example, that her new ideas were used not only in markets and technologies but also in scientific information: how people contributed new ideas and how all the various resources had to be managed in order to stimulate and master new ideas.

When she considered what the organization might not have if her position was scrapped, she came to the conclusion that the organization would lose its research direction. She was surprised about this at first because she had always considered that her boss, the manufacturing director, was mainly responsible for overall direction. However, upon reflection, she saw that he depended very heavily upon her specialist knowledge and how this might be applied to commercial ends.

When Mary considered the question: 'What am I expected to achieve in my job by my boss, my subordinates, my working colleagues, my external relationships?', she found that all parties with whom she had relationships would have a slightly different expectation. Although this was confusing at first, she accepted this as being a natural outcome of a job's role. In many respects, what people expected of Mary was the traditional role of a manager. She was expected to lead her team, to control and monitor, to allocate resources and to plan for new developments. Mary was quite happy with these expectations but she wanted her role to be marked by a more dynamic energy. She committed herself to accepting the traditional views of other people's expectations, but she decided to set very stretching performance goals for herself and her team.

Mary was very impressed with the 80/20 rule and after asking the question, 'From all the areas of my job which are the key areas that will account for the major part of my performance?'. She decided that her key performance areas were:

(1) Research direction and policy.
(2) Scientific and technological information.
(3) Patent development and protection.
(4) New product innovations.
(5) Development cost management.
(6) Availability of development resources.
(7) Staff and personal development.

Before she finally decided that this was her listing for the next year she quickly checked the logic of the performance areas. Essentially these areas were suggesting that as R&D manager she should decide where to go; check that this was feasible and valid; ensure that resources were available and controlled; check that the right people were in the right place at the right time; and finally that all these were to be channelled into new products. She decided that this made a lot of sense and so finally accepted her performance areas.

Mary questioned whether a planning horizon of one year was appropriate for her? One of her new products had a development cycle of about three years but the greater part of her work had cycles of one year or less. In many respects this was a reflection of the size of the company where development expenditure had to show a return as quickly as possible in order to ensure the continuing viability of the company. All things considered, she decided on one year as her planning horizon; she could accommodate the longer term projects into this cycle at the appropriate points. She noted that her job was very much concerned with a rapidly changing business and technological environment and she considered that her performance areas and performance objectives should be reviewed on a six-monthly rolling basis. This would ensure that her one-year planning would be constantly updated in the light of changing circumstances.

Before she considered her performance objectives in detail, Mary reflected upon the key factors that seemed to be affecting her job. In many respects these key factors would affect her performance objectives. She did not think it was sensible to set performance objectives unless there was a framework within which these objectives could be integrated. The major concerns she identified, which could affect her job and the company, were a series of external environment and internal control issues. Over the next year she would have to address:

(1) The rise in demands for increased product safety.
(2) The impact of the newer technologies.
(3) The need to transfer technology to other countries.
(4) The need to launch products successfully.
(5) Tighter development cost and control.
(6) The need to take a fresh view of development staff outlook.

Mary now felt she was ready for her first attempt at defining her performance objectives. This first attempt was very good. She decided to highlight the performance objectives by using simple, key words to get the basic idea of the goal established. Once she had done this she could rework the performance objective into more specific statements.

Her first attempt at setting her performance objectives is shown in Table 7.1.

Mary reviewed her general performance objectives and was convinced that, if she could achieve these objectives within the planning year, then her job would be better balanced and richer and she would have a clear idea of the various priorities of her efforts and time. Whereas in the past Mary had tended to concentrate on new product introductions and technology trends as the main parts of her job, she was now very certain that her job was broader and that parts of her job which she had given lower priority to, for example patent protection and staff development, were now very important. Bearing in mind her original problem of erratic achievement, Mary was pleased that she had developed a systematic and logical overview of her performance areas and objectives.

She now continued to make her performance objectives more specific. To help her to be more specific she considered a number of aspects:

(1) Was the objective stretching enough?
(2) What was the best completion date?

Table 7.1 Mary Mathews — Performance objectives

Performance area	General performance objective
(1) Research direction and policy	(1) Better product safety (2) Ensure R&D meets market needs
(2) Scientific and technological information	(3) Better systems for market knowledge (4) More reliable technology forecasting
(3) Patent development and protection	(5) Contain abuse of patents (6) Improve technological transfer
(4) New product innovations	(7) Introduce product 'Y' (8) Progress product 'Z' towards market launch
(5) Development cost management	(9) Keep to the budget on safety development costs (10) Better method of managing budget appropriation
(6) Availability of development resource	(11) New laboratory for fundamental research (12) Better information system for project teams
(7) Staff and personal development	(13) More progressive staff development and training (14) Improve my knowledge of business management

She began with a general statement of her first objective.

For a general statement of her first performance objective 'Better Product Safety', she was concerned to take account of the trends towards improved product safety of pharmaceuticals and the new statutory safety standards which were to be progressively introduced over a period of years. She considered that her objective should be to meet these standards prior to their formal introduction and in order to stretch herself and the department, *all* products in development should attain outline approval rather than only the specified sensitive products. She considered that, if she could achieve this by January 1986, she and her department would be well on the way to meeting the introduction of new standards.

Mary continued the process of specification with a general statement of her second performance objective 'Ensure R&D Meets Market Needs'. For this objective Mary needed to consider how technologies were changing over a period of time and how markets were developing in response to new technologies and new health needs. Balancing research and marketing was

always a difficult problem and she thought that she should specify the technologies that were appearing and specify the forecast market trends. If she could relate these two major aspects and circulate her ideas, then this would be a significant step forward. Mary was happy to include a number of relevant technologies in her studies. This she thought would be stretching enough and would be a good achievement. Much of the information was available but it needed to be organized and written up. She thought she could achieve this by August 1985 and this would give her plenty of time to replan for the future.

Mary continued with her performance objective specification and the results of her deliberations are shown in Fig. 7.2. Mary was happy with her final statements of the performance objective as shown in column 3 of the table. Although clearly the objective could be even more specific, Mary guarded against this at this stage. She remembered the advice about keeping the vision and richness of a performance objective and not reducing it down to excessive numbers and measurements. She thought her level of specification was practical and matched her style of work.

Mary's next task was to translate her performance objectives into a year plan and to do this she needed broadly to specify how much time each particular objective would need for achievement. Upon examining her objective she found that all objectives apart from objective 9 (her budget objective) were, in fact, of a project type. This is typical for an R&D manager because much of the work is concerned with project management. For all of her project objectives Mary estimated roughly how long each objective would take and drew up her first attempt at the year plan (Fig. 7.3).

Assigning priorities to the objectives was a process of Mary's judgement in assessing the consequences if objectives were *not* achieved. It was clear to Mary that certain objectives were essential to her achievement, inasmuch as if these were not completed on time then her performance would be questioned. Other objectives however were important but they could be delayed or deferred without serious consequence to her personal reputation in the job. Her deliberations on priorities led her to assign priorities on the 'first attempt' year plan.

Mary examined her year plan to identify any potential conflicts of priorities over the year. January and February were fairly easy to manage but March, April and May were potential problem months with projects ending and starting. June and July were slightly easier but August and September and October would need to be closely watched because high priority projects would be nearing completion. November, December and January would be relatively easy months but by this time she would need to plan constructively for the following year and she would need to use this last quarter for her 1986 plans.

Mary remembered the golden rule about BRINGING FORWARD her projects and she revised her year plan in order to relieve the two main potential priority conflict periods. Her revised year plan is shown in Fig. 7.4.

When revising her year plan Mary also considered her delegation plan for the year. It was clear to her that objectives 2, 3, 4, 12 and 13 could be delegated as WHOLE JOBS to her subordinates, and objectives 1 and 6 could be delegated as a PART JOB to her senior subordinates. Clearly she would have to control these very closely but nonetheless the work would be good

Performance area/ Objective No.	General statement of performance objective	Final statement of performance objective
Research direction and policy		
Objective No. 1	Better product safety	All new products in development to meet new safety standards by January 1986
Objective No. 2	Ensure R&D meets market needs	All identified and relevant technologies to be explored and related to forecast market trends and opportunities by August 1985
Scientific and technological information		
Objective No. 3	Better system for market knowledge	Introduce continuous system for assessing market trends and opportunity and competitor knowledge by May 1985
Objective No. 4	More reliable technology forecasting	Introduce an appropriate technology forecasting system by May 1985
Patent development and protection		
Objective No. 5	Contain abuse of patents	Contain abuse of patents on product X by September 1985
Objective No. 6	Improve technology transfer	Pursue licensing agreements on new products to be completed by January 1986
New product innovation		
Objective No. 7	Introduce product 'Y'	Ensure all tests and development work on product 'Y' completed for market launch by August 1985
Objective No. 8	Progress product 'Z'	All product safety tests on product 'Z' to be completed and accepted by product safety committee by October 1985
Development cost management		
Objective No. 9	Keep to budget on safety development costs	Ensure that development costs on safety standards programme do not exceed £1.3m in budget year 1984/5
Objective No. 10	Better method of managing budget appropriation	Complete introduction of 'portfolio balancing' method of development costs planning by June 1985
Availability of development resources		
Objective No. 11	New laboratory for fundamental research	Commission new laboratory facility for fundamental research by May 1985
Objective No. 12	Better information system for project teams	Complete programme of micro-computerization facilities for all project team by September 1985
Staff and departmental development		
Objective No. 13	More progressive staff development and training	Introduce programme of development and training for all scientific staff by March 1985
Objective No. 14	Improve my knowledge of business management	Complete general management development course by December 1985

Fig. 7.2   Mary's Performance Objective worksheet

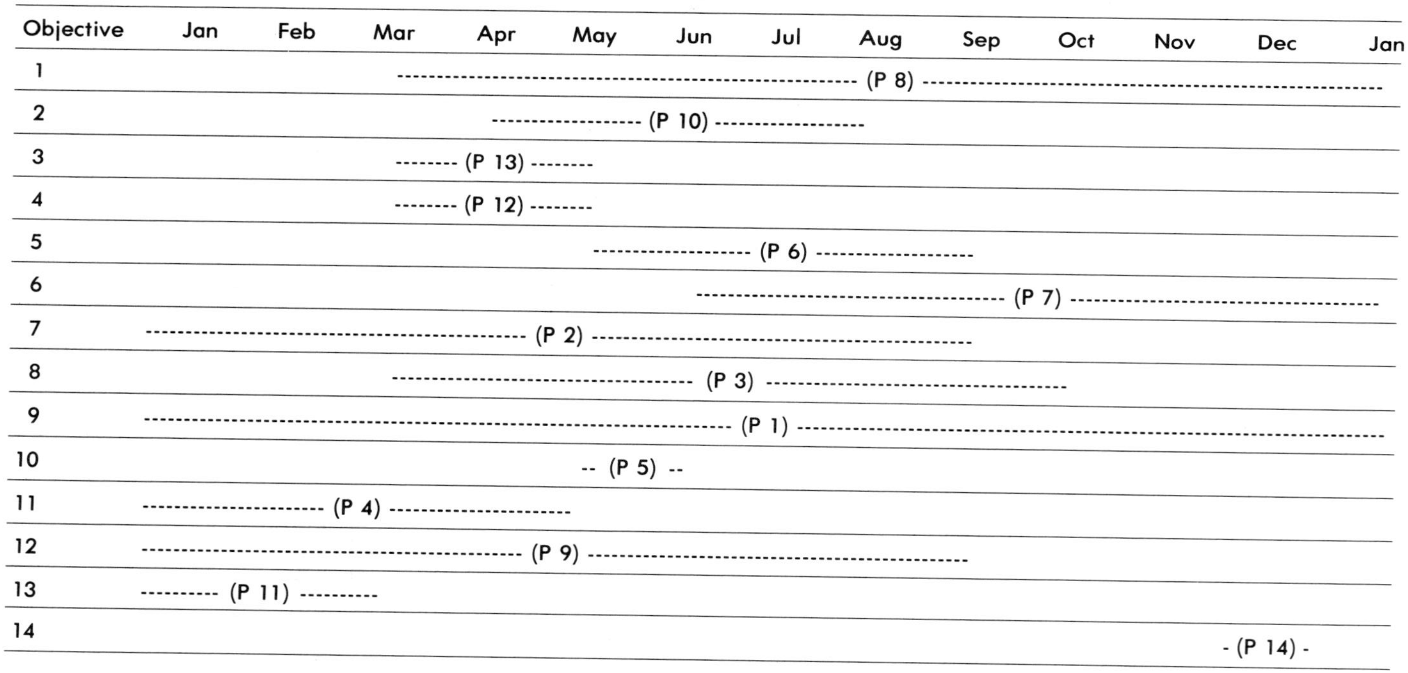

Fig. 7.3 Mary's year plan — first attempt

The figure is a Gantt-style chart titled "Mary's revised plan," showing Objectives 1–14 across the months January to January (Jan, Feb, Mar, Apr, May, Jun, Jul, Aug, Sep, Oct, Nov, Dec, Jan).

Objective	Jan	Feb	Mar	Apr	May	Jun	Jul	Aug	Sep	Oct	Nov	Dec	Jan
1								DELEGATE (P 8)					
2				DELEGATE (P 10)									
3		DELEGATE (P 13)											
4		DELEGATE (P 12)											
5				(P 6)									
6								DELEGATE (P 7)					
7				(P 2)									
8					(P 3)								
9					(P 1)								
10				(P 5)									
11			(P 4)										
12					DELEGATE (P 9)								
13		(P 11)											
14												(P 14)	

Fig. 7.4 Mary's revised plan

development work for her senior subordinates. All her other objectives she would have to complete herself with support from her team.

Mary's final task was to translate her year plan into key points in her appropriate month plans and as she revised her monthly plans at a more detailed level she would continue to look ahead to ensure that her year plan was on track.

Mary reflected upon what she had learnt about job planning. She identified five key learning points.

(i) Good job planning does not need highly detailed objectives but broad objectives sufficient to give sound approximate direction and a broad specification of start and finished time.

(ii) All objectives need to be assigned a priority rating. This ensures that priority conflicts can be managed AHEAD, normally by BRINGING FORWARD work.

(iii) Planned delegation is essential to a manager's performance.

(iv) Performance can be managed very effectively by a broad, flexible approach to job planning. Details are not required.

(v) A manager does not have to plan a long way ahead in detail. The year plan is a broad specification primarily to identify priority conflicts and delegation. Detail planning is only required on a MONTHLY PLANNING level. Monthly plans are on a rolling basis and as they are created and revised, the manager only needs to look a little ahead (say 2–3 months) to ensure that the year plan is intact.

Worksheet 7.1   Performance areas

Central Question:	*What am I expected to achieve in my job?*
Probing Question 1:	What unique contribution does my job make to the organization?
Probing Question 2:	What would the organization not achieve if my job was not performed?
Probing Question 3:	What am I expected to achieve in my job, by my boss, my subordinates, my working colleagues, my external relationships?
Probing Question 4:	For all the areas of my job, which are the key areas that will account for the major part of my performance?

Performance Area 1:

Performance Area 2:

Performance Area 3:

Performance Area 4:

Performance Area 5:

Performance Area 6:

Performance Area 7:

Performance Area 8:

Worksheet 7.2   Key factors

List all the key factors that may have an impact upon your job over the next year.

FACTOR 1:

FACTOR 2:

FACTOR 3:

FACTOR 4:

FACTOR 5:

FACTOR 6:

FACTOR 7:

Worksheet 7.3   Performance objectives

*Performance area
and objectives*

*General performance
objective*

*Final statement of
performance objective*

Worksheet 7.4   Year plan

Objective	1	2	3	4	5	6	7	8	9	10	11	12	1
1													
2													
3													
4													
5													
6													
7													
8													
9													
10													
11													
12													
13													
14													

8
Developing monthly and daily plans

In the last chapter we discussed how managers can clarify their jobs in terms of performance. We also developed the technique for setting performance objectives for a planning period of one year. In this chapter we intend to take the next important step which is to develop the disciplines for managing your performance on a monthly and daily basis.

Monthly planning

It is very important to state at the outset a very critical observation about managers. *No manager has the capability to time plan his job for more than a month.* Why is this the case? It is totally unrealistic to expect a manager to plan in detail for a long time period (say) one year. A manager's job is very dynamic. The very essence of the job is to manage many events, some very serious for the organization, on a day-to-day basis.

We know from experience that about 15% of the top priority work actually arrives at the manager's desk *on the day it needs to be completed.* This day-to-day, top priority work comes in the form of questions, queries, emergencies, requests for management information, personnel problems, machine breakdowns, etc. Very little of this day-to-day, top priority work is foreseeable or capable of being planned for, other than at the contingency level.

Another very important aspect of a manager's job is that he or she needs to have contact with the outside world. These outside contacts are people, customers, competitors, suppliers, distributors and so on. Any event or person outside a manager's job is essentially outside the control of the manager and the manager's job is to react to these external demands on the organization. Here again, very few of these external events are foreseeable or capable of being planned other than at the contingency level.

Another reason for not time planning for a long period is the events within the organization itself. All organizations re-organize their structures and policies and for a large organization these changes are almost continuous. Its very nature is to change. All organizations endeavour to follow some form of competitive strategy and of course strategies are changed radically or are in a continuous state of evolution. The types of internal change are endless: managers are promoted, leave or join the organization; new investment or product plans are announced; new ventures fail dismally or show unexpected and rapid growth and so on. Although some of these events are foreseeable, certainly at a senior management level, for the typical manager in the organization they are events that arrive almost without warning and immediate response is requested.

Finally, every manager knows that what can go wrong will go wrong: machines break down; staff are ill; suppliers are late on delivery; customers have difficulties with their new equipment; competitors bring out a high cost, exciting promotional campaign and so on. Whatever your job, events will happen around you when you are least expecting them and when you are least prepared. It is a fact of commercial life!

So we can see from the above examples that a manager's job, in the main, is to REACT to events and to modify OBJECTIVES. If this is the case then is it reasonable to PLAN? Not only is it reasonable to plan but it is essential, for no other reason than because *events will change your direction*. This is the essential dilemma in the manager's position. Because events will change your direction the only means of stabilizing your performance and ensuring that you and the organization are pointing and working in the right direction is to plan the *CORE* of your performance and to modify this CORE PLAN only if it is absolutely essential to do so. The knack for managing performance is not to OVER-REACT.

Let us return to the original proposition: *No manager has the capability to plan his job for more than a month*. If so many events will change a manager's job then to plan for a longer term than a month is unrealistic. As you saw in the previous chapter, it is perfectly feasible and necessary to have a broad view of what is likely to happen over the year because this provides many benefits in terms of resource planning, managing priorities and delegation planning. This year plan, at this broad level is in fact your CORE PLAN. This is what you intend to achieve over the year, *but* subject to the day-to-day events which will occur during the year. No manager could *detail* this year plan other than by planning one month ahead in more detail and reviewing each monthly plan in the light of his CORE or YEAR PLAN as he progressses through the year.

This leads to another aspect of monthly planning. We saw from the examples of changing events above that many events are not foreseeable nor capable of being planned other than at a contingency level. Contingency planning is a strong feature in a monthly plan. From working with managers on their job planning I now believe that about 50–70% of a manager's job is of the contingency nature. This 50% includes the 15% top priority work that comes in on any particular day. This suggests that between 30% and 50% of a manager's job is capable of being specified and scheduled for a month ahead.

Let us now pick up a concept we raised in Chapter 2. We saw in Chapter 2 that there is a tendency for a manager to allow *more* time for his *low priority work* than for his *high priority work*. Our experience suggests that a manager devotes about 40% of his time to high priority work and about 60% to his low priority work. The main reason for this is his lack of planning and poor diary control. To redress this situation we need to make a personal policy decision to devote more time to high priority work and to establish the disciplines of better monthly planning and diary control.

Managing our time for high priority work must be a feature of the monthly plan. The 'A' time concept, which suggests that we will allocate adequate time AHEAD to devote to 'A' priority work needs to be scheduled into the monthly plan. Only by scheduling 'A' time ahead will we ensure that we devote more time to top priority work.

We are now in a position to state the basic STRUCTURE of a monthly plan. It contains the following basic elements:

(i) A schedule of specified activities that relate to the progress of the objectives in the CORE or YEAR PLAN.
(ii) Unspecified activities that will occur during the month, due to the contingency nature of the job.
(iii) A specification of 'A' time for the month.

These three elements are combined. Firstly we schedule 'A' time for the month ahead. Secondly we schedule the specified activities from the CORE or YEAR PLAN into 'A' time and unspecified activities slot into contingency. Figure 8.1 shows an example of one week from a monthly plan.

There are a number of points that need explanation on this diagram: 'A' time; specified activity, unspecified activity.

'A' time is a technique for ensuring that more of our time is devoted to top priority work. My normal recommendation is to schedule 'A' time for the morning of the working week. Firstly this ensures that we always have a MINIMUM of 50% of our time devoted to top priority work. Secondly it provides a means of scheduling our top priority activities taken from the CORE or YEAR PLAN and thirdly it ensures that low priority work is not started before top priority work at the start of the day. This latter point is critical because very typically a manager will begin his day with low priority work and this is a major reason for delay in high priority work.

There are only two rules about 'A' time. It must be *continuous* time and it must be about 50% of your time. Managers allocate their 'A' time in different ways. Some allocate whole days, some allocate afternoons and often managers allocate combinations of mornings, afternoons or whole days. The general aim is to allocate roughly one half of the working week. My personal recommendation for 'A' time in the mornings is due to my previously stated logic that top priority should come before low priority work.

Another point about 'A' time is that it only acts as a MINIMUM time. If you start a top priority activity during 'A' time then you don't stop working on this activity when you come to the end of 'A' time. Clearly you carry on until you have finished. Also, 'A' time is not

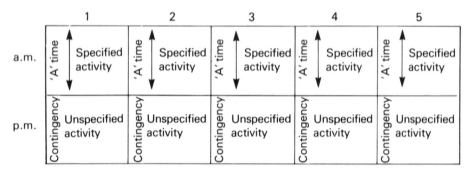

Fig. 8.1   One week from a monthly plan

devoted solely to one activity. Very typically 'A' time will contain a number of different types of high priority work. Even when you are working on a scheduled 'A' time activity you still need to respond to outside events or urgent demands. If these events or demands are top priority then you make a judgement to do the work at the time or tack it on to the end of your 'A' time. If the event or demand is low priority then you defer it until later in the day.

'A' time can contain a variety of activities. It contains meetings on top priority work. It contains planning meetings between yourself, your secretary and your staff. It contains delegation reviews, individual working sessions, dealing with top priority correspondence, top priority telephone calls and so on. Any activity that relates to your top priority work or your core performance from the yearly plan.

Finally 'A' time will not *always* contain a specified activity from your CORE PLAN. Although I have stressed in previous paragraphs that 'A' time is for scheduling specified activities this is because I believe that to *stretch* your performance to the maximum you need to specify activities ahead and allocate time for their completion. However I recognize that there will be many occasions when it will be impossible to know in advance what the activity will be. Also, sometimes a major, top priority activity will arrive on your desk that will displace any scheduled activity you intended to complete. For this reason it is always wise to leave some of your 'A' time without a specified activity as an extra buffer against any major contingency.

In summary, 'A' time is a simple but powerful technique that has provided managers with a means of controlling their top performance work. The benefits are:

  (i) It ensures that a *minimum* of 50% of your time is devoted to top priority work.
 (ii) It allows you to schedule your top priority activities over the monthly plan. This ensures that your core performance is maintained for the year.

(iii) It provides the discipline of continuously clarifying and gaining experience in managing your priorities because 'A' time will automatically *ask you* if the work you are doing or intending to do is top priority.
 (iv) If you allocate 'A' time in the morning it will ensure that you never put low priority work in front of top priority work.
  (v) It provides the basis for effective diary control (see later).
 (vi) It provides the basis for developing effective daily disciplines (see later).

We mentioned in the paragraph above that *SPECIFIED ACTIVITIES* can be a variety of activities each relating to your top priority work, e.g. meetings, delegation review, job planning, et. How do we know what the content of the activity will be? We gain insight into the specification of activities by remembering that your performance objectives are of two types: CONTINUOUS and PROJECT.

Activities relating to CONTINUOUS objectives are continuous activities. With continuous activities you don't specify the ACTUAL content but you do specify the time you will devote to the content.

For example a production manager, when he reviews the production from the night shift and makes a morning visit around the production plant, will not know the detail of what he has to deal with until the day arrives. However he does know that he has to allocate time to this morning review. A salesman will not know his sales call plan in detail until he has allocated some time to his call planning. So in this example call planning is a continuous activity that needs to be scheduled if the salesman is to achieve his overall performance objective of profitable sales.

There are other types of continuous activities where the actual contents will not be known but time has to be allocated to them. Job planning time with your secretary is a continuous top priority activity which can be specified only by the time you allocate it. Your own job planning time, top priority telephone calls, top priority reading time, top priority correspondence and so on are all examples of continuous activities that are essential to your achievement of top performance. None of these can be specified in detail — only by the time you are prepared to allocate for them.

Activities relating to PROJECT objectives are project activities. With project activities you can specify both the content of the activity and the time you have estimated for the completion of the activity. I recommend that you take a very flexible approach to project activities. Project management is a technique that provides many benefits for managers; however it is a rigid discipline best used in the fields of research, engineering, production and new product development where tight project and resource control is essential. From a broader viewpoint, project management purely provides the typical manager with a discipline for thinking about the month ahead.

The basic concept of project management is very simple. To achieve an objective you need to complete a logical sequence of activities. Some of the activities will be dependent upon completing previous activities and some will be independent of previous activities. These independent activities can be completed in parallel with other activities.

For each activity you can estimate the time required to complete it. If you need to achieve an objective by a certain time, then you will need to arrange the activities in such a way that the sum of the times they take falls within the deadline.

This basic concept of project management is the essential discipline for managers. You achieve project objectives by thinking about the project activities that need to be completed *AND* the logical sequence for completing these activities.

From this point we leave the rigid discipline of project management but build on the basic concept highlighted above. Managers are very flexible creatures. Because they have to respond to day-to-day events they like to plan in a very flexible manner. They make very rough time estimates based upon their previous experience and they tend to think in terms of total time for a whole set of activities rather than individual time for an individual activity. They are also not too greatly concerned with a logical sequence and they use their judgement to create roughly a sequence that will achieve a deadline. In essence, managers use a very 'broad brush' technique of project management.

In the previous chapter you will remember that we used very rough estimates of the total time it will take to achieve a project objective. When we developed the year plan we only specified the *month* of starting the project and the *month* of finishing the project. In principle we were using the 'broad brush' approach to project management which is very natural to a manager because it relies heavily upon judgement and our natural ability to 'rough' plan.

Specifying month project activities is an extension of this natural ability. At the *beginning* of a month when a project *starts* you identify the major activities that need to be completed in that month. You need only make a rough judgement about the activities and a rough judgement about the time. The *two* critical factors are that you START at the beginning of the month you have allocated in your year plan and that you schedule into your month plan your rough judgements of the activities. As you review your month plan on a daily basis you will adjust your judgements and a you review your month plan in relation to your year plan you will again adjust your judgements to suit the project deadline.

Finally let us look at UNSPECIFIED ACTIVITIES. Basically the time you have allocated for unspecified activities is the time remaining after the allocation of 'A' time. On the monthly plan it provides for the contingency time your job requires.

Monthly events and reviews

When a manager is developing the monthly plan there are a number of events and reviews that need to be scheduled into 'A' time on a continuous basis.

In the chapter on managing people we saw that regular reviews of progress and performance are an essential feature in leadership, teamwork and delegation. The nature of your job will dictate how regular these review meetings should be. All managers need a *minimum* of one review meeting with their team per month. I normally find that this monthly review meeting follows a general plan. If you have a secretary, make a point of inviting her. She is part of the team and she needs to know what is going on.

(i) A briefing on the performance and achievements of the team in the previous month.
(ii) A briefing on the key problems and issues that each direct report had to deal with in the previous month.
(iii) A review of the key objectives and activities for the month ahead for the business and each direct report.
(iv) A review of likely problem areas that are foreseeable.

(v) A reminder on any major meetings that are scheduled ahead.

(vi) A reminder on individual delegation reviews that have been scheduled.

(vii) A short PIP (Performance Improvement Planning) session on the successes and failings of the previous month and the objectives for the next month. As we mentioned in Chapter 4 — Managing People, PIP sessions are always associated with teamwork development rather than technical progress.

Another regular review is the one with your boss. Again this is normally, or should be, a scheduled event in your 'A' time. The timing and format would follow the above review with your own direct reports. Depending upon your own job circumstances you may need to schedule a broad based staff meeting or board meetings on a monthly basis.

Like all meetings these review meetings need preparation and de-briefing. Short preparation times and de-briefing time need to be scheduled into your monthly plan. Providing you allow plenty of time between preparation and the meeting and use your secretary effectively you will find that you can prepare well but in a short time.

Another very important and regular event in your monthly plan is your own monthly planning session. During this session you update and revise your monthly plan on a 4-week rolling basis. You adjust your activities to ensure that deadlines are met, delegation is planned, and you build in the major events and contingencies that have arisen. In my own experience I find that this monthly planning session lasts for about 45 minutes and it is normally undertaken prior to the monthly review meeting with direct reports. It is worthwhile making this point about monthly planning sessions very clearly. Your monthly plan is a 4-week rolling plan that is updated on a weekly basis.

Finally, you need to schedule a time for reminding yourself about the delegation reviews that have been arranged. Your monthly planning session highlights the key tasks that are to be delegated; however, you need to remind yourself about the tasks that have already been delegated and are coming up for review. You will remember that delegation review is an essential aspect of ensuring that delegation is crisp and that subordinates are effectively managed. In my own experience I check on arranged delegation reviews prior to the review meeting with direct reports. You will note that during this review meeting the team are gently reminded about delegation reviews that have been arranged.

As a general summary of this section on monthly planning let me bring together the essential structure of a monthly plan. Clearly there are 4-weeks to the monthly plan but I will use the example of one week. This is shown in Fig. 8.2.

	MONDAY	TUESDAY	WEDNESDAY	THURSDAY	FRIDAY
a.m.	↑ 'A' time ↓ Monthly plan / Delegation review / Review meeting / De-brief	↑ 'A' time ↓ Scheduled activity	↑ 'A' time ↓ Scheduled activity	↑ 'A' time ↓ Scheduled activity	↑ 'A' time ↓ Schedule activity
			LUNCH		
p.m.	Contingency — 'A' time extension — Low priority work	Contingency — 'A' time extension — Low priority work	Contingency — 'A' time extension — Low priority work	Contingency — 'A' time extension — Low priority work	Contingency — 'A' time extension — Low priority work

Fig. 8.2   Structure of a monthly plan — example of one week

Daily plans and disciplines

Let me start this section on daily plans and daily disciplines by stating what I believe to be an area of notorious weakness in managers. The typical manager has *completely abdicated any control over his diary*. Managers are so weak in this area that it is a wonder they achieve any real performance at all. The major weakness is that they use their diaries solely for *appointments* and *meetings*. Why am I so forceful on this point?

Take your own diary and look at what it contains. If you are a typical manager it will contain only appointments and scheduled meetings. How are you going to use the time in your diary that has not yet been allocated?

Let me demonstrate how quickly I can abuse your time management and also how other people abuse it.

Take any two days in your diary about four weeks ahead. These are shown in Fig. 8.3.

More than likely the two days you have chosen are completely FREE of appointments and meetings. If I telephone you today and say 'May I come and see you in about four weeks?' you will look at your two days and immediately say to yourself 'It looks as though I am free'. I also know that as we talk you will not question me *too much* about the priority of my visit. You will have a general idea but you will not be able to assess the impact of my visit on your priorities because you will not know what you will or should be doing on the day. Because you have an empty space you would probably say to me 'Yes, Mr Noon, what time have you in mind?' Again, because you look as though you are free you will let me specify the time of the visit. Finally, I also know that if you are the typical manager we will agree the START of the meeting but you will not ask me how long the meeting will take. You will be completely clueless as to whether I will be with you for 15 minutes, 30 minutes or even 90 minutes. You will ASSUME that I will be with you for a minimum of 20 minutes and a maximum of 60 minutes. What has happened here?

(1) I am into your diary.
(2) I am in at a time convenient to me.
(3) I am in without your knowing the impact on your priorities.
(4) I am in for an unspecified time.

Who is controlling your diary? I am! Don't think your secretary would do any better. In fact she will do far worse. If you are a typical manager with a typical secretary, then she will look at your office diary about four weeks ahead, see that it is free and book me in immediately. She will say two additional things to me. 'Yes, Mr Brown is free on that day' and as a safeguard she will say 'I will confirm this appointment with you'. Now, apart from the four points above I know you are free all day (at the moment). I also know that you have very, very little idea about the purpose of my visit and if I play my cards right then *you* will confirm the appointment to *me*. This makes it more difficult for you to break the appointment. Do you now see what I mean about abdicating control of your own diary? However, this is only the beginning!

Tomorrow, a manager of equal status, Mr Jones, sends you a memo. He wants you to attend a meeting on a project that has some bearing on your responsibilities. The meeting is scheduled for four weeks ahead. If your peer is a typical manager he will be brief in his memo and he will specify the START time of the meeting but not the FINISH time. Again you open your diary, see you are FREE on the day in question and again you will schedule the meeting. Figure 8.4 shows what your diary now looks like for those two days ahead in four weeks time.

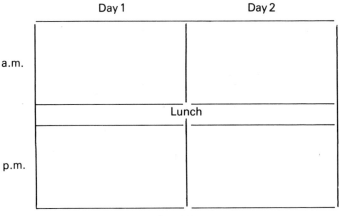

Fig. 8.3

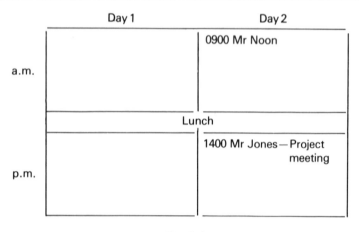

Fig. 8.4

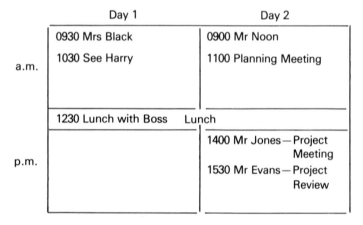

Fig. 8.5

What do we now know about your diary?

(1) Mr Noon and Mr Jones are in.
(2) They are in at times convenient to them.
(3) They are both in without your knowing the impact on your priorities at the time.
(4) They are in for unspecified times.

In fact, if you are a typical manager, this abysmal time and performance management goes on and on. Imagine you are now not four weeks away but three weeks away from the two days. Your diary will now look like Fig. 8.5.

One week away from the 2 days and it looks like Fig. 8.6.

And finally, you are now *actually* at DAY 1 looking at your diary and it looks like Fig. 8.7.

How do you now feel about these two days? You're busy! Now here is the final BLOW for you. *You are*
actually at the start of day 1 and if you were now to allocate a priority rating to your activities for the two days you would find that the vast majority are of lower priority than the essential top priority work that needs to be completed over the two days.

This is what I call RESIDUAL TIME MANAGEMENT. You will COMPLETE your TOP PRIORITY work in the time you have *left* after you have abdicated control of your diary.

Do you recognize this phenomenon? If you are a typical manager then this is happening every day of your working life. This is why the typical manager spends 40% of his time on top priority work and 60% on low priority work. It comes about solely because the manager has abdicated control of his diary and because he does not exercise the essential monthly and daily disciplines of planning and self management for job performance.

	Day 1	Day 2
a.m.	0930 Mrs Black 1030 See Harry	0900 Mr Noon 1100 Planning Meeting

p.m.	1230 Lunch with Boss
	1400 Budget Meeting
	1530 Visit Depot for
	     Maintenance Meeting
		1230 Lunch with Kathy
		1400 Mr Jones — Project
		                    Meeting
		1530 Mr Evans — Project
		                   Review
		1630 Mr Arnold

Fig. 8.6

	Day 1	Day 2
a.m.	0930 Mrs Black 1030 See Harry 1100 See accountant on budgets	0900 Mr Noon 1100 Planning Meeting 1215 See John

p.m.	1230 Lunch with Boss
	1400 Budget Meeting
	1530 Visit Depot for
	     Maintenance Meeting
		1230 Lunch with Kathy
		1400 Mr Jones — Project
		                    Meeting
		1530 Mr Evans — Project
		                   Review
		1630 Mr Arnold

Fig. 8.7

How can we control this situation and gain control over our own performance and time? There are two important disciplines:

(1) Diary entries must always be checked for priority and time allocation.
(2) Your diary events need to be of greater variety and more fully associated with managing your job and performance.

Let us take the first point. When you receive a request for a meeting or an appointment you *must* always say to yourself: *What is the PRIORITY of this request?* and, *If I accept this request how will it affect my priorities at the time?*

Both of these question are very reasonable. However they are impossible to answer *unless* you are aware of your priorities and aware of the priority activities that are likely to be undertaken at the time. Never assume that you are FREE however far in advance the request is made. You are not FREE because you will be managing your top priority work.

Also, *never* let a request enter your diary unless you know how long the meeting or appointment will take. Try to break the bad habit of thinking in terms of 'round numbers' of time. Most managers assume 30 minutes for appointments and 60 minutes for meetings, when 20 and 45 minutes are more reasonable and 'crisper' for your time management.

Finally, try and ensure that *you* specify the time. Top priority events go into 'A' time whereas low priority events are entered into your contingency time and as a general preference at the end of the working day.

The second discipline needs greater explanation. Presently you probably use your diary for appointments and meetings. In fact these are only part of your job. As you have been reading this book you will have noticed that many types of activity need to be completed if you are to perform well. Most of these activities relate to your TOTAL performance in your job. If you use your diary well you will be using it to manage your performance. This point is a critical one for diary control. Here are the main performance events that need to be scheduled in your diary.

Top Priority Events

    (i) Job planning with your secretary.
    (ii) 'A' priority correspondence.
    (iii) 'A' time for top priority work:

        — continuous activities specified only by time.
        — project activities specified by content and time.

    (iv) 'A' priority telephone work.
    (v) 'A' priority reading.
    (vi) 'A' priority meetings/preparation and de-briefing.
    (vii) 'A' priority appointments.
    (viii) Delegation reviews.
    (ix) PIP sessions.
    (x) Your personal job planning session.

This listing has an important function. I have found from my own experience and from working with managers on their self-management discipline that the listing acts as a *reminder* about the events that make up their total performance. Changing your diary control habits is in fact fairly easy.

For about 2–3 weeks you schedule your diary events quite methodically. Very quickly the new diary control habits establish themselves and you become much more acutely aware of the most appropriate daily plan for your job. Once this awareness is achieved and the new diary control habit formed you then find you CONTROL your diary without having to schedule all the events. Basically you establish the mental aspect of the discipline and you can then reduce the physical aspect of writing and scheduling the daily events.

Clearly you need to be quite flexible in your approach to your daily discipline. For my own circumstances I have now refined my own daily disciplines and their relation with my monthly planning as follows:

FROM THE MONTHLY PLAN

(1) From my monthly plan I physically transfer my 'A' time into my daily plan. I use an A5 self management system rather than a dairy (see later) and I make the transfer by drawing with yellow highlighter to indicate 'A' time. If you use a diary, draw a pencil line over the appropriate hours.

(2) From my monthly plan I physically transfer into the 'A' time any monthly events e.g. review meetings, etc. and any specified activities that are scheduled for the month. These events and activities form the basis of the main priorities of the day.

FOR EACH DAILY PLAN

(3) I mentally schedule 'JOB REVIEW' time. This is normally about 10 minutes and I review the top priority work that has to be completed or progressed on the day. I physically list the priorities of the day.

(4) I mentally schedule 'SECRETARY' time. This is normally about 15 minutes. During this time I review with my secretary the work of the day and the imminent work so that she can plan her own time. Normally my own job planning session from the previous working day forms the basis of the imminent work. 'SECRETARY' time must be a CONSISTENT feature of your working day. Try not to confuse 'SECRETARY' time with correspondence but always focus upon job planning.

(5) I mentally schedule 'A' PRIORITY CORRESPONDENCE time. This can vary in length but normally is about 30 minutes.

(6) I mentally schedule 'A' PRIORITY TELEPHONE time. Again this varies in time. The primary purpose of 'A' PRIORITY TELEPHONE time is to begin the telephone work of the day. You will remember from the section on telephone handling (Chapter 6) that on 'A' priority telephone calls you persist until you have the information you require.

(7) I mentally schedule CONTINUOUS ACTIVITY time. Again this can vary in length but normally takes about 30 minutes. During this time I review the business performance and other aspects of my CONTINUOUS OBJECTIVES.

(8) As noted previously, all continuous activities of which I know the actual content I will physically schedule, and all project activities will be physically scheduled.

(9) For all meetings and appointments, I check on priority and length of time. When I enter the event, whenever possible, I allocate a 15-minute preparation session prior to the meeting and a 15-minute de-briefing session after the meeting. As a rule of thumb I have found that 15 minutes is a suitable allocation. It may take longer to prepare or shorter but they average out. Normally I try to allocate the preparation session about two days in advance of the meeting or appointment and the de-briefing session immediately after the meeting or appointment.

(10) All delegation reviews are physically scheduled.

(11) I mentally schedule my own job planning time. This normally takes 15–30 minutes a day. During this time I review the priorities of the day, the monthly plan and any imminent deadlines, update the monthly plans and delegation reviews.

(12) I mentally schedule 'A' PRIORITY READING time. This normally takes about 15 minutes a day. Clearly more reading will take place during the day which is associated directly with the work on hand.

As with any manager, my day can vary. Sometimes I am away from the office all day on business. Many days I am away on consultancy and training work. Those 'field' days tend to have a structure dictated by the business of the day. However as a *preference* I will structure each day as close as possible to the DAILY PLAN and DISCIPLINE. In diagrammatic form my preferred day structure is as shown in Fig. 8.8.

To complement the DAILY PLAN I also have a few key disciplines (or habits) that I maintain as consistently as possible given the circumstances.

(1) Clarify and commit myself to my priorities. DO IT NOW! is a key discipline and drive hard to get the best results for my top priority work.

(2) Use my secretary as fully and as effectively as possible.

(3) Control my *own* diary and 'A' time.

(4) Think through delegation, delegate and don't HOVER, and check DELEGATION BACK. Be consistent on delegation and reviews.

(5) As stated above, allocate preparation and de-briefing time for meetings and appointments.

(6) Handle 'A' priority interruption and telephone

calls *at the time* if appropriate but defer any lower priority interruption and telephone calls to the end of the day.

(7) Always persist with 'A' priority telephone calls.

(8) Commit myself to *START* on any large or difficult matters or projects. Only by starting can you eventually plan for the work.

(9) On team projects, fully involve myself at the beginning to ensure DIRECTION, INVOLVEMENT and HARMONY, then as quickly as possible reduce my active involvement so that I can manage the team project.

(10) Keep a CLEAR DESK policy and be ruthless with paperwork.

(11) Always keep an eye on my monthly plan.

(12) Check any tendencies to procrastinate.

(13) Try to listen hard when appropriate.

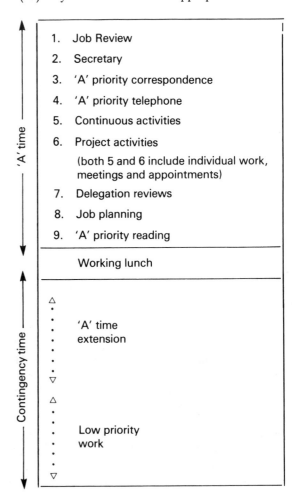

Fig. 8.8 Daily structure

(14) Involve staff as much as possible in the direction of the business and decisions affecting them.

(15) Resolve conflicts or personal matters at the time.

I have no expectation that a manager should have a daily plan and disciplines that follow those for my own personal circumstances. Clearly each manager has his or her job circumstances to manage. The point about DAILY PLANS and DISCIPLINES is that each manager requires them for his own job. I have stated my plan and disciplines as an example only. What is so clear about a manager, managing himself, is that without a discipline top priority work falls both in quality and quantity. Managing yourself is a skill that you need to develop because without the skill your job will manage you and other people will control your time.

Self management support systems

I mentioned previously that I do not use a diary but a system. The system is a proprietary one distributed by BUSINESS TIME/SYSTEM of London.

Diaries do not have the flexibility nor the range to cover your self-management and the purpose of a system is to provide you with a set of tools to assist with managing yourself and your job.

The principle behind the system is very simple. Managers use a number of aids. They use a diary, a telephone directory, a 'to do' list, yearly planning aids, short term planning forms, notebooks, desk notepaper, filing systems, accounting forms, project management forms, expense forms, etc. A manager will use all these aids in various parts of his job.

The system brings all these aids together into a neat, A5, comprehensive workbook that acts as a work centre and, on occasions, as a portable office. Each system is adapted to a manager's job and used mainly for managing top priority work and ensuring day-to-day effectiveness. Systems are flexible and cover a range of activities.

The system has a focus on the four priorities of self management: delegation, meetings, time planning and personal organization.

The A5 workbook has a number of key sections:

Section One   ACTIVITIES
This section is your 'to do' listing. It is a listing of activities by date of entry, description, priority and delegation.

As you go through your day any activity that needs your attention is entered into the ACTIVITIES section.

Section Two   OVERVIEW
This section contains your planning forms. It contains your yearly plan, your project plans and your monthly plans.

All the various planning forms are supplied and you use this section to create and revise your job plans.

Section Three   DAILY PLAN
This section contains your daily schedule of activities (similar to your diary), your 'aide memoire' for activities and following up telephone calls, correspondence and activities. It also contains your notes and 'scribbles' of the day in the form of a daily journal.

Section Four   DATABANK
This section contains 10 indexed sub-sections. Seven of the sub-sections relate to your key performance areas in your job so you can 'file' the key information, documents and plans relating to your performance.

It also contains 3 sub-sections on FINANCIAL, PERSONAL and IDEAS BANK. The financial sub-section contains any financial information of expenses or accounts. The personal sub-section contains any personal or social information. The ideas bank is a chronological listing of ideas which are recorded as an 'aide memoire' for future follow-up.

Section Five   INFORMATION
Whereas the DATABANK relates to information very specific to your job, the INFORMATION section contains more general information about your company. For example it may contain price lists, product range, internal communication or organization charts.

Section Six   MISCELLANEOUS
This section is normally used as a general notebook.

Section Seven   DIRECTORY
This section contains an A-Z register of people, addresses and telephone numbers.

Section Eight   CARD HOLDER
This contains a set of clear view
plastic wallets for credit cards and
business cards.

Each system is looseleaf. Each is supplied with a storage
box of approximately 700 pre-printed forms which are
used in various sections of the workbook. The work-
books have vinyl or leather covers and are supplied with
propelling pencils, highlighter and calculators, depending on the model.

The range of pre-printed forms is extensive. They
include amongst the most commonly used:

Activity checklist
Yearly overview
Project overview
Monthly plans
Weekly plans
Daily plans
3 column accounting
Vehicle expenses
Project management
Meetings checklist
Reports
Notes
Delegation reviews
Lined paper
Graph paper
Matrix paper
Entertainment expenses
Expense envelopes
Sales graphs
Plain paper
Tracing paper

Many hundreds of thousands of managers now use
these systems worldwide and, indeed, many thousands
of organizations in both private and public sectors sup-
ply their managers with the system and self management
training.

There are many benefits to using a system:

(1) A system acts as a central workbook for all the key
plans and information relating to your job.
(2) The system is portable and is used when you are
travelling, waiting or at home. Because it contains
all your priority information you are never without the information you need to carry out your
job.
(3) The system contains all the necessary forms for
planning your job.
(4) The system acts as an aid to your daily disciplines.
(5) The system acts as an 'aide memoire' to ensure

quick follow-up and a guide against a faulty
memory.
(6) The system assists with better meetings, managing your priorities, project planning, delegation
and many other aspects of management.
(7) You are never without your telephone directory.
(8) The system helps you keep track of all your finances and expenses.
(9) The system helps you considerably to keep a
CLEAR DESK policy, because it curtails the
generation of numerous notes and jottings you
make yourself.

Finally, as an example of its use, this is how I use my
system:

(1) My ACTIVITIES section contains a running list
of all the key activities that enter my job. Activities
that I need to follow up, such as telephone calls, I
transfer to my daily plan section for the appropriate day. Activities I need to work on I transfer
to the activity lists for the appropriate day. Activities I have delegated are transferred to the delegation review section in my databank.
(2) My OVERVIEW section contains my yearly plan
and my monthly plans.
(3) My DAILY PLAN section contains my 'A' time
and activity schedule, top priority work for the
day, follow-up activities and journal of the key
decisions and information of the day.
(4) My DATABANK section contains priority files
and general information files. The 10 sub-sections
of my databank are arranged as follows:

(i) My general notebook.
(ii) A record of business meetings.
(iii) A record of delegated work by task, person
and review time.
(iv) Business development plans/activities.
(v) Promotions and agency.
(vi) Budgets and financial performance/board
reports.
(vii) Contracts and agreements.
(viii) Personal and staff development.
(ix) Consultancy clients.
(x) Ideas bank.

(5) My INFORMATION section contains general
business information.
(6) My MISCELLANEOUS section contains my
general notebook.
(7) My DIRECTORY section contains information
about people I meet in business, addresses and
telephone numbers.

(8) My CARD HOLDER section contains credit cards and my own business cards.

If you wish to receive more information about the self management system then please contact the author at BUSINESS TIME/SYSTEM, KNIGHTWAY HOUSE, 20 SOHO SQUARE, LONDON W1V 6DT. TELEPHONE 01-439-2299.

Summary of key ideas, action points and disciplines

Throughout the book I have highlighted many action points and disciplines for improving your performance as a manager and for using your time to best effect. In this chapter we will bring together all the major ideas into a summary of action and disciplines.

Chapter 1: Assessing your work style

Your performance at work is conditioned by four major aspects of your workstyle. Your workstyle is very much the summation of all the things you do at work and, particularly, how you cope with your workload. The four key aspects of your workstyle are:

(1) How you manage your work behaviour.
(2) How you manage your work planning.
(3) How you manage your tendency to procrastinate.
(4) How you manage your work stress.

WORK BEHAVIOUR

Let us look at your work behaviour. This is conditioned by your DRIVES and MOTIVATIONS. There are two extremes of work behaviour at opposite ends of a continuum.

TYPE 'A' ⟷ TYPE 'B'

All managers have a combination of TYPES 'A' and 'B' behaviour and all have a *tendency* towards one of the two extremes. TYPE 'A' is action driven and the manager wishes to achieve a great deal in the shortest possible time whereas, in contrast, the TYPE 'B' manager is relatively unhurried, relaxed and calm and his or her aspirations to achieve 'more in less time' are much more subdued than with the TYPE 'A' manager. Sometimes managers will change their work behaviour as they progress through their career or when they work in different departments or change organizations.

You also find that organizations have a work behaviour similar to TYPES 'A' and 'B'. Organizations which are very close to a competitive marketplace tend to be TYPE 'A' whereas those not highly affected by competition tend to be TYPE 'B'. Interestingly there is a general trend towards developing TYPE 'A' organizations as the general level of competition and need for higher productivity increases. The significant factor in organizational change is when a TYPE 'B' organization gets into trouble in the market place and/or a new chief executive arrives who is a strong TYPE 'A' manager. Both these factors bring about change very rapidly and a TYPE 'A' manager is strongly placed to benefit from this change.

Neither TYPE 'A' nor 'B' is a preferred work behaviour — it depends upon your organization's style of work and the competitiveness of your business environment. However it is important to know your tendency because this normally highlights some fundamental problem areas in your management of your performance and time.

PROBLEM AREAS FOR TYPE 'A' MANAGERS

TYPE 'A' managers tend to meet a number of problems if they are not careful to manage their work style. These are the typical problem areas:

(1) They tend to have difficulty CONTROLLING the amount of work they handle. They are very quick to say YES! and slow to say NO!

(2) They tend to have difficulty DELEGATING their work and even if they do delegate they tend to be imprecise in the task setting, too quick to plan the delegation and indisciplined in the delegation follow-up.

(3) They tend to have difficulty in ASSESSING PRIORITY of work. Everything they handle is TOP PRIORITY and consequently they allocate their time to tasks without thinking about their overall achievement.

(4) They tend to be POOR PLANNERS of their work. Work control, delegation and priority assessment all combine to put TYPE 'A' managers under time pressure and of course it is very difficult to plan when *EVERYTHING* needs to be done. Also associated with TYPE 'A' managers is the lack of ability to stand back from their jobs so that they can attempt to plan.

(5) They tend to be very much concerned with QUANTITY of work at the expense of QUALITY. TYPE 'A' managers tend to trade off quality for quantity whenever there is a difficult or time pressing situation.

(6) They tend to experience difficulties in managing their INTERPERSONAL RELATIONS. They can be poor communicators and poor listeners. They tend to be quick in their dealings with people and very often their subordinates will complain about a lack of awareness of what their TYPE 'A' boss wants to achieve and the quality level expected.

(7) They can be ERRATIC in their performance. Because they have a strong FUTURE orientation they don't necessarily get satisfaction from the job in hand but the next job! These submerged frustrations can lead to lack of consistency in performance.

(8) Finally, they manage their job by DEADLINES. The volume of work which they are prepared to accept combined with other factors above lead to a constant work pressure that necessitates very tight deadlines and often crises or firefighting.

Given these potential problem areas for the TYPE 'A'

manager here are the *key* action points for keeping the worse tendencies under check:

ACTION POINTS FOR TYPE 'A' MANAGERS

(1) Work hard at creating performance objectives and priorities. Decide on what you want to achieve and stick to this and no more.

(2) Develop the key skills at delegation planning and delegation reviews SLOW DOWN! Your delegation will improve substantially if you *THINK ABOUT IT*.

(3) Begin to plan your work and time more effectively. Focus *only* on your top priority work, delegate more and keep a firm grip on work control.

(4) Begin to set higher QUALITY objectives. Don't trade off too quickly QUALITY against QUANTITY whenever you get into trouble.

(5) Make absolutely clear to your working team what you want to achieve. Spend more time talking to your team about PERFORMANCE. Try to be more sensitive to your team and spend more time making sure that communications about objectives are clearly understood.

(6) Learn to relax with yourself. You are very good so you don't have to prove it every minute of the day.

(7) Get off the DEADLINE treadmill. Plan your work so you know the proper schedule for your work and the proper resources and staff you'll need. Make certain you stop your CRISIS management affecting all your team. Give them time to plan to react.

PROBLEM AREAS FOR THE TYPE 'B' MANAGERS

Typical problem areas for TYPE 'B' managers are:

(1) They tend to under-achieve if they don't stretch themselves to perform higher. They can often say NO! in such an effective way that they screen out any extra work.

(2) They can become complacent about their performance. They can rest heavily upon their track record and their relaxed and calm style of work such that they are perfectly satisfied with their present performance.

(3) They can be poor planners because they are not under pressure to plan their work or their time.

(4) Like the TYPE 'A' manager, they can have difficulty in assessing their priorities. They tend to assess their work by high quality rather than high

quantity and they have difficulty in SELECT-ING the right quality level for the job at hand.

(5) They can be very broad in their outlook and often they can become impractical and irrelevant. Pragmatism and expediency are not their constant companions.

(6) They can be very imprecise in their delegation. They tend to be woolly in their task briefing.

(7) They tend to have too little control over their work team. They are slow to sanction or discipline and too accepting of low performance in the team as a whole.

ACTION POINTS FOR THE TYPE 'B' MANAGERS

(1) Work hard at setting higher and more stretching performance objectives. Decide on what you want to do and DRIVE HARD to achieve.

(2) Begin to plan your work and time more effectively. Increase your workload and put pressure on yourself to plan.

(3) Don't perform *all* your work at a *high* quality level. Learn to be more selective about quality and accept that your low priority work can be successful at a much lower level of quality.

(4) Accept that pragmatism and expediency are the constant companions of a manager who is performing well at a high level of output.

(5) Tighten up control of your team. Stretch your team to achieve more by allowing more TASK orientation rather than PEOPLE orientation and don't forget, make your delegation much more crisp.

As a final action point on work behaviour, if you are responsible for changing your organization don't forget the general trend from TYPE 'B' to 'A' organization. If you are changing from TYPE 'B' to TYPE 'A' then make certain, by effective training, that your managers don't inadvertently pick up the weaknesses of the TYPE 'A' manager. If you don't control this then your changed organization will probably be poor at PRIORITIES, PLANNING, WORK CONTROL, COMMUNICATION and lower in QUALITY output.

WORK PLANNING

To achieve at a consistent and high level it is imperative for a manager to plan his or her work. Planning applies to job objectives and scheduling activities but it also applies to planning your personal organization and your time at the daily level. Planning means deciding in advance what to do, how to do it and who is to do it. Planning can't predict the future but it provides a creative process that has the flexibility to cope with change and the unexpected event.

Work planning must meet 4 criteria of it is to be successful.

(1) Planning needs to be flexible. Realistic objectives are set and reviewed in the light of changing circumstances. The more circumstances are changing the more the need to plan.

(2) Planning must be directed at achievable objectives which are capable of being defined and, importantly, communicated to others around you.

(3) Planning must concentrate on effective use of resources and effective use of time.

(4) Planning must be reviewed consistently and adapted. Objectives don't change but your plans to achieve objectives will change.

All managers recognize the need to plan their work. Some, however, will reject planning or plan without commitment. Here are some of the key reasons why planning fails for some managers.

(1) Managers lack commitment to their plans. Today's crises are more important (and comfortable!) than tomorrow's opportunities.

(2) Managers don't have a general strategy for their job and performance. They see their job in a narrow light with short time scales.

(3) Managers don't set objectives or they set objectives which lack definition and are incapable of achievement.

(4) Managers over-plan and become bogged down in detail and procrastination.

(5) Managers rely heavily upon experience. Everything they meet they have met before and they become short sighted about their experience.

(6) Managers resist change and planning tends to stimulate change.

Some managers may have all or some of these attitudes which restrict simple work planning. In total these attitudes indicate a lack of vision and positive approach to performance. The key action for a manager is to develop a more positive attitude to work planning. Here are the key action points:

ACTION POINTS FOR POSITIVE ATTITUDES TO PLANNING

(1) You must commit yourself to planning and implementing your plans.
(2) You must use a planning system which is simple and practical. It needs to be flexible.
(3) You must organize yourself for planning. You need to define objectives and put your plans into action. Planning needs time for organization and review.
(4) You must communicate your plans and what you intend to achieve.
(5) You must link long-term planning with short-term planning. Work planning is about what you want to achieve over the year and what you are doing TODAY.
(6) You must accept change and benefit from it. Always see the benefits and plan to achieve these benefits.

PROCRASTINATION

Procrastination needs to be managed because it is a strong impediment to our performance. Procrastination has a positive role in checking our forward drive. It also has a strong negative role by our inability to overcome obstacles, or indeed, by placing obstacles in our own way.

All managers procrastinate and the only differences between managers is the type of things they procrastinate on and the strength of their procrastination. All managers will have recognized that:

(1) They procrastinate on unpleasant tasks.
(2) They procrastinate on matters concerned with people.
(3) They procrastinate on difficult telephone calls.
(4) They procrastinate on large projects or jobs which don't fit the natural activity pattern of the job.
(5) They procrastinate on unfamiliar jobs or jobs that are risky.
(6) They procrastinate when many small jobs build up into a large task.
(7) They procrastinate whenever an activity is 'public' and likely to affect their self-esteem.

Procrastination is based on SELF DOUBT or a fear of failure, so any task which is doubtful or if a manager is not confident of success is a candidate for procrastination.

Managers procrastinate in different ways. Here are some typical examples of procrastination:

Self-doubter	Whatever the manager's successfully track record the manager lacks confidence to succeed and he suffers from a general level of procrastination.
Perfectionist	The manager sets far too high a quality or quantity goal and finds that he or she is not going to succeed. After this recognition there is a tendency to procrastinate. Perfectionist procrastinators are very good STARTERS but poor FINISHERS. The TYPE 'B' manager is a typical candidate for perfectionism. PERFECTIONIST PROCRASTINATORS delay at the end of work.
Rebel	The manager constantly needs to demonstrate to himself and others that he has no fear of failure. He accepts large jobs and difficult jobs in short time sales. However he or she is a very poor STARTER and a good FINISHER. The TYPE 'A' manager tends to be a REBEL procrastinator. He's slow to start and plan and loves DEADLINES. REBEL PROCRASTINATORS delay at the beginning of work.
Socializer	Here a general level of procrastination creeps in by the excessive amount of time spent in gossip, distractions, trivial tasks and lengthy non-work conversations.
Day dreamer	Again a general level of procrastination can be seen. The manager lacks commitment and drive and tends to have difficulty in keeping concentration high and focused on top priority work.
Priority inverter	This is a typical procrastinator. Here the manager will put low priority work in front of high priority work. Very often this occurs at the beginning of the work day.

ACTION POINTS FOR THE PROCRASTINATOR

(1) Accept that procrastination is common and that you can solve the problem. Don't doubt your capability — get on and succeed.
(2) You don't procrastinate in every area of your job. Make a log of a day's procrastination and you will find that you procrastinate in a certain area or on a

particular type of problem. When you know the problem, work hard not to procrastinate in these problem areas. Check which type of procrastinator you are by studying the text.

(3) Procrastination is solved by doing *little* things, rather than *big* things. Always commit yourself to START a task, then you can plan and the finish will look after itself.

(4) DO IT NOW! is the most powerful technique you can use. Always START a task.

(5) Get into the SINGLE HANDLING habit. Pick work up to complete or progress not just to have a look at it. Do jobs once and once only.

(6) Never put low priority work in front of high priority work.

(7) Keep your socializing down to the level of good working relationships, but no more.

WORK STRESSS

Work stress is the 'wear and tear' of working life. If work stress is prolonged it can be dangerous to health. However stress also leads to poor performance through low motivation, low confidence, poor communication, low trust, low involvement with working colleagues and a low concern for achievement.

Managers face work stress in three key areas:

(1) *Work Overload*
This is when a manager has too much to do or too much of the work is too difficult to do. All managers cope with this very positively; however if it is prolonged then stress will occur. Also stress can occur if a manager is underloaded. The knack is to get the right balance as a constant stimulation. Your optimum stress is when you feel exhilaration, high motivation, sharp perception, mental alertness, high energy, a realistic analysis of problems, sound relationships and calmness under pressure.

(2) *The Manager's Role*
High participation leads to high performance. However, many managers are not fully aware of what is expected of them. There are four main problem areas:
   (i) when a manager is not clear about the job.
   (ii) when conflicts of priority are placed on the manager.
   (iii) when people problems are not dealt with effectively.
   (iv) when the organization suffers from weak structure and procedures.

(3) *Personal Relationships*
Management depends upon good working relationships. Poor relationships with your boss lead to pressure to perform, criticism, less involvement and participation. Poor relationships with your subordinates lead to poor work control and team achievement, restricted delegation, low loyalty, poor communication. Poor relationships with your peers lead to internal competition, low communication and involvement and inter-department politics.

All managers react to stress differently, some are stress resistant whilst others can buckle very quickly. It is also true that different situations will stress managers differently. Whatever the level and type of stress it needs to be managed so that performance is high. Here are the key action points for keeping stress at bay and performance high:

ACTION POINTS FOR THE WORK STRESSED

(1) Seek to achieve and maintain the right workload balance — not too much and not too little. A key skill is to plan your workload ahead.

(2) Make certain you know what your job is. Sit down with your boss and subordinates and clarify what is to be achieved and how it is to be achieved.

(3) Remember that the good boss is the boss who actively manages the people around them. Think through how to involve people in decisions, ensure proper participation, allow discretion to your work team and establish good informal and formal communications between yourself and your team.

(4) Manage the priority conflicts around. Keep your job priority conflicts under control and learn to say NO! nicely to your boss.

(5) Share your problems as well as your answers. Your work team is your strength and sharing problems is the basis of good communications.

(6) When faced with a stress situation, remain calm, get the facts, change to adapt to the situation and get on with that new situation. Don't dig your heels in!

(7) Finally, don't forget the strength of your family. They can solve problems as well as listen to your success.

Chapter 2: Assessing your performance and time management

Most managers have a false impression of how they use their time and how it affects their performance. My own research and experience of working with many thousand managers suggests that the typical manager can improve his or her output by at least 10% and save time by as much as 20–30% in a typical working day.

There are many reasons for this potential. Managers can improve their job planning and in particular they can devote more time to top priority work and less time to low priority work. Very typically a manager will spend between 30 and 40% of his time on 'A' priority work and the remainder on lower priority work. Managers also have the potential for more effective meetings, 'crisper' delegation and a potential for developing much keener disciplines for controlling their time and ensuring effective workflow and organization.

The first step in correcting your false impression and identifying your potential is to write a TIME REPORT. This is a 3-day log of your activities which is assessed using four techniques.

The four assessment techniques are:

(1) Performance Assessment
(2) Time Category Assessment
(3) Key Time Question Assessment
(4) Preferred Day Assessment

PERFORMANCE ASSESSMENT

This technique aims to assess whether the performance objectives of the day were, in fact, achieved. Many managers don't set objectives for the day, nor establish their key priorities, nor commit themselves to drive hard to achieve their priority objectives.

A managers' day is made up of different types of priorities:

'A' priorities are highly essential activities which must be completed or progressed substantially.
'B' priorities are less essential activities which can be deferred because the time element is less critical and the impact on job performance is lower.
'C' priorities are non-essential activities which can be scrapped, screened out, handled by other people or handled at low priority times.
'X' priorities are activities which require immediate attention. They may be queries, requests for informa-

tion, crises and emergencies, boss demands or interruption. You can have 'AX', 'BX' or 'CX' priorities.

One of the golden rules of time management is based on the PARETO or 80/20 rule. This suggests that 80% of your performance will come from 20% of your activities and 20% or your performance will come from 80% of your activities.

When you assess your own time usage and your own performance in the day you will find that the majority of your time has been spent on lower priority work. To establish this assessment you do the following on your time logs:

(i) For each activity calculate the time you spent on it.
(ii) For each activity assign a ABCX priority.
(iii) Sum the total time spent on ABCX priorities as a percentage of the total day.
(iv) Ask a very frank question about your 'A' priority activities 'Did I achieve what I intended to achieve?'
(v) Estimate the time you could have saved, by better discipline and control, on each low priority activity.
(vi) Make a judgement about your achievement on the day, how much 'continuous' time you spent on your top priority work, how you controlled your low priority work and how much 'total' time you could have devoted to high priority work if you had exercised better control and discipline.

When you go through this assessment you will find that you are not spending enough time on your top priority work in order to achieve, and that the majority of time (could be as high as 60 or 70%) will be spent on low priority work of which you could have saved at least 20% by better control and disciplines.

TIME CATEGORY ASSESSMENT

This is a simple technique whereby you sum the total amount of time (in percentages) you spend in certain categories of activities. Typical categories are: meetings; telephone; secretary; correspondence; project work; report writing; reading, etc. Each manager will have different categories and different times; however, you do find that managers spent at least 40–50% of a typical day in some sort of meeting. More senior managers will spend at least 70% of the day in meetings.

When you have listed your categories, then any major users of time are critical categories for your self management. If you made an assessment of the amount of time you save by 'crisper' management of these activities you would find that your time saving could be between 20 and 30%. The four priority areas for time saving and better self management are: delegation, meetings, planning and personal organization.

KEY TIME QUESTION ASSESSMENT

This technique is a detailed look at each of the main activities of the day. Each activity is reviewed against five key time questions:

    (i) What was the purpose of the activity?
    (ii) Who were the people in the activity?
    (iii) How was the activity delegated?
    (iv) How was the activity scheduled?
    (v) How was the activity tried?

The first question establishes whether the activity was a necessary one in order to achieve your objectives and whether the time used was well spent. The second question establishes whether the people involved had the right skills and experiences to assist you in achieving the task and whether the team management and spirit were adequate for top performance. The third question establishes whether you delegated well or indeed did you delegate when you could have delegated? This question leads on to many important issues about delegation planning, definition of tasks and delegation reviewing. Another side to this question is whether the activity was delegated to you by your boss: this question leads on to your management of your boss and how effectively your boss manages himself. The fourth question establishes your ability to plan your time effectively and how you control your diary and the planning lead time for your activities. The fifth question establishes whether the activity was well timed in the day for your personal productivity and whether you are able to manage your time in 'continuous' blocks rather than short, haphazard periods. From this detailed questioning you gain many insights into your basic performance management problems and how time has a substantial impact upon what you can achieve. Of all your resources, time needs to be managed carefully and very effectively.

PREFERRED DAY ASSESSMENT

All managers have a productivity cycle throughout the day. Some are at their best in the morning whilst others are at their best in the late afternoon. Also each manager has a preference for their working hours and the types of activities which are scheduled during these hours. The

knack for high performance is to manage your 'A' time for you 'A' priority work, to ensure sufficient job planning time and to ensure that you have sufficient time for contingencies that will arise in the day. If these 'preferences' are matched to your productivity cycle then you can consistently achieve at your highest level. Preferred Day Assessment is therefore mainly concerned with how much match you have between your 'A' time, your 'A' priority work and your high period on your productivity cycle. It is also concerned with the effectiveness of your regular daily disciplines and scheduling.

Your TIME REPORT is your basic document for assessing *exactly* how you manage your performance and how you use time. As you progress through the assessment of your TIME REPORT you identify all the problem areas that need your active attention. When all these problem areas are identified you can then make your judgement about how you can improve and where you should improve. When you have collected together all these improvements you then have your IMPROVEMENT PLAN for your self management and your time management.

Chapter 3: Writing your improvement plan

Your improvement plan is personal to you. It will contain problem areas and action points which are based upon your present style of management and disciplines as they apply to your present job circumstances.

Although your plan is personal you are likely to find that it has many improvement areas which are common to other managers. Here are the key points taken from a typical improvement plan for a middle manager with a direct report team of six younger managers and a secretary. You'll probably find that you have many improvements in common:

TYPICAL IMPROVEMENT PLAN

(1) Establish a job planning system that is flexible, capable of change and dealing with contingencies.
(2) Sit down with your boss and establish clearer objectives, standards of work and more specific time scales.
(3) Develop a 'broad brush' year plan to check on performance, resources, managing priorities and delegation planning.

(4) Develop the discipline of monthly planning.

(5) On a daily basis, establish 'A' time to ensure that the majority of my time is allocated to 'A' priority work. Make certain that 'A' time is continuous time matched to my highest period in my daily productivity cycle.

(6) Make certain that I don't schedule 'A' priority work in the gaps *left* after low priority work. Schedule my 'A' priority work FIRST and do it FIRST *then* schedule my low priority work SECOND and do it SECOND. Manage low priority work for MINIMUM TIME to do the activities.

(7) Keep my 'A' time clear of interruptions from low priority work by screening out (by secretary) or by deferring into low priority time.

(8) Commit myself to protecting my 'A' time and briefing my secretary on how to protect it.

(9) Establish more effective diary control by vetting entries for priority and time duration. Schedule in my diary *all* aspects of my job performance and not just meetings and appointments. Keep my diary under my control.

(10) Plan into my diary the time I will need for job planning with my secretary, job planning time for me, and all 'A' priority activities.

(11) List my 'A' priorities of the day and commit myself to achieve them. DRIVE FOR RESULTS!

(12) Check my procrastination. Ensure that I don't put low priority work FIRST, don't set objectives I can't achieve, start EARLY on large and difficult jobs and commit myself to DO IT NOW! and SINGLE HANDLING of work.

(13) Use my secretary more effectively. Delegate all 'C' and some 'B' priority work. Establish routine work procedures and 'A' time control. Involve my secretary more and allocate 'A' priority time to our job planning on a regular daily basis.

(14) Manage my boss more effectively. Discuss with him the quality of his delegation and his time management and how it affects me. Learn to say NO! nicely and effectively.

(15) Improve my meetings management substantially. Ensure better planning and organization. Improve my chairmanship and discussion leading. Keep meetings as short as possible. Schedule 'B' priority meetings into low priority time and always allow a buffer between meetings.

(16) Improve my team management. Spend more time developing the team to ensure better direction, involvement and harmony.

(17) Improve my personal, desk and filing organization. Commit myself to a CLEAR DESK policy.

(18) Improve my telephone handling skills. Separate telephone calls into 'A' priority and low priority both for incoming and outgoing.

(19) Improve my personal communication skills. Aim for better organization of my reading and writing and pay much more attention to my listening and speaking.

(20) Manage my work stress more effectively. Exercise more control over my workload and aim to improve my job clarity and personal relationships with people around me.

(21) Commit myself, by the above improvements, to achieving an increase in output of at least 10% and an overall time saving of 20% of my present activities. Use this time saved for more output.

This typical improvement plan can be broken into a number of distinct topics:

(i) How we manage and work with people.
(ii) How we improve our personal communications.
(iii) How we process our workflow.
(iv) How we plan our objectives.
(v) How we plan our short-term activities.

These topics are covered in the following sections. The IMPROVEMENT PLAN identifies where we need to improve and the following section shows how we can achieve these improvements.

Chapter 4: Managing people

How you manage your performance and time is affected by people — your boss, your subordinates, your peers and your external relationships. Bearing in mind that people are critical to a manager's performance, we need to look at four major topics: Leadership Development, Teamwork Development, Delegation and Performance Improvement Planning.

LEADERSHIP DEVELOPMENT

Good leadership comes from a combination of two important factors: leadership personality and leadership process. These two factors will be further conditioned by your power and authority in the situation and your professional or technical experience.

Leadership personality is built on a number of factors:

(1) *The Planning Factor*: The ability to organize and

plan people, resources and time plus the ability to plan and organize yourself.

(2) *The Doing Factor*: The drive to achieve objectives and the drive for action.

(3) *The Visionary Factor*: The ability to create and pursue a vision of the future and to seek and take opportunities that arise within that vision.

(4) *The Influencing Factor*: The ability to communicate with other people by various means plus the ability to influence and persuade other people about your ideas and decisions.

(5) *The People Factor*: The sensitivity to understand people and their needs and abilities and the ability to exercise social skills in many different situations.

(6) *The Stability Factor*: The ability to maintain emotional stability and resilience and to show honesty and integrity.

(7) *The Hard Work Factor*: The natural ability to be enthusiastic about work and to maintain this enthusiasm over long hours and in difficult situations.

(8) *The Ideas Factor*: The natural expression of ideas, creativity and imagination and the ability to develop new ways.

(9) *The Risk Taking Factor*: The ability to accept, seek and adapt to change and to make risky decisions.

In addition to a leadership personality, a leader has to perform certain tasks in order to keep a work team on the correct course. These essential tasks are:

(1) Defining the objectives for a work team so the team can harness its resources.

(2) Planning the activities of the team so that the objectives will be achieved.

(3) Briefing the team so that all team members know the objectives for themselves and other team members.

(4) Controlling the work of the team in a quiet and restrained manner with the emphasis of work control on the team itself.

(5) Evaluating the future situations such that changes are planned for and so that they may have minimal impact on the work of the team.

(6) Motivating the team towards the objectives.

(7) Organizing the team so that work is well delegated and communications are effective.

(8) Setting an example is critical. The team leader needs to 'do' and 'be' what he expects in others.

Your leadership personality has two major components. Component one is concerned with the DIREC-TION you create and communicate to the team. Component two is concerned with your ability to create FOLLOWSHIP in your team. You achieve your performance objectives because you have created the right DIRECTION and have motivated and managed the proper FOLLOWSHIP.

Your leadership process breaks down into 2 stages. The first stage is concerned with getting the team STARTED and the second stage is concerned with the CONTINUOUS management of the team.

For successful performance and good time management you need firstly to create the right DIRECTION and *spend* time on actively STARTING the team. Then you need to change your active involvement substantially by *reducing* your time in the activities and concentrate on developing FOLLOWSHIP and CONTINUOUS management of the team. The key skill for the manager is to ENSURE that he changes gear from ACTIVITY INVOLVEMENT to MANAGEMENT OF THE TEAM at the right time. This change to a 'helicopter view' is essential for good time management.

TEAMWORK DEVELOPMENT

Your leadership ability is the basic foundation for your teamwork development. For teamwork to be effective *all* the members of the team need to work well together and you need to generate the right team spirit that will allow the team to manage itself well.

Teams develop a good team spirit when three factors are developed. Firstly the team depend very heavily upon the DIRECTION of the team leader. Objectives need to be defined, communicated and established so that the team knows it will achieve. It is also critical that team members participate in the creation of this direction. Secondly a team works well when it is INVOLVED in the day-to-day decision making. As long as direction is clear and achieveable, the quality of the team's decision will be superior to any one individual (including the team leader!) This is often a bitter pill for the autocratic manager to swallow. Thirdly, the HARMONY of the team needs constant attention. Without harmony the team will develop its own continuous conflict and all the indisciplines of personality difficulties and lack of cooperation.

Given these three factors, here are the key action points for teamwork development.

(i) Take time to talk through with your team the three factors of DIRECTION, INVOLVE-MENT and HARMONY.

(ii) Whenever a team is established, clarify at the

outset whether any team member has a special expertise or knowledge about the task at hand.

(iii) Work with the team to establish a clear statement of the objectives, the level of quality and the time for achievement.

(iv) Always ensure that there is agreement on policy. Delay any movement forward by the team until policy agreement is established. Without agreement on policy, detail disagreements will arise and upset teamwork.

(v) During teamwork discussions take a 'helicopter view'. Ensure that discussions are logical and well managed. Establish FACTS first, then INTERPRETATION of the facts and finally CONCLUSIONS based on the interruption. Avoid the natural tendency to jump from FACTS to CONCLUSIONS. This is the natural breeding ground for red herrings!

(vi) Seek to develop a team atmosphere where feelings can be expressed and team members are involved in decision making.

(vii) Seek harmony and seek to resolve conflict at the time by: cooperation, avoiding aggression, avoiding ultimatums, never voting to resolve conflict, avoiding personal attacks, and effectively listening to the views of others.

(viii) Finally, if you are the team leader then manage the team actively — it is expected of you. Always take the 'helicopter view' when you know the team is working well.

Bad teamwork lowers performance and wastes time for you and all the team members, so without good teamwork you'll never achieve at your highest potental nor manage your time in the most effective way.

EFFECTIVE DELEGATION

Delegation is a key skill for a manager. For the successful senior manager it appears that there are five key factors that make effective delegation.

(i) *Delegation Planning* Successful senior managers plan their own performance by planning their delegation well ahead.

(ii) *Delegation Precision* Successful senior managers spend time ensuring that tasks are well defined and agreed.

(iii) *Delegation Review* Successful senior managers are pedantic over their reviewing of delegated tasks.

(iv) *'Hands Off' Approach* Successful senior managers let their subordinates get on with the job. They don't HOVER and they check DELEGATION BACK.

(v) *Risk and Time* Successful senior managers always assess the risk of failure and the *latest* time when a task should be taken back if failure is possible.

Although these are key factors for successful managers you find that delegation skill needs quite substantial improvement for the typical manager. Here are some of the signs that indicate that delegation is poor.

(i) When you have difficulty in asking a subordinate to perform a task because of that subordinate's dominant personality.

(ii) When you have difficulty accepting the ideas and approaches of other people and you generally assess them as less effective than your own approach.

(iii) When you have a strong tendency to do things yourself because you feel it is quicker and of better quality.

(iv) When you mistrust the skills and judgements of other people and you fear that mistakes will occur if other people do not perform as well as you do.

(v) When you have a high leaning towards detail, precision and well defined situations and this leaning affects your attitude to your job.

(vi) When you feel you work longer and harder than your subordinates and because of this you have little time to train them.

(vii) When your job has a high proportion of menial tasks or routine matters which could quite easily be done by other people.

Improving delegation comes from developing more positive attitudes towards delegation and improving your skill in the process of delegation. Here are the key action points.

POSITIVE ATTITUDES

(i) Delegation is a key skill in my job and one that needs developing fully. Delegation is one of the 'rights' of my job.

(ii) Delegation is an essential method of developing the skill and judgement of my subordinates.

(iii) Delegation requires a trust in other people's idas and approach and an acceptance that their mistakes will be my responsibility.

(iv) Delegation means I do not 'do it myself' thereby 'wasting myself' and my time.

(v) Delegation means I have to spend *more* time on delegation in order to produce *more* time for my work and improving my performance.

(vi) Delegation means I have to follow a sound way of delegating.

THE SOUND WAY OF DELEGATING

(i) Always ask yourself if this job could be done better by somebody else and if I were not doing this job now what more important job could I be doing.

(ii) Always think through the work to be delegated very carefully. Establish the key objectives and standards of performance, the time required and the key skills and resources required.

(iii) Consult and select a subordinate who has the skills to perform the work. If these skills are not available then these skills will need to be developed. This means you need to plan your delegation in advance.

(iv) Always check on whether the subordinate will have a number of bosses when the work is undertaken. If more than one boss then be wary of conflicts of priority.

(v) Determine the limits of authority that are being delegated — how much money, people, time, resources, etc. These need to be clear before the work starts.

(vi) Always delegate a WHOLE job rather than a PART job. Make certain that the boring or bad work is not the only work you delegate.

(vii) Always talk through with your subordinate how the work is to be controlled, how it will be manned, by whom, when, what results are expected and how these are to be monitored along the way. When broad controls have been established then leave the subordinate to it — don't hover and question.

(viii) In all delegation establish clear delegation review times and schedule these in your diary. Clearly establish what you expect to have been achieved by the review date.

(ix) When a job is under way, monitor the type of questions and consultation you are getting from the subordinate. When the subordinate raises a problem, ask for the solution. Be wary of too much consultation, otherwise the job will be delegated back to you.

(x) Whenever the work is completed successfully then praise in public. Whenever it does wrong, then think what *you* did or did not do to let it go wrong and work through with the subordinate how to correct the error. Praise in public but always correct or sanction in private.

PERFORMANCE IMPROVEMENT PLANNING

Performance Improvement Planning or PIP for short, is a simple but important concept. It is based on the simple idea that a team improves, rapidly and substantially, by reviewing its successes and failures and setting new objectives to build on the successes and remedy the failures. As the team completes a task, it reviews its performance, and eventually, over a series of reviews, it builds up a robust set of rules for high performance. The technique is remarkable inasmuch as within five or six reviews it has developed such a level of confidence and team spirit that it knows it will succeed on the next task, whatever its nature and difficulty.

PIP is a continuous part of management. Normally PIP sessions of about 15 minutes are added on to technical progress meetings or possibly 1-hour PIP sessions are undertaken each month. A PIP session has four main stages:

Stage 1: Reviewing the tasks the team has worked on, allow the team to identify any significant factors that have contributed successfully to the task and any significant factors that have impeded the task.

Stage 2: From the success and failure factors, select those which are practical to keep and those which need to be removed.

Stage 3: Agree with the team its objectives for building on the success factors and dispensing with the failure factors.

Stage 4: Agree with the team how each individual will act or work differently to achieve the objectives.

Here are some of the typical areas that are often discussed in a PIP session:

(i) Lack of clarity on the overall direction and strategy of the team to achieve its objectives.

(ii) Lack of understanding on objectives and how the team or individuals are to be measured on their success or failure.

(iii) The need to invest time in developing and agreeing objectives and standards of performance.

(iv) The need to recognize expertise in the team.

(v) The need to listen effectively within the group.

(vi) The need to concentrate on priorities of work and the need for the team to manage its time by its priority objectives and tasks.

(vii) The need to manage effectively the processing of work within the team. For example, meetings management, chairmanship, delegation skills, interruptions management, personal organization.

(viii) The need for involvement and harmony in the team.

PIP sessions are normally, as you can see from the above, mainly concerned with performance and time management. They are very important for establishing 'codes of practice' for how the team wants to manage itself more effectively.

Chapter 5: Managing your communications

Working with people means that communication skills are critical. In fact managers spend 70% of their time in four main methods of communication: speaking, listening, reading and writing.

EFFECTIVE SPEAKING

Some managers have the natural gift of speaking in a confident and authoritative manner. For many managers speaking has to be developed if communications are to be improved. Here are the golden rules of speaking:

(1) *Speaking is very important*: Speaking with confidence and authority is an important measure of a manager's capability in the job. Apart from better communication, speaking can make a manager's reputation. It can also destroy it.

(2) *Speaking is about the strength of your enthusiasm*: Speaking is effective only when you let your enthusiasm and commitment *DRIVE* your ideas, spoken word, gestures and actions. Speaking starts deep inside the mind and the body and effective communication comes when the whole body talks with confidence and authority.

(3) *Speaking is about your right to assert yourself*: Assertion is the balance between being passive and being aggressive. You have a right to speak but you must not undersell or oversell yourself.

(4) *Speaking is about the simplicity of your ideas*: Communication breaks down when you are complicated. Long words, abstract ideas, technical jargon interfere with communication. The key skill is to put substantial ideas into the simplest form.

(5) *Speaking is brief*: No manager gains from speaking too much or too long. Only talk when you have something important to say. Think about it, say it and shut up!

(6) Never underestimate your audience, and learn to 'read' them by their eye contact and facial gestures. Never take your eyes off your audience's eyes because their interest will fade.

(7) *Speaking is about rhythm, stress and interest*: You generate interest by following the model: CONCEPT-EXAMPLE-OPINION-KEY COMMUNICATION POINT. This is the 'WHAT' of speaking. The 'HOW' of speaking is your rhythm, which is PAUSE, SLOW, QUICK and your stress which you use at key times by raising the VOLUME and by FACIAL and BODY GESTURES.

(8) *Speaking is about visual aids*: The greatest aid a manager has is his flip chart. Visuals are the picture of your mind. Be bold, draw your ideas as you speak them.

(9) *Speaking is about NEVERS*: Never be passive or submissive; never show aggression; never be impatient; never fear an audience; never hide an error; never apologize for speaking; never hide your hands in your pockets; never fold your arms across your chest; never look at the floor. All these and more show that you are uneasy and not enthusiastic and committed to what you are saying.

(10) *Speaking is about knowing your subject*: Always prepare well. You are speaking because you *know more* than your listeners.

These golden rules apply to all forms of managerial speaking. How about management presentations? Here are the nine most common failings in a presentation and the key action points for improving.

(1) *The manager is not BOLD enough*: Speak with enthusiasm and commitment. Concentrate on the 'HOW' as well as the 'WHAT'. Engage a higher gear when you are presenting.

(2) *The manager rejects the audience*: Research your audience and know it well. Build rapport and common experience at the start and always keep eye contact by sweeping across the audience and resting for a moment on individuals.

(3) *The manager suffers and shows nerves*: Nerves are important to you because they ensure that you get into high gear. The first four minutes of the presentation are the time you need to manage your nerves. Here are some of the key signs of nerves: nervous smile; hands in pockets; telling jokes; crossing your legs or arms; dry mouth; speaking too slowly or quickly; looking at the floor; making comments about how dull the presentation will be; rushing to your first visual aid; standing with your back to the audience.

(4) *The manager doesn't use visual aids*: Simple and active visual aids are best. Use them often but make them clear and explain them.

(5) *The manager speaks for too long*: The longest presentation you should make is 20 minutes. No presentation should contain more than five main points of about three minutes each.

(6) *The manager tries to be clever rather than simple*: If you want to lose your audience then talk over their heads. Be simple and pragmatic.

(7) *The manager is poorly prepared*: You need five times your speaking time for your preparation time. This is a minimum figure. Never write a presentation and never read a presentation. Rehearsals are about thinking and logic of the presentation.

(8) *The manager doesn't demonstrate a logic in the presentation*: Show the audience where you are going and always summarize the key communication points of the presentation.

(9) *The manager tends to waffle*: If you haven't prepared well, you have no logic in the presentation and you have insufficient knowledge, then you'll waffle.

EFFECTIVE LISTENING

The skill of listening is important. Apart from improving understanding and communication, listening also has a symbolic value. It demonstrates to your subordinates your style of management. It does this because most managers listens more effectively to their bosses rather than their subordinates. Good listening is one of the key signs of a good boss. The six factors in a good and bad boss are:

Good boss
(1) Ability to give clear direction.
(2) Ability to involve managers in decision making.
(3) Ability to give the subordinates freedom to achieve in the way they want to achieve.

(4) High technical or professional expertise in the area.
(5) Fairness in dealings with the subordinate.
(6) Ability to listen well and give time to listening.

Bad boss
(1) Lack of direction for the subordinates.
(2) Autocratic decision making.
(3) Too close a control of the subordinate's actions and decisions.
(4) Low technical or professional expertise.
(5) Lack of consistency in dealing with subordinates.
(6) Inability to listen and always too busy to listen.

The first five factors are governed by your leadership and teamwork skills but listening is important. Good leadership and teamwork cannot be developed without listening.

There are certain areas where you need to listen very hard and search for understanding. These areas are:

(i) When you are contemplating action or a decision. Listen carefully to the words of others.
(ii) When you are about to argue or criticize.
(iii) When anybody wishes to talk over a sensitive or personal issue.
(iv) Whenever a new idea, direction or concept is raised.
(v) Whenever you are approached by a subordinate.

You also need to listen well in meetings. It is here that the GAP SEARCHING phenomenon occurs. GAP SEARCHING is when you are listening to a speaker but an idea enters your head. You then stop listening and start searching for a gap to interrupt the speaker. GAP SEARCHING is very common and in fact most time in meetings is spent gap searching rather than listening. Apart from low communication gap searching always drags the discussion back towards the start of the meeting.

Here are some general action points for improving your listening:

(1) Be prepared to listen. Being interested and attentive and trying hard to understand is imperative to good listening.
(2) Listen to ideas and not words.
(3) Be on your guard against distractions. Concentrate solely on the speaker.
(4) Be wary of your prejudices, they interfere with your listening.
(5) Stimulate the speaker with attending, following and responding skills. You demonstrate attention

by body gestures of being alert and open. You demonstrate following by giving short encouragements like 'Oh! I see, right', etc. and by asking open-ended questions. You demonstrate response by summarizing the facts and the feelings of the speaker.

(6) Don't search for gaps. Let the speaker finish and always bear in mind that the good listener understands the need for silence.

EFFECTIVE READING

Business reading is now so demanding of time and concentration that even the most seasoned of businessmen find it a chore. As with other aspects of time management the 80/20 principle applies. The plain fact of the matter is that we read too much low priority reading matter and not enough high priority reading matter. The knack is to be selective and process your reading in a systematic and speedy manner.

INCREASING READING SPEED

You can increase your reading speed from an average of 200 and 300 words per minute to 600 to 700 words per minute by correcting regression. Regression means that your eye travels backwards rather than forwards over the line. To correct regression you DRIVE your eyes forward and read thought patterns and not words. Another bad habit we picked up as children is the need to speak the words in our own mind. This is known as sub-vocalization. You can improve your reading speed by using a pointer under a line of words. Move the pointer quickly and this will train your eyes to pick up thought patterns. Increase the speed of the pointer as you progress. Don't worry about comprehension because it normally *improves* as you increase your reading speed. Also don't worry about having to read quickly all the time. When you have developed quicker reading speeds, select the reading speed appropriate to the reading task.

REDUCING READING LOAD

Reducing your reading load is based upon 'A' priority reading and low priority reading. To sort your reading into priority use the SCANNING technique. Range your eyes quickly over the contents pages, summaries, opening and closing paragraphs and conclusions, and focus upon KEY WORDS associated with your job priorities. Sort your reading into A B C priority piles.

Use the SKIM technique on your 'A' priority, delegate for comment your 'B' priority pile and throw away your 'C' priority pile. Ensure that it is screened out of your system.

The SKIMMING technique is needed for 'A' priority reading in order to establish any points of interest and any area for further reading in more depth. To SKIM read we:

(i) Read at our most rapid rate.
(ii) Read the title, contents and summary.
(iii) Scan the headings and sub-headings.
(iv) Read the first and last paragraph of major sections.
(v) Read the first and last sentence of any major paragraph.
(vi) Read the conclusions carefully.

IMPROVING CONCENTRATION AND MEMORY

Concentration means you have focused your attention on the reading material so that you understand the key points. Here are some guidelines for improving your concentration for reading:

(i) Set aside 15 minutes as a daily discipline to sort and read 'A' priority reading material.
(ii) Clear your desk of any work.
(iii) Place the reading material on your desk and ensure that distractions are minimized for 15 minutes.
(iv) Now you can start. Say to yourself 'Now I must concentrate' and 'I must finish this reading within this reading session'. Make a strong effort to keep your attention on the reading.

Basically your concentration is improved by the discipline of time and by setting an objective to achieve in the time.

Your memory has two stages. Short term memory lasts for about 24 hours but only 20% of what you read will remain after 24 hours. After 24 hours you have a very inefficient long-term memory and unless you constantly review reading material you will forget the vast majority of it very quickly.

To improve your memory you need to focus upon key points and create a mental picture of the overall theme of these key points. If you physically draw the picture of the theme and key points then you will reinforce your memory. You can also use this picture for reviewing and improving your long term memory.

EFFECTIVE WRITING

Business writing needs discipline if you are going to communicate well. Here are the four key principles of business writing.

(i) Write for your reader's ACTION.
(ii) Keep your writing SHORT.
(iii) Keep it SIMPLE.
(iv) Only write when you need to RECORD or CIRCULATE.

Writing for your reader's ACTION means that you have thought through what action you are taking or wish to take and what action you wish the reader to take. The presentation and structure of all your points need to focus on this action.

Keeping your writing SHORT and SIMPLE means that you write as you speak. Don't write long words, long sentences or long paragraphs, because you don't speak that way. Here is a very simple technique for achieving better clarity. The technique is called the CLARITY INDEX.

(i) Choose a sample of 100 words.
(ii) Count the number of major punctuation marks (. ; : ! ?).
(iii) Divide the 100 words by the number of major punctuation marks. This gives you the average length of a sentence.
(iv) Count the number of words with three or more syllables and work out the percentage of long words to the 100 words in the sample.
(v) Add the average sentence length to the percentage of long words (disregard the % sign).
(vi) This gives the CLARITY INDEX.

People in conversation have a clarity index of 30. The clarity index of the quality national press is 30. As a general guide for business writing aim for the following:

business memos	20–25 index
business letters	23–28 index
business reports	30–35 index
business articles and books	35–40 index

When you write a business report write it for SKIM READING. Basically this means your report should have a distinct style and structure.

(1) Clearly defined titled, contents pages, summary and section headings.
(2) The first and last paragraphs of major sections should contain the important points.
(3) Each report should have detailed conclusions, recommendations and actions.

Aim to circulate your summary of the report and not the whole report. A summary for circulation needs only the title, the author, the content list, the key points laid out in a clearly headed sequence and a full listing of the recommendations or actions. A circulating summary should be no more than two or three pages.

Here are the key action points for business writing:

(1) Think before you write and think about ACTION.
(2) Write only if it is absolutely necessary to RECORD or CIRCULATE.
(3) Write about ACTION.
(4) Always write for the reader and ASSUME the reader will SKIM READ.
(5) Keep it short and simple — aim for a clarity index of 30.
(6) Write as you speak and aim for a friendly but matter of fact style.
(7) When you write a report, write for SKIM READING.
(8) Only circulate a well written management summary of your report. This is the only way you can ensure that your report findings will be read promptly.

Chapter 6: Managing your work flow

How you process your work or manage your work flow has a significant impact on your performance and time. Unfortunately it is in this area that many managers have developed very bad habits.

EFFECTIVE MEETINGS

Meetings between people are the largest user of time. Most managers will spend at least 40% of their time in meetings and most senior managers will spend at least 60–70% of their time. We must use this time well and we must substantially improve on our present management in this area. The aim is to be better planned and crisper in our management. Here are the 'seven deadly sins' of meetings:

(1) Meetings do not have a purpose.
(2) Too many people at the meeting.
(3) Meetings do not have agendas or have bad agendas.
(4) People do not prepare for meetings.

(5) Timekeeping is poor.

(6) Chairman (if any) exercises poor control of the discussion.

(7) Action of the meeting is unclear.

To make meetings more effective we need to abide by a number of golden rules:

(1) *Concentrate the meeting on a considered and easily understood purpose*: Lack of purpose tends to come about because we have *too many* purposes within the same meetings. Managers overlap meetings about progress, briefing, team building, problem solving, decision making, risk sharing, planning and ideas generation. As you overlap these types of meeting the purposes become unclear, the number of people increases and time increases. Concentrate a meeting on one or a few purposes and also state the purpose of the meeting in about five or six words.

(2) *Attend a meeting only if it is absolutely necessary and important*: Question the habit of meetings because many meetings are, in fact, unnecessary and unjustifiable in terms of people and time devoted to them. It is very good practice to justify the COSTS of a meeting against the purpose. Never call a meeting where the costs are not justified and never attend a meeting where your costs are not justified.

(3) *Limit people at a meeting to only those who are relevant*: Let the purpose of the meeting justify the people attending. Try not to combine briefing meetings with other types of meeting because participant number increases and confuses the discussion on decisions, problems, risks, etc. Try not to use a meeting for decision-making participation or involvement. Try to seek alternative means based on a 'one-to-one' meeting.

(4) *Always ensure that your meeting has an agenda*: The agenda must always describe the PURPOSE, describe what is to be discussed, what is to be achieved and what is to be prepared by the participants. It must also state the time of START and FINISH. Always put the IMPORTANT items first and always try to seek to start the meeting with a rapport-building item. Always plan an agenda in advance and circulate it in advance.

(5) *Always ensure preparation for the meeting*: If you have planned your agenda well and circulate it in advance there can be no excuse for lack of preparation. It can only mean lack of commitment or lack of self management. Always identify preparation by name of the participant.

(6) *Always ensure good time keeping*: Always publish the START and FINISH times. It is a good rule for the chairman to establish in his or her mind how much time is to be allowed per agenda item. Keep your time management matched to the priority of the items. The chairman should never restart a meeting for late arrivals, and always start on time. Try to aim for a 20% reduction in the time of your meetings from their present time. This is perfectly feasible and it will make the meetings management crisper.

(7) *Good chairmanship is critical to the success of a meeting*: Meetings with effective chairmanship are superior to meetings which have no chairman or weak chairmanship. The chairman should control the 'HOW' of the meeting as well as making a contribution to the business discussion. Chairmanship is a skilled job and here are some of the key mistakes of poor chairmanship.

(i) Failure to state the purpose of the meeting.

(ii) Failure to start and finish on time.

(iii) Failure to ensure agreement on policy before detail discussion.

(iv) Failure to manage conflict between individuals.

(v) Failure to proportion the time spent on high priority items and low priority items.

(vi) Failure to lead a discussion. Establish FACTS then INTERPRETATION of facts then CONCLUSION based on INTERPRETATION.

(vii) Failure to control red herrings and discussion off the point.

(viii) Failure to stop 'meetings within meetings'.

(ix) Failure to ensure all participants are contributing.

(x) Failure to ensure effective listening and minimizing gap searching.

(xi) Failure to control interruptions.

(xii) Failure to summarize agreements, actions and accountability for actions.

(8) *All actions should be clearly stated and agreed*: The function of the meeting is to achieve ACTION. Action minutes must describe WHAT, WHO, WHEN. The chairman must always summarize the action minutes and gain agreement.

Finally, meetings are so important to performance and time management that you need to establish a 'code of practice' for your working team. The code of practice is an agreed method (based on the golden rules above) which your team will use. You can't control people outside your team but you control inside your team.

WORKING WITH YOUR SECRETARY

Secretaries are a great potential which is rarely tapped to the full. Your performance, efficiency and time management depends very greatly upon the quality of the working relationship you have established.

Here are the guiding principles for using your secretary more effectively.

(1) Stretch your secretary more in terms of her performance. Your secretary is part of your management team and very capable of handling more important work.

(2) Treat your secretary with greater consideration and warmth. You will never have high performance from her *for your benefit* unless you have a sound personal relationship.

(3) Involve your secretary more in the business. In particular involve her in your job planning. Have regular daily planning sessions.

(4) Train yourself to use your secretary and train her in the basics of management.

(5) Consult more on how you both can improve performance. Make these performance reviews a regular feature of your relationship.

Here is a plan of action for improving your joint performance. Use the plan as an agenda for your first performance review.

(1) Brief your secretary on the business, its plans, its markets, its trends, etc. Brief your secretary on the organization and how your job fits into the overall organization and strategy.

(2) Brief your secretary on your objectives, year plan, key activities and priorities. Concentrate on the priorities and how you can both manage them more effectively.

(3) Work through with your secretary the management of your 'A' time and your daily disciplines. Pay particular attention to how 'A' time should be protected and how she can help to ensure 'continuous' time for 'A' time.

(4) Establish a weekly planning session for longer term work and a regular daily planning session for the immediate tasks and priorities. Don't confuse planning with correspondence.

(5) Establish an 'A' priority objective or activity for your secretary to be trained to manage.

(6) Delegate more 'B' priority work and let your

secretary manage all your 'C' priority work. Brief your secretary on how to recognize priorities of work and screen out low priority work.

(7) Work out how she can handle all routine work and all work when you are absent. Look at all your systems and procedures and seek to improve them such that you are less involved in routine work on a day-to-day basis.

(8) Establish how visitors are to be handled so that you both create a good image of effectiveness and high performance. Look at your telephone manner and your telephone handling habits. Work out a gentle reminder system for overstay visitors.

(9) Work out your best desk organization and your filing procedures and systems. Let your secretary handle your IN and OUT trays so she can screen work. Your basic office system should be URGENT, TO DO, FILE, ABEYANCE and MAIL. A clear desk and clear office is a priority for both of you.

(10) Work through standards of typed work. Look at presentation and agree a procedure where she manages her own quality of work.

(11) Look at your personal relationship. Are trust, confidence, warmth and good temper all consistent parts of your relationship?

(12) Establish a training plan for your secretary so she becomes more familiar with your professional expertise and more familiar with the basics of management. As a matter of course, review your secretary's performance as you would any other subordinate. Let these reviews form the basis of her training plan.

(13) Talk about your bad habits and seek to improve. These are the typical bad habits of a manager: lack of advance preparation of correspondence; untidy desk; knowledge of whereabouts; lack of praise; not keeping appointments; avoiding return telephone calls; white lies; holding onto work at your desk; lack of planning.

(14) Work through how your secretary can handle all your travel arrangements and your basic expenses.

(15) Talk through very carefully how you want to manage meetings and how she can assist.

(16) Talk through how she can assist in your delegation reviewing. Establish an abeyance system so that you are reminded on delegation review.

(17) Talk through how your secretary can assist in the management of your reading and information search.

DESK ORGANIZATION

Some managers work in a complete shambles, with desks piled high and untidy, and very inefficient, filing systems. Other managers are neat and with well organized filing. Which are you? It is very important to recognize that YOUR DESK IS FOR WORKING ON, NOT FOR STORAGE.

Apart from the value judgement — an untidy desk is an untidy mind — which may or may not be true, there are more important considerations. An untidy desk and filing system SLOWS work down and SLOWS down action. It leads to error and it leads to procrastination. It leads to confusion over priorities. Remember that an untidy manager can be 3 to 5 days BEHIND a tidy manager.

Poor organization is generated by 2 factors: poor discipline and volume of paperwork. Here are the combinations and the desk organization styles:

Cause	Effect
Messy worker/	Full desk of stored work
High paperwork	Disorganized storage/filing
Neat worker/	Clear desk as a matter of discipline
High paperwork	Neat, effective storage/filing
Messy worker/	Desk used for storage
Low paperwork	Informal storage/filing
Neat worker/	Very clear desk
Low paperwork	Neat, informal storage/filing

It is important to recognize that poor organization is generated mainly by poor discipline rather than by volume of paperwork. However to get yourself organized you need two important attitudes:

(1) Have a CLEAR DESK policy.
(2) Be ruthless with paperwork.

Keeping a clear desk comes from discipline. Don't store work on your desk, use it for work! Work awaiting attention should be stored AWAY from the desk. Sort your work into priorities and HANDLE WORK ONCE ONLY. Your basic office system should be URGENT, TO DO, FILE, ABEYANCE, MAIL. Let your secretary handle IN and OUT.

Being ruthless with paperwork is essential. Only create 'A' priority paperwork. Low priority paperwork should be recycled. Aim for short correspondence and reports. Circulate only summaries of reports. Reduce your reading to top priority matter. Let your secretary screen out low priority paperwork. Finally, throw paperwork AWAY! Only 20% of what you keep is relevant.

Here are the key action points for better desk organization:

(1) The root of your problem is your discipline and your commitment to a CLEAR DESK POLICY.
(2) Keep important papers in clearly titled manilla folders. One folder per project or item.
(3) Set up an URGENT, TO DO, FILE, ABEYANCE, MAIL system. Let your secretary handle IN and OUT.
(4) Let your secretary manage a single file point where all work is stored.
(5) Never use your desk to STORE. Keep on your desk only the work in hand. When work is finished put it back in STORE.
(6) Pick up work ONCE, and ONCE ONLY. Develop the attitude of single handling.
(7) Allocate in your diary one hour per month to ruthlessly reducing paperwork to the absolute top priority material.

CONTROLLING INTERRUPTIONS

Interruptions are the most frequent cause of complaint at work. Interruptions drain away time very quickly and are a reason why the lesser part of time is spent on top priority work.

Managers have an ambivalent attitude towards interruptions. They dislike them but they also like them. Interruptions provide a 'pace' to the day and provide a distraction from working on a single task. Also, because interruptions are from people, they provide a very necessary socializing element to work. These are some of the reasons why we don't manage our interruptions.

Interruptions come about because we give PRIORITY to the interrupter over the work at hand. We do this for relief from a single task, from procrastination, from common courtesy and from automatic response to people's requests.

You can follow two main strategies in dealing with interruption.

Firstly, you can establish 'A' time and commit yourself to managing it well. All interruptions, other than 'A' priority interruptions are screened out either by your secretary, by operating a CLOSED DOOR policy or by working away from your normal place of work.

Secondly, you can attempt to accumulate interruptions into a time which is convenient for you. Accept all interruptions but immediately ask the question 'Should I deal with it now?' If yes — do it. If no, defer it to a later time. 'A' priority interruptions you handle now and low priority interruptions you defer into low priority time.

To handle visitors to your work space you need only IMMEDIATELY STAND UP as they enter. This is a very bold body signal which ensures that the interruptions will last less than two minutes. If you are working on 'A' priority work never offer a seat, this will only length the interruption.

Your strategies on interruption will not work all the time but they work for the majority. Don't forget you don't want to get rid of all your interruptions, because you like them! Here is an action plan.

(1) Establish your 'A' time and publish it to your boss, peers and subordinates. If you have a secretary then brief her to protect 'A' time.
(2) In 'A' time never give prior right to the interruptions. If it's an 'A' priority interruption then handle it. If low priority then defer it to low priority time. Let your secretary screen your interruptions.
(3) In 'A' time always stand up when a visitor (even your boss!) enters your work space.
(4) Establish with your work team a 'code of practice' on interruptions. In simple terms 'no interruptions in 'A' time'.

HANDLING YOUR TELEPHONE

These are the major irritants on business telephone calls that stand in the way of your work flow:

(1) The person is not available.
(2) People ringing back are never prompt.
(3) People don't have the information available.
(4) You are put on HOLD.
(5) You talk too long on low priority matters.
(6) People prefer meetings to long telephone calls.
(7) Secretaries are not briefed to handle low priority matters.

Here is an action plan for more effective telephoning:

'A' PRIORITY CALLS

(1) Batch your 'A' priority calls and do them at the start of 'A' time.
(2) Make a note about purpose and actions on your calls.
(3) Make your first call, never go on hold but ring back. Put the call to the end of the list. Make the next call, and so on.
(4) If a person is engaged, leave the message that you will ring back at a set time but state the purpose and action.
(5) When you are put through, state your name and

purpose straightaway. If the information is not available then ring back at your stated time.
(6) Never rely on being called back. With 'A' priority calls you must always control the time when you ring and always persist with your ringing until you have the information.

LOW PRIORITY CALLS

(1) Batch your low priority calls and do them towards the end of the day.
(2) Never go on HOLD but put these calls to the end of your list.
(3) If a person is engaged then suggest that the secretary handle the matter. If not, ask the person to ring you back the following afternoon (not in 'A' time).
(4) Always state your name, purpose and action to the secretary or manager when you are put through.
(5) Don't rely upon being called back but with low priority calls it doesn't matter. Never persist with low priority calls.

Try to get into the habit of long telephone calls instead of meetings for 'A' priority work. Ring at the start of your 'A' time and suggest a meeting over the phone. Agree the purpose and key points and fix a telephone appointment. Ring at the stated time.

For incoming calls, handle all 'A' priority calls at the time. Defer all low priority calls into low priority time, either by your secretary screening or you deferring. Let your secretary handle more of the low priority matters over the phone.

Two final points. Always keep a telephone directory handy and don't handle calls or work for your subordinates. If you have regular callers make sure your subordinate deals with the right person straightaway.

Chapter 7: Developing your objectives and year plan

A very common problem for managers is the lack of planning for their job. Planning breaks into two major sections. This section will deal with job objectives and creating an overview of the year. The next section will deal with monthly and daily planning.

You can develop sound job objectives by a 3-step process: developing performance areas; developing key factors; developing objectives.

STEP ONE: PERFORMING AREAS

Your performance areas relate to the output of your job. They are the general areas of results for which you are responsible. The purpose of performance areas is to focus where your efforts and time should be used most effectively. Performance areas are brief and general statements of about five or six key words maximum. Normally a manager has between four and eight performance areas. Here is an example for a production manager:

(1) Production levels and schedules.
(2) Production costs and controls.
(3) Quality level and methods.
(4) Stock levels and costs.
(5) Delivery times.
(6) Machine utilization.
(7) Staff development.

You clarify your performance areas by answering four key questions. All these questions focus upon what you are expected to achieve in your job.

Question 1: What UNIQUE contribution does your job make to the organization?
Question 2: What would the organization NOT achieve if your job was not performed?
Question 3: What am I expected to achieve in my job, by my boss, my subordinates, my peers, and my external relationships?
Question 4: From all the areas of my job, which are the key areas that will account for the major part of my performance?

Here is another example for a Managing Director of a manufacturing company:

(1) Corporate direction and leadership.
(2) Market standing and strategy.
(3) Organization and management development.
(4) Corporate image and external relations.
(5) Return on investment.
(6) Product innovation and technological position.
(7) Availability of the right resources.
(8) Staff and personal development.

STEP TWO: KEY FACTORS

Key factors give more focus for your objectives. Whereas performance areas remain stable your objectives will change from year to year depending on the key factors affecting your job and organization. Therefore key factors help to define your objectives for a planning period of one year.

Key factors tend to be opportunities, threats, resource constraints or organizational difficulties. Here are some examples:

change of company ownership
loss of clients
lack of investment capital
loss of skilled personnel
weak management

You normally find that a manager has about 4–8 key factors affecting his job over the next year and these will affect the nature and level of his objectives.

STEP THREE: PERFORMANCE OBJECTIVES

Objectives are a statement of what you will achieve over the year. They need to be clear so you can communicate them. They also need to be achievable and capable of being turned into a series of activities.

Objectives need a TIME for achievement. Objectives need a DESCRIPTION concerned with 'how well' or 'how much' you will achieve. Objectives can be QUANTITATIVE and measured in numbers or QUALITATIVE and measured by values or judgements.

Objectives need to be STRETCHING. They need to be realistic but put the manager on track for top performance. Normally for each performance area you define you will find either one or two objectives. Therefore a manager is capable of achieving between eight and sixteen well defined objectives in his job.

Here are two examples of objectives taken from an R&D manager's job:

(1) Ensure all tests and development work on product 'Y' are completed for market launch by August 1985.
(2) All product safety tests on product 'Z' to be completed and accepted by the Product Safety Committee by October 1985.

When you have developed and listed your objectives you can take your first look at PRIORITIES.

OBJECTIVES AND PRIORITIES

One of the reasons for defining objectives is so that you can assign a priority to each of the objectives. This is an important step because you can now search your year plan of objectives for PRIORITY CONFLICTS.

Your objectives may be CONTINUOUS. These are permanent parts of your job which extend continuously over time, e.g. sales development. They may also be PROJECTS. These are temporary parts of your job with a distinct START and FINISH over the year.

Too many managers manage their priorities in the short term. This is dangerous. PRIORITY CONFLICTS normally develop about 2–3 months AHEAD. If you take a short-term view then you'll miss the conflict and all you can do is respond.

Priority conflicts are always built into your year plan by the nature of *close deadlines* and a manager's lack of planning and tendency to DELAY work. Delay is an important feature because it *compounds* the priority conflict and leads to low priority work taking precedence over high priority work.

The knack in managing priority conflicts is to BRING WORK FORWARD. You do this simply by scheduling your year plan such that priority conflicts based on close deadlines are relieved by bringing work forward in the year. This is such a simple rule but many managers are oblivious to it.

Here are the correct sequence of stages for developing your objectives, your year plan and managing your priorities.

Stage 1   Develop your performance areas.
Stage 2   Identify the key factors affecting your performance over the year.
Stage 3   Develop one or two objectives for each performance area. Ensure that each is described and allocated a time frame.
Stage 4   Examine which objectives are CONTINUOUS and PROJECT.
Stage 5   Draw up a rough plan of the year showing start and finish times. Draw these on graph paper.
Stage 6   Assign to each objective a priority number. Try to be specific and avoid equal priority rankings.
Stage 7   Examine the plan and identify any conflicts of priority AHEAD. Normally these conflicts are indicated by CLOSE deadlines or when low priority objectives can interfere with high priority objectives.
Stage 8   Assume a factor of delay and examine how these priority conflicts can be heightened or new priority conflicts created.
Stage 9   Examine which objectives can be brought FORWARD in order to reduce or remove conflict.
Stage 10 Examine which objectives can be delegated in WHOLE or PART and make plans to delegate.
Stage 11 Ensure that your final year plan of objectives and delegation are planned to START in the appropriate monthly plan.

Please note how we have introduced delegation planning and monthly planning into the planning sequence.

Chapter 8: Developing your monthly and daily plan

The purpose of developing your broad year plan is so that you establish your objectives and resources. Also you manage your priorities and your delegation planning at this level. How you develop your year plan will always be a 'broad brush' approach and your detail planning will occur at the monthly and daily levels.

It is important to state that NO MANAGER HAS THE CAPABILITY TO TIME PLAN HIS JOB FOR MORE THAN A MONTH AHEAD.

This must be the case because we know that about 15% of top priority work actually arrives on the day it has to be handled. Also managers deal with the outside world and this is out of your control. Another reason is that organizations change their structure and their strategies either radically or by evolving. Also what can go wrong will go wrong. A manager's job is about CHANGE and managing this change. This is the essential dilemma in a manager's job. The more the job is subject to change the more the need to plan. Whatever the change you need to ensure that the CORE of your performance is achieved. You will have to REACT and modify your objectives but the knack for top performance is not to OVER-REACT and not to change your objectives unless it is absolutely essential to do so.

Given the year plan, the monthly plan provides more detail and provides the level of reaction you need in your job. Contingency planning is a strong feature of the monthly plan. From experience, between 50% and 70% of the manager's job needs to be contingency. This includes the 15% 'A' priority work that comes in on the day. Another important feature of the monthly plan is 'A' time. This is the time you are prepared to allocate AHEAD for the 'A' priority work.

The monthly plan has a basic structure (Fig. 9.1):

(i)   It contains a schedule for specified activity that relates to the year plan.
(ii) It contains contingency time.
(iii) It contains a specification of 'A' time.

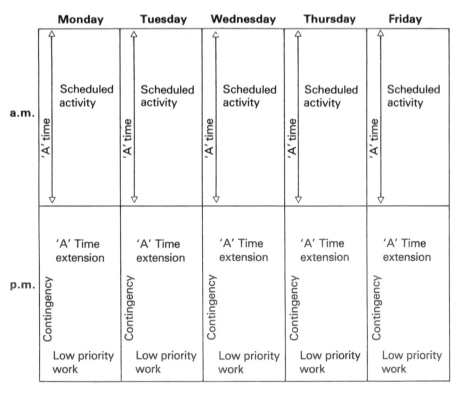

	Monday	Tuesday	Wednesday	Thursday	Friday
a.m.	↑ 'A' time ↓ Scheduled activity	↑ 'A' time ↓ Scheduled activity	↑ 'A' time ↓ Scheduled activity	↑ 'A' time ↓ Scheduled activity	↑ 'A' time ↓ Scheduled activity
p.m.	'A' Time extension / Contingency / Low priority work	'A' Time extension / Contingency / Low priority work	'A' Time extension / Contingency / Low priority work	'A' Time extension / Contingency / Low priority work	'A' Time extension / Contingency / Low priority work

Fig. 9.1   Monthly plan structure

MORE ABOUT 'A' TIME

'A' time is to ensure that you devote the majority of your time to top priority work. Preferably schedule 'A' time for the morning. This ensures that we have a minimum of 50% of our time for top priority work. It also ensures that we specify scheduled activities from our year plan and that low priority work is not put in front of high priority work.

'A' time needs to be continuous time, i.e. a 'block' of time. If you don't finish 'A' priority work in the morning then extend 'A' time into the afternoon. 'A' time is not one activity — it is all the activities that make up your top priority work. Try to plan as much scheduled activity into your 'A' time as you can when you review your monthly plan on a weekly basis.

Here are the benefits of 'A' time.

(i) It ensures that a *minimum* of 50% of your time is devoted to top priority work.
(ii) It allows you to schedule your top priority activities over the monthly plan. This ensures that you stay on track with your year plan.
(iii) It provides a discipline of continuously clarifying

and gaining experience in managing your priorities because 'A' time will question *you* if the work you are doing is top priority.
(iv) If you allocate 'A' time in the morning it will ensure that you never put low priority work in front of high priority work.
(v) 'A' time is the basis for effective diary control.
(vi) 'A' time is the basis of effective daily disciplines.

MORE ABOUT SPECIFIED ACTIVITIES

If you have a CONTINUOUS OBJECTIVE you have a CONTINUOUS ACTIVITY. By the nature of these continuous activities you can't specify the actual content until the day in question but you *can* specify the amount of time you will allocate to these continuous activities when they arise. Your own job planning, planning with your secretary, 'A' priority correspondence are all examples of continuous activities.

If you have a PROJECT OBJECTIVE you have a PROJECT ACTIVITY. With these you can specify both the actual content and your estimate of the time needed to complete. You need to be very flexible with project activities. If you are rigid and rely upon project management techniques you will OVER-PLAN. Make only rough time estimates and rough judgements about the logical sequence of activities. However you *must* follow three disciplines:

(1) Always *START* a project at the beginning of the month on your year plan.
(2) Always schedule into your monthly plan your ROUGH JUDGEMENTS OF ACTIVITIES.
(3) Always review your monthly plan on a rolling basis. Each week revise and update your monthly plan and each day keep an eye on your schedule and activities.

MORE ABOUT UNSPECIFIED ACTIVITIES

After you have allocated 'A' time what you have left is your CONTINGENCY TIME. You can't schedule this time nor the activities however contingency time will be used in a number of ways.

(i) Your 'A' time will extend into it.
(ii) Some of your 'A' priority work that comes in the day will use the time.
(iii) You will use it for low priority work.
(iv) You will use it for working at a slow pace.
(v) You will use it for handling low priority calls and interruptions that you deferred from 'A' time.

MONTHLY EVENTS AND REVIEWS

On your monthly plan you will also schedule regular monthly events and review meetings with staff and boss. These are normally scheduled into 'A' time. Each week you also need to schedule your review of the working plan and a period for reminding yourself on delegation review.

DAILY PLANS AND DISCIPLINES

Daily planning and disciplines are a notorious area for managers. This mainly comes about because of poor monthly planning and a complete abdication of any control over the manager's diary.

Most managers use their diary solely for meetings and appointments. How are you going to use the rest of your time?

Let me show you how weak your diary control is. Choose two days in your diary about four weeks ahead.

You have probably chosen two days that are free. If I telephone you now and ask for an appointment for some time over those two days you won't question me too strongly about the priority of the meeting from your point of view because you will not know what you will be doing at the time. You will look at your diary and think you are free. Also I know we will agree the START of the appointment but not mention the FINISH of the appointment. You will assume the finish time. I also know that I could specify the time I wanted to come, because again you say to yourself that you are free. All this is very reasonable and happens to every manager every working day. However this is what has happened:

(i) I am in your diary.
(ii) I am in at a time convenient to me.
(iii) I am in without your knowing how important my visit is to *your* priorities at the time.
(iv) I am in for an unspecified time.

Who is controlling your diary? I am!

I am only one example. Tomorrow another manager rings you up and he is in your diary, and so on. Three weeks away from the two days and other people are in your diary; two weeks away and more people are in your diary; one week away and more people. *Finally* when you arrive at the two days in question; *when you assess the priorities of your diary activities for the two days you will find that the vast majority are of lower priority than the essential top priority work that needs to be completed over the two days.*

This is what I all RESIDUAL TIME MANAGEMENT. YOU WILL COMPLETE YOUR TOP PRIORITY WORK IN THE SPACE YOU HAVE LEFT AFTER OTHER PEOPLE HAVE STOLEN YOUR TIME. This is why you spend 40% of your time on top priority work and 60% on low priority work.

Here are the two daily disciplines for getting back in control:

Discipline one: Be careful about diary events

(i) When you receive a request for a meeting or appointment ask yourself two questions: What is the priority of this request? and, If I accept what will be the impact on my priorities at the time?
(ii) Never assume that you are FREE or not BUSY. You will be busy managing your top priority work.
(iii) Always have a specified FINISH time.

(iv) Always try and ensure that *you* specify the time. Top priority work in 'A' time and low priority work in low priority time.

Discipline two: Schedule more top priority activities

Here are the top priority activities that you need to schedule into your diary mentally or physically. In total they represent your top performance.

(i) Job review time to review the top priority work of the day.
(ii) Job planning time with your secretary.
(iii) 'A' priority correspondence.
(iv) 'A' priority telephone calls.
(v) 'A' priority continuous activity time.
(vi) 'A' priority project activities.
(vii) 'A' priority meetings and appointments.
(ix) Job planning time with yourself.
(x) 'A' priority reading.

Think through your daily planning and daily disciplines and think constructively about whether you have a structure for your day for better overall performance. You will have your own job circumstances but use·the daily plan shown in Fig. 9.2 as a starting point.

SELF MANAGEMENT SUPPORT SYSTEMS

Although you may use a diary for your self management you will find that it is not flexible nor capable of providing the range of support you need for effective self management.

Have you considered using a BUSINESS TIME/ SYSTEM? This is a self management support system that brings together into a neat A5 workbook all the aids you need.

The A5 workbook has 8 major sections:

Section One   *Activities*
               This is your 'to do' list by date, priority, delegation.

Section Two   *Overview*
               This contains your yearly, project and monthly plans.

Section Three *Daily Plan*
               This is your daily schedule and your 'aide memoire' for priority activity and follow-ups.

Section Four   *Databank*
               This contains 10 sub-sections for the key parts of your job. Here you file your key information and plans for each part of your job.

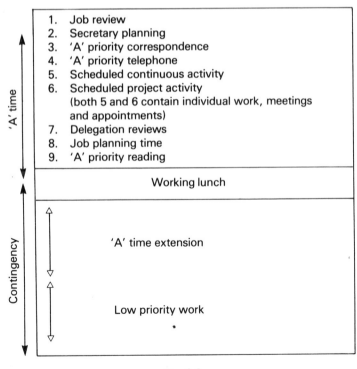

1. Job review
2. Secretary planning
3. 'A' priority correspondence
4. 'A' priority telephone
5. Scheduled continuous activity
6. Scheduled project activity
   (both 5 and 6 contain individual work, meetings and appointments)
7. Delegation reviews
8. Job planning time
9. 'A' priority reading

'A' time

Working lunch

Contingency

'A' time extension

Low priority work

Fig. 9.2

Section Five   *Information*
               This contains general information
               about your company or organization.
Section Six   *Miscellaneous*
               This is your general notebook.
Section Seven *Directory*
               This is an A-Z register of people,
               addresses and telephone numbers.
Section Eight *Card Holder*
               This contains your credit and
               business cards.

Each system is loose leaf and comes supplied with 700 pre-printed forms.

Each system is easily adapted to your job. The A5 format means you can use your own forms as well as the pre-printed ones. Many hundreds of thousands of managers are now using these systems.

Here are the key benefits:

(1) The system acts as a central workbook for all your key plans and information.
(2) The system is portable and can be used when travelling, waiting or at home. You are never without your top priority information.
(3) The system contains all the forms you need for your job.
(4) The system acts as an aid to your daily disciplines.
(5) The system acts as an 'aide memoire' to ensure quick follow-up and a guard against a faulty memory.
(6) The system helps you to set and maintain better priorities, better meetings, better delegation, better project planning and many other aspects of your self management.
(7) You are never without your telephone directory.
(8) You can keep track of finances and expenses.
(9) The system helps you to keep a CLEAR DESK policy because it curtails the generation of jottings and scrap notes.

If you wish to obtain more information about Business Time/System then please contact the author at Business Time/System, Knightway House, 20 Soho Square, London W1V 6DT. Telephone 01-439-2299.

Index